AT HOME with the WORD® 2022

Sunday Scriptures and Scripture Insights

Year C

Sherri Brown

Maribeth Howell, OP

Edrianne Ezell

Teresa Marshall-Patterson

Also available in a Large-Print Edition

LTP

LITURGY
TRAINING
PUBLICATIONS

Nihil Obstat
Rev. Mr. Daniel G. Welter, JD
Chancellor
Archdiocese of Chicago
March 24, 2021

Imprimatur
Most Rev. Robert G. Casey
Vicar General
Archdiocese of Chicago
March 24, 2021

Published by the authority of the Committee on Divine Worship, United States Conference of Catholic Bishops.

Prayers in the introductions to each liturgical time are adapted from *Prayers for Sundays and Seasons, Year C* by Peter Scagnelli, Chicago: Liturgy Training Publications, 1998.

AT HOME WITH THE WORD® 2022 © 2021 Archdiocese of Chicago: Liturgy Training Publications, 3949 South Racine Avenue, Chicago, IL 60609; 800-933-1800; fax: 800-933-7094; email: orders@ltp.org; website: www.LTP.org. All rights reserved.

This book was edited by Mary G. Fox. Michael A. Dodd was the production editor, Anna Manhart was the cover designer, Anne Fritzinger was the interior designer, and Kari Nicholls was the production artist.

The cover art for this year's *At Home with the Word*® is by James B. Janknegt. The interior art is by Kathy Ann Sullivan.

Printed in the United States of America

ISBN 978-1-61671-606-6

AHW22

Welcome to At Home with the Word® 2022

THE AUTHORS OF THE INTRODUCTIONS

Marielle Frigge, OSB, taught Scripture and theology for thirty-three years at Mount Marty College in Yankton, South Dakota, and is now formation director for Sacred Heart Monastery. Michael Cameron teaches Scripture and history of Christianity in the theology department at the University of Portland in Oregon.

SCRIPTURE READINGS

For each Sunday, you will find the three readings and responsorial psalm from the *Lectionary for Mass*, from which readings are proclaimed in Roman Catholic churches in the United States.

SCRIPTURE INSIGHTS

Two authors have written Scripture Insights for 2022. Sherri Brown, PHD, is associate professor of New Testament at Creighton University, Omaha, Nebraska. Her doctorate in biblical studies is from the Catholic University of America. She is the author of *Apostles to the Apostles: The Role of Women in the Gospel of John* (Grand Rapids: Baker Academic, forthcoming 2022); *Come and See: Discipleship in the Gospel of John* (Mahwah, NJ: Paulist Press, 2021); and *God's Promise: Covenant Relationship in John* (Mahwah, NJ: Paulist Press, 2014). She cowrote the textbooks *Interpreting the Gospel and Letters of John* and *Interpreting the New Testament* with Francis J. Moloney (Grand Rapids: Eerdmans, 2017, 2019). Dr. Brown wrote the Scripture Insights from the First Sunday of Advent through the Fourth Sunday of Easter.

Maribeth Howell is a Dominican Sister of Adrian, Michigan. She has taught Old Testament at Kenrick Seminary, in St. Louis, Missouri; St. Mary Seminary, in Wickliffe, Ohio; and Aquinas Institute of Theology, in St. Louis, Missouri, where she is professor emerita of biblical studies. Her PHD and STD are from the Catholic University of Leuven, Belgium. She is the translator of the Psalms in *Dominican Praise* and has written a variety of articles and contributed chapters in several academic and pastoral publications. Sister Howell wrote the Scripture Insights from the Fifth Sunday of Easter through the Solemnity of Our Lord Jesus Christ, King of the Universe.

PRACTICE OF FAITH, HOPE, CHARITY

Two authors wrote the Practice of Faith, Hope, or Charity. Edrianne Ezell, MDIV, a freelance writer, is a former campus minister at the Eastern Illinois University Newman Center, Charleston, Illinois. She earned her master of divinity degree from Weston Jesuit School of Theology and her bachelor of arts degree in English and studies of religion from the University of Michigan. Edrianne wrote the practices from the Fifth Sunday of Easter through the Solemnity of Our Lord Jesus Christ, King of the Universe.

Teresa Marshall-Patterson facilitates the Christian initiation process and liturgical ministries at St. Vincent de Paul Catholic Church in Andover, Kansas. She is the author of *We Learn About Our Parish Church* (LTP, 2010). Her master of arts in pastoral ministries is from St. Mary's University, Winona, Minnesota, and her master of arts in communications is from Wichita State University, Kansas. She wrote the practices from the First Sunday of Advent through the Fourth Sunday of Easter.

ADDITIONAL DOWNLOADABLE QUESTIONS AND ACTIVITIES

Download additional questions and activities for three audiences: families, Christian initiation groups, and other adult groups. The link http://www.ltp.org /ahw will take you to the *At Home with the Word®* Extra Content page. Click on the desired audience: Adult Faith-Sharing Groups, Christian Initiation Groups, or Families.

WEEKDAY READINGS

See the opening of each liturgical time for a list of Scripture texts read at Mass on weekdays and on feasts falling on weekdays.

ART FOR 2022

On the cover, James B. Janknegt has illustrated Mary Magdalene running to tell the disciples that Christ has risen. The reading is from Matthew 28:1–10, proclaimed at the Easter Vigil. In the interior art, Kathy Ann Sullivan uses a scratch-board technique to evoke the liturgical seasons, from our ancestors on the Jesse tree to the oil lamps for Ordinary Time in the fall.

Table of Contents

Lent

The Sacred Paschal Triduum

Easter Time

Ordinary Time, Summer

Ordinary Time, Autumn

The Lectionary

By Marielle Frigge, OSB

WHAT IS A LECTIONARY?

The word *lectionary* comes from the Latin word *legere*, "to read," and names a collection of Scripture readings from both the Old and New Testaments that are proclaimed throughout the liturgical year in a particular order. Christian lectionaries were in use already in the fourth century, but before the invention of the printing press in the mid-fifteenth century, readings differed from place to place. Printing allowed for a more standardized lectionary, so that Catholics around the world could hear the same Bible readings at Mass on any given day.

However, in the four centuries before the Second Vatican Council (1963–65), the lectionary had a somewhat limited ability to touch the faith lives of Catholics. Most could not understand what was read because Scripture readings as well as the prayers of the Mass were proclaimed in Latin. Further, because the lectionary of that time used only particular selections from the Bible repeated year after year, Catholics received a restricted exposure to the riches of Scripture.

GIFTS OF THE SECOND VATICAN COUNCIL

After the Second Vatican Council, not only were the biblical readings made available in the language of the people, but the structure of the lectionary was expanded as well. These changes resulted from a fresh understanding of the role of Scripture in the liturgy. Returning to the ancient understanding that Christ is present in the Scriptures, the Council Fathers further emphasized that the Eucharist nourishes God's people at two tables: the proclaimed Word of God and the Eucharistic banquet. For this reason, the revised Lectionary includes much more Scripture. Rather than repeating a yearly pattern, it includes a three-year cycle for Sundays and a two-year cycle for weekdays. Through this expanded array of selections, it aims to present the broad sweep of the salvation story, arranged purposefully around the liturgical year with the four major liturgical seasons of Advent, Christmas Time, Lent, and Easter Time punctuating the many weeks of Ordinary Time.

These great liturgical seasons instruct the faithful in the most significant aspects of salvation history. The liturgical year begins with Advent, expressing the ancient longing and hope of God's covenant people for redemption. Christmas Time celebrates the Incarnation of the Lord, God's Word of salvation fully present and active in the world, made flesh in Jesus the Christ. During Lent, the Scripture readings call Christians to deeper conversion: to amend their ways of failing to respond to God's saving Word, to cultivate greater intimacy with God, and to rejoice that he never ceases to offer life-changing mercy. These Scriptures about conversion speak powerfully to those preparing for initiation. Easter Time proclaims the paschal mystery, the redeeming death and resurrection of Jesus Christ. That mystery leads us into life in divine Spirit, poured out upon all the faithful at Pentecost, sending us out to serve. In addition to highlighting the liturgical seasons, the lectionary illuminates other key mysteries of Catholic faith in solemnities such as the Most Holy Trinity, the Most Holy Body and Blood of Christ, the Assumption of the Blessed Virgin Mary, and in feasts such as the Presentation of the Lord and the Exaltation of the Holy Cross.

FOUR SUNDAY SCRIPTURE SELECTIONS

At Home with the Word® provides all four Scripture passages of each Sunday: a selection from the Old Testament (except during Easter Time when we hear from Acts of the Apostles); a responsorial psalm or canticle; a New Testament reading from one of the letters, the Acts of the Apostles, or Revelation; and, most important, a Gospel passage. Each year of the three-year cycle draws from a particular Gospel account: Matthew in Year A, Mark in Year B, and Luke in Year C. The Gospel of John, so highly symbolic and profound, is heard in the liturgical seasons. The lectionary includes readings from John on several Sundays of Lent, during the Sacred Paschal Triduum, and most Sundays of Easter Time. Because Mark is the shortest Gospel account, some Sundays of Ordinary Time in Year B use passages from John.

The pattern of today's Catholic lectionary has served as a model for lectionaries of several other Christian churches. As a result, Catholics and many Protestants hear the same Scripture passages proclaimed on Sundays. The biblical Word of God thus draws them closer.

Understanding how the four Scripture passages of each Sunday are related can help us appreciate how the lectionary invites Christians to understand, ponder, and integrate the message of God's Word. The first reading from the Old Testament usually bears some connection to the Gospel passage, often by means of a significant person, event, or image. Rooted in the ancient practice of the Jewish synagogue, the responsorial, which follows the first reading, is usually from a psalm and represents the people's response to God's Word in the first reading. In this way the first two Scripture passages mirror a theme woven throughout the Bible: God always takes the initiative to address humankind, speaking a Word that invites a response from God's people. The responsorial may also illustrate or clarify what the first reading proclaims, or may be related to the liturgical season, and thus is intended to foster meditation on the Word of God.

Frequently the second reading, always from the New Testament, follows the ancient practice of *lectio continua* (Latin for "continuous reading"), so that on each Sunday we hear important selections in order from a particular book. For example, the second reading is often an excerpt from one of the letters of St. Paul, and by continuous reading over several Sundays, the lectionary presents some of his major theological insights in a particular letter.

During Ordinary Time the lectionary presents continuous reading in the Gospels also, allowing us to see each evangelist's distinctive way of unfolding the Gospel story. For example, in Year A, from the Fourteenth Sunday in Ordinary Time to the end of the liturgical year in November, we hear the Gospel of Matthew from chapter 11 through chapter 25. Not every verse of Matthew is included, and occasionally a Sunday solemnity or feast requires a reading from a different Gospel, but continuous reading relates major aspects of Matthew's narrative, just as it does for Mark's in Year B and Luke's in Year C. Over time, through continuous reading, we can become familiar with the particular content and qualities of each Gospel account.

THE LECTIONARY AS A VISUAL SIGN

The lectionary nourishes us with its words proclaimed in the liturgy—the Lord's own voice speaking to his people. It also nourishes us as a visual sign of the Lord's presence among us. The United States Conference of Catholic Bishops reminds Catholics that gestures and physical objects used in liturgy are "signs by which Christians express and deepen their relationship to God" (*Built of Living Stones: Art, Architecture, and Worship,* 23). Although the lectionary's proper place during the liturgy is on the ambo (the special podium from which readings are proclaimed), a part of the lectionary—the Gospel readings—has been made into a separate Book of the Gospels. That book, often richly decorated, may be carried in the entrance procession on Sundays and holydays. It is placed on the altar at the beginning of Mass and then, when the assembly rises to sing the Alleluia, the Gospel reader may processes with the book to the ambo, accompanied by servers holding candles. In response to the deacon or priest's introduction to the Gospel reading, the people respond, signing their forehead, lips, and heart with a small cross. Observing such signs and ceremonies, one could not miss the special reverence we give to the Word of God—especially in the Gospel.

In the bishops' teaching about the ambo, from which the Scriptures are proclaimed, we find an apt crystallization of the Church's conviction about the role of Scripture in the Mass. Urging that the ambo should be of a size and placement that draws attention to the sacred Word, the document says, "Here the Christian community encounters the living Lord in the word of God and prepares itself for the 'breaking of the bread' and the mission to live the word that will be proclaimed" (*Built of Living Stones,* 61).

Introduction to the Gospel according to Luke

by Michael Cameron

The Gospel according to Luke, together with its sequel, the Acts of the Apostles, presents a breathtaking narrative of early Christianity, from Gabriel announcing the birth of John the Baptist in Jerusalem to the apostle Paul announcing the Gospel of Jesus in Rome. This majestically conceived, magnificently crafted epic makes up about a quarter of the New Testament.

Luke was a second-generation Christian who may have been a Gentile admirer of Judaism before his conversion. He was well educated, traveled widely, wrote excellent Greek, and was influenced by contemporary modes of writing history. He echoes the atmosphere, the language, and at times even the style of the Old Testament. Luke tells us directly that he is handing on what contemporaries of Jesus have reported (1:1–4). Writing about fifty years after Jesus' time, he incorporates many stories and sayings from Mark, from a source also known to Matthew, and from his own traditions. Nevertheless, he shapes the traditions according to his own rich perspective.

Luke is a theologian with a historical bent, possessing a strong sense of the salvation story's development through three phases of time. *The time of Israel* is the period of "the law and the prophets" (16:16) from the creation to the appearance of John the Baptist. The entire Old Testament portrayed Israel growing in the knowledge of God and awaiting the future "redemption of Jerusalem" (2:38). Luke's account represents this time poetically through the infancy narrative (chapters 1 and 2), with its unforgettable characters who represent Old Testament piety at its best. *The time of Jesus* encompasses his baptism to his ascension (chapters 3 to 24), when salvation is definitively accomplished in the words and works of the messiah, especially his death and resurrection in Jerusalem (24:44–47). Luke accentuates the dramatic immediacy of salvation by a strategic use of the word *today* (fulfillment "today," 4:21; salvation "today," 19:9; paradise "today," 23:43). *The time of the church* stretches from Pentecost until Jesus returns. Anticipated in 24:48, this period begins to unfold in the 28 chapters of Acts of the Apostles.

Luke's work has a distinctive, sweet air, a beautiful mildness. His naturally humane outlook finds deep resonance with Jesus' concern for people's healing and salvation. In contrast to Mark's rough prophet, Matthew's wise teacher, and John's mystical divine, Luke's Jesus is the herald of healing peace. From the early scene announcing "liberty to captives" (4:17–19) to the last healing of the slave of the high priest who arrested him (22:50–51), Luke's Jesus is the good and gentle Savior. At the same time, Luke is blunt about Jesus' severe demands on those who become his disciples (14:25–33; 17:7–10), who must take up their cross daily (9:23) and leave everything to follow him, a favorite idea (5:11, 28; 14:33).

Luke is an exquisite storyteller, with a keen eye for deep characters, pungent storylines, poignant ironies, and heartwarming endings. As with all such masters, his pen's slightest stroke speaks volumes, as when Jesus agonizes while the disciples sleep "from grief" (22:45), or Peter denies Jesus a third time and "the Lord turned and looked at Peter" (22:61). Luke's arresting vignettes anticipate the stained glass storytelling of great medieval cathedrals. It is not accidental that artists have often rendered Luke as a portrait painter, or that the Church has made Luke patron saint of artists.

Luke contains certain features that the other Gospel accounts omit or mention only in passing. Joy is a distinct emphasis (1:14, 47; 2:10; 10:17, 21; 15:7, 10; 19:37; 24:41), as are prayer (3:21; 6:12; 11:5–8; 18:1–8; 23:46), the Holy Spirit (1:15, 41, 67; 2:27; 4:18; 10:21; 11:13), Jesus' friendships with women (7:36–50; 8:2–3; 10:38–42; 23:27–31; 23:55), and his teaching on hospitality (9:49–50; 10:25–37; 14:12–14; 15:4) and right attitude about wealth (6:24–25; 12:13–21; 16:19–31). If Luke's account of the Gospel had somehow not survived, our loss would be incalculable.

Luke alone gives us the stories of Jesus' infancy narrative, including the birth of John the Baptist, the angel Gabriel's annunciation to Mary (1:26–38), and her visitation to Elizabeth (1:39–45); the liturgical songs of Mary (1:46–55, the Magnificat) and Zechariah (1:67–79, the Benedictus); he draws images of the crowded inn at Bethlehem, Jesus lying in the manger, shepherds frightened by angels singing "Peace on Earth" (2:1–20), hoary Simeon exclaiming his praise (2:28–32, the Nunc Dimittis), old Anna prophesying redemption, (2:36–38), the young Jesus cross-examining the scholars (2:46), and Mary keeping in her heart the mysteries about her son (2:19, 51).

Luke's memorable characters include the judgmental Pharisee Simon (7:39–47), the hungry learner Mary (10:39), the repentant taxman Zacchaeus (19:1–10), and the distraught disciple Cleopas (24:18–24). Special dramas abound: Jesus raised up a widow's only son at his funeral, then "gave him to his mother" (7:11–17), healed the woman bent double for eighteen years (13:10–17), and cured ten lepers among whom the Samaritan alone returned to say thanks (17:11–19). He painted a host of affecting scenes: Jesus reading in his home synagogue (4:16–20), Peter repenting at Jesus' knees (5:8), the woman bathing Jesus' feet with her tears (7:38), Jesus praying with sweat "like drops of blood" (22:44).

Further, Luke transmitted many unique sayings of Jesus: "One's life does not consist of possessions" (12:15). "Do not be afraid any longer, little flock" (12:32). "The kingdom of God is among you" (17:21). "Father, forgive them, they know not what they do" (23:34). "Today you will be with me in Paradise" (23:43). And many well-known parables are found only in Luke: the good Samaritan (10:29–37), the woman's lost coin (15:8–10), the prodigal son (15:11–32), the rich man and Lazarus (16:19–31), the widow and the unjust judge (18:1–8), the Pharisee and the tax collector (18:9–14).

Luke's first sentences in the prologue (1:1–4) address an otherwise unknown figure named Theophilus (the name means "God's friend"), who symbolizes any Christian seeking a deeper understanding of Jesus. For each reader who takes up his "orderly sequence" with serious intent, Luke has a single stirring aim. Literally translated, it reads, "that you may come to know a deep assurance about the teachings you have received."

Prayer before Reading the Word

In this and every year,
in this and every place,
O God everlasting,
your Word resounds in the wilderness of Advent,
calling us to stand upon the height
and to behold the splendor of your beauty.

Fill in the valleys of our neglect;
bring low our mountains of self-centeredness.
Prepare in our hearts
your way of righteousness and peace.
Let our love become a harvest of goodness,
which you will bring to completion
for the day of Christ Jesus,
who was, who is, and who is to come,
your Son who lives and reigns with you
in the unity of the Holy Spirit,
God, for ever and ever. Amen.

Prayer after Reading the Word

God of holiness,
whose promises stand through all generations,
fulfill the longings of a humanity
weighed down by confusion and burdened
                with fear.

Raise up our heads and strengthen our hearts,
that we may proclaim to all people
the Good News of your presence in our midst.
May we delight to share with them
your peace, which surpasses all understanding.

Through our Lord Jesus Christ, your Son,
who lives and reigns with you
in the unity of the Holy Spirit,
God, for ever and ever. Amen.

Weekday Readings

November 29: *Isaiah 2:1–5; Matthew 8:5–11*

November 30: Feast of St. Andrew, Apostle
   Romans 10:9–18; Matthew 4:18–22

December 1: *Isaiah 25:6–10a; Matthew 15:29–37*

December 2: *Isaiah 26:1–6; Matthew 7:21, 24–27*

December 3: *Isaiah 29:17–24; Matthew 9:27–31*

December 4: *Isaiah 30:19–21, 23–26;*
   Matthew 9:35—10:1, 5a, 6–8

December 6: *Isaiah 35:1–10; Luke 5:17–26*

December 7: *Isaiah 40:1–11; Matthew 18:12–14*

December 8: Solemnity of the Immaculate Conception
   of the Blessed Virgin Mary
   Genesis 3:9–15, 20; Ephesians 1:3–6, 11–12;
   Luke 1:26–38

December 9: *Isaiah 41:13–20; Matthew 11:11–15*

December 10: *Isaiah 48:17–19; Matthew 11:16–19*

December 11: *Sirach 48:1–4, 9–11; Matthew 17:9a, 10–13*

December 13: *Numbers 24:2–7, 15–17a; Matthew 21:23–27*

December 14: *Zephaniah 3:1–2, 9–13; Matthew 21:28–32*

December 15: *Isaiah 45:6c–8, 18, 21c–25; Luke 7:18b–23*

December 16: *Isaiah 54:1–10; Luke 7:24–30*

December 17: *Genesis 49:2, 8–10; Matthew 1:1–17*

December 18: *Jeremiah 23:5–8; Matthew 1:18–25*

December 20: *Isaiah 7:10–14; Luke 1:26–38*

December 21: *Song of Songs 2:8–14 or Zephaniah 3:14–18a;*
   Luke 1:39–45

December 22: *1 Samuel 1:24–28; Luke 1:46–56*

December 23: *Malachi 3:1–4, 23–24; Luke 1:57–66*

December 24: *Morning 2 Samuel 7:1–5, 8b–12, 14a, 16;*
   Luke 1:67–79

READING I *Jeremiah 33:14–16*

The days are coming, says the LORD, when I will fulfill the promise I made to the house of Israel and Judah. In those days, in that time, I will raise up for David a just shoot; he shall do what is right and just in the land. In those days Judah shall be safe and Jerusalem shall dwell secure; this is what they shall call her: "The LORD our justice."

RESPONSORIAL PSALM
Psalm 25:4–5, 8–9, 10, 14 (1b)

R. To you, O Lord, I lift my soul.

Your ways, O LORD, make known to me;
   teach me your paths,
guide me in your truth and teach me,
   for you are God my savior,
   and for you I wait all the day. R.

Good and upright is the LORD;
   thus he shows sinners the way.
He guides the humble to justice,
   and teaches the humble his way. R.

All the paths of the LORD are kindness
    and constancy
   toward those who keep his covenant and
    his decrees.
The friendship of the LORD is with those who
    fear him,
   and his covenant, for their instruction. R.

READING II *1 Thessalonians 3:12—4:2*

Brothers and sisters: May the Lord make you increase and abound in love for one another and for all, just as we have for you, so as to strengthen your hearts, to be blameless in holiness before our God and Father at the coming of our Lord Jesus with all his holy ones. Amen.

Finally, brothers and sisters, we earnestly ask and exhort you in the Lord Jesus that, as you received from us how you should conduct yourselves to please God—and as you are conducting yourselves—you do so even more. For you know what instructions we gave you through the Lord Jesus.

GOSPEL *Luke 21:25–28, 34–36*

Jesus said to his disciples: "There will be signs in the sun, the moon, and the stars, and on earth nations will be in dismay, perplexed by the roaring of the sea and the waves. People will die of fright in anticipation of what is coming upon the world, for the powers of the heavens will be shaken. And then they will see the Son of Man coming in a cloud with power and great glory. But when these signs begin to happen, stand erect and raise your heads because your redemption is at hand.

"Beware that your hearts do not become drowsy from carousing and drunkenness and the anxieties of daily life, and that day catch you by surprise like a trap. For that day will assault everyone who lives on the face of the earth. Be vigilant at all times and pray that you have the strength to escape the tribulations that are imminent and to stand before the Son of Man."

Practice of Hope

The Gospel tells us that "people will die of fright in anticipation of what is coming." Today's reading from Luke may bring to mind terrifying images from movies. A doomsday scenario, however, is not the point of the reading. At the start of the Advent season, Luke provides a sense of hope. The awaited Christ child is a gift to us and is our pathway to living forever with God. This Christ child also is the Son of Man, who will be seen "coming in a cloud with power and great glory." ◆ If you have not already done so, acquire materials that will help to lead you spiritually through this liturgical season. Consider Liturgy Training Publications' calendar resources that include seasonal explanations and notations for the saints. ◆ Make or purchase an Advent wreath to celebrate the season. ◆ Embrace the journey through this season of the liturgical year and try not to allow "the anxieties of daily life" to distract you.

Download more questions and activities for families, Christian initiation groups, and other adult groups at http://www.ltp.org/ahw.

Scripture Insights

On this First Sunday of Advent, Christians begin preparing for the coming of the messiah. The word *advent* comes from the Latin *adventus*, which means "arrival." The Advent season allows us to prepare for a dual arrival: the coming of the messiah into the world through the birth of Jesus and the second coming of the risen Christ in glory. Our readings cross both expectations.

In a time of suffering for the people of Judah, Jeremiah looks forward with hope to God's fulfilling the promise of the Davidic covenant. The time is coming, says he, for God to raise up his Anointed One from the line of David to redeem Israel to return justice to the land and its people. The psalmist follows, developing the essence of this covenantal relationship by petitioning God to continue teaching his ways and remember his fidelity, righteousness, and mercy. The hope is for an abiding, life-giving relationship, made manifest in the coming gift of the Christ.

The New Testament readings spring from the lived reality of this relationship in history. Paul pleads for help for God's people to abound in love, manifesting that of God the Father in the gift of Jesus the Son through loving care for creation and one another. How we choose to act and interact with one another should reflect this relationship. The hope now is for the time to come, as Jesus expounds in Luke's Gospel. Jesus calls disciples of all time to stand strong in the face of fear and distraction. Life in covenant relationship with the One who created us and the One who redeemed us is the longer, possibly harder road, but the journey is worth the effort in hope for a destination in union.

◆ Finding hope amid suffering is difficult. How do your relationships with God and your loved ones help you meet this challenge?

◆ How might the seduction of immediate gratification and comfort be the most dangerous threat of all in our quest to live in right relationship with God?

◆ Reflect on Paul's teaching. How might you better manifest God's love by how you care for others in the coming year?

READING I *Baruch 5:1–9*

Jerusalem, take off your robe of mourning
>   and misery;
> put on the splendor of glory from
>   God forever:
wrapped in the cloak of justice from God,
> bear on your head the mitre
>   that displays the glory of the eternal name.
For God will show all the earth your splendor:
> you will be named by God forever
>   the peace of justice, the glory
>   of God's worship.

Up, Jerusalem! stand upon the heights;
> look to the east and see your children
gathered from the east and the west
>   at the word of the Holy One,
> rejoicing that they are remembered by God.
Led away on foot by their enemies they left you:
> but God will bring them back to you
>   borne aloft in glory as on royal thrones.
For God has commanded
>   that every lofty mountain be made low,
and that the age-old depths and gorges
>   be filled to level ground,
> that Israel may advance secure in the glory
>   of God.
The forests and every fragrant kind of tree
>   have overshadowed Israel at God's command;
for God is leading Israel in joy
>   by the light of his glory,
> with his mercy and justice for company.

RESPONSORIAL PSALM
Psalm 126:1–2, 2–3, 4–5, 6 (3)

R. The Lord has done great things for us; we are
>   filled with joy.

When the LORD brought back the captives of Zion,
> we were like men dreaming.
Then our mouth was filled with laughter,
> and our tongue with rejoicing. R.

Then they said among the nations,
> "The LORD has done great things for them."
The LORD has done great things for us;
> we are glad indeed. R.

Restore our fortunes, O LORD,
> like the torrents in the southern desert.
Those who sow in tears
> shall reap rejoicing. R.

Although they go forth weeping,
> carrying the seed to be sown,
they shall come back rejoicing,
> carrying their sheaves. R.

READING II *Philippians 1:4–6, 8–11*

Brothers and sisters: I pray always with joy in my every prayer for all of you, because of your partnership for the gospel from the first day until now. I am confident of this, that the one who began a good work in you will continue to complete it until the day of Christ Jesus. God is my witness, how I long for all of you with the affection of Christ Jesus. And this is my prayer: that your love may increase ever more and more in knowledge and every kind of perception, to discern what is of value, so that you may be pure and blameless for the day of Christ, filled with the fruit of righteousness that comes through Jesus Christ for the glory and praise of God.

GOSPEL *Luke 3:1–6*

In the fifteenth year of the reign of Tiberius Caesar, when Pontius Pilate was governor of Judea, and Herod was tetrarch of Galilee, and his brother Philip tetrarch of the region of Ituraea and Trachonitis, and Lysanias was tetrarch of Abilene, during the high priesthood of Annas and Caiaphas, the word of God came to John the son of Zechariah in the desert. John went throughout the whole region of the Jordan, proclaiming a baptism of repentance for the forgiveness of sins, as it is written in the book of the words of the prophet Isaiah: / *A voice of one crying out in the desert: / "Prepare the way of the Lord, / make straight his paths. / Every valley shall be filled / and every mountain and hill shall be made low. / The winding roads shall be made straight, / and the rough ways made smooth, / and all flesh shall see the salvation of God."*

Practice of Charity

In today's first reading, Baruch, considered the scribe of the prophet Jeremiah, provides messages of hope to the Israelites exiled in Babylon. Enslavement and the destruction of their temple had devastated these exiles. Jeremiah gives them reason to rejoice through the despair. God has commanded that "every lofty mountain be made low" so that Israel could "advance secure in the glory of God." ◆ During this busy season of preparation, look for reasons to be thankful for the abundance in your life. ◆ Find ways to give generously to people who might be struggling in some way. Perhaps you may have an opportunity to lend a listening ear to someone who recently lost a family member or friend. ◆ Consider a simpler celebration of Christmas that reflects the importance of gathering loved ones rather than on acquiring new gadgets and clothes.

Download more questions and activities for families, Christian initiation groups, and other adult groups at http://www.ltp.org/ahw.

Scripture Insights

On this Second Sunday of Advent, Luke's Gospel introduces the adult John and his mission (in the words of the prophet Isaiah) to "prepare the way of the Lord" (3:4). His is the voice crying out in the desert, and he is the one who baptizes those coming to him in repentance and moving toward a new direction. A way of preparing for the coming of the messiah when all "shall see the salvation of God" (3:6) is presented to those who are attentive and courageous enough to reflect on their lives and their way of proceeding, in relationship both with God and with other people.

The reading from Paul encompasses his thanksgiving, a component he typically adds to the conventional Greco-Roman letter. Paul expresses his joy with the Philippians at their lived manifestation of the good news. The timeless summons of his prayer is for everyone to strive for the good of all. Seeking to find and be our best selves includes discerning what is truly of value. This is the hard work also bidden by the psalmist and envisioned by Baruch. The restoration of God's people after the exile is described as tears that lead to joy. The mercy and justice of God guide those in covenant with him to be accountable in what they believe and do. This is the path to authentic satisfaction.

These readings lead us to examine our lives, relationships, and vocations as we prepare for the fullness promised in the coming of the messiah: union with God. Advent gives us the opportunity to do the work God gifts to us in our lives.

◆ Are you as just as you could be? Are there relationships in your life that you need to reexamine?

◆ Are you as joyous as you could be? Are there gifts in your life that you are called to recognize and act on in new ways?

◆ How can you take advantage of the Advent season to do some hard work on your life and relationships?

December 12, 2021 THIRD SUNDAY OF ADVENT

READING I *Zephaniah 3:14–18a*

Shout for joy, O daughter Zion!
　　Sing joyfully, O Israel!
Be glad and exult with all your heart,
　　O daughter Jerusalem!
The LORD has removed the judgment
　　　　against you,
　　he has turned away your enemies;
the King of Israel, the LORD, is in your midst,
　　you have no further misfortune to fear.
On that day, it shall be said to Jerusalem:
　　Fear not, O Zion, be not discouraged!
The LORD, your God, is in your midst,
　　a mighty savior;
he will rejoice over you with gladness,
　　and renew you in his love,
he will sing joyfully because of you,
　　as one sings at festivals.

RESPONSORIAL PSALM
Isaiah 12:2–3, 4, 5–6 (6)

R. Cry out with joy and gladness:
　　for among you is the great and Holy One
　　　　of Israel.

God indeed is my savior;
　　I am confident and unafraid.
My strength and my courage is the LORD,
　　and he has been my savior.
With joy you will draw water
　　at the fountain of salvation.　R.

Give thanks to the LORD, acclaim his name;
　　among the nations make known his deeds,
　　proclaim how exalted is his name.　R.

Sing praise to the LORD for his
　　　　glorious achievement;
　　let this be known throughout all the earth.
Shout with exultation, O city of Zion,
　　for great in your midst
　　is the Holy One of Israel!　R.

READING II *Philippians 4:4–7*

Brothers and sisters: Rejoice in the Lord always. I shall say it again: rejoice! Your kindness should be known to all. The Lord is near. Have no anxiety at all, but in everything, by prayer and petition, with thanksgiving, make your requests known to God. Then the peace of God that surpasses all understanding will guard your hearts and minds in Christ Jesus.

GOSPEL *Luke 3:10–18*

The crowds asked John the Baptist, "What should we do?" He said to them in reply, "Whoever has two cloaks should share with the person who has none. And whoever has food should do likewise." Even tax collectors came to be baptized and they said to him, "Teacher, what should we do?" He answered them, "Stop collecting more than what is prescribed." Soldiers also asked him, "And what is it that we should do?" He told them, "Do not practice extortion, do not falsely accuse anyone, and be satisfied with your wages."

Now the people were filled with expectation, and all were asking in their hearts whether John might be the Christ. John answered them all, saying, "I am baptizing you with water, but one mightier than I is coming. I am not worthy to loosen the thongs of his sandals. He will baptize you with the Holy Spirit and fire. His winnowing fan is in his hand to clear his threshing floor and to gather the wheat into his barn, but the chaff he will burn with unquenchable fire." Exhorting them in many other ways, he preached good news to the people.

Practice of Faith

John the Baptist gave sage advice in today's Gospel to the crowds surrounding him. As a result, even the tax collectors—considered to be ruthless and dishonest—were willing to be baptized and reformed. Luke tells us that the people considered John as a possible messiah because of his strong message of change and charity. ◆ For this Advent season, think about an organization to which your family can contribute items or time to help. ◆ Find your baptismal certificate or photographs and video of the event (and perhaps those of family members). Talk about that day and the meaning of this membership in the Body of Christ. ◆ If you don't already have one, consider placing a bowl of blessed holy water in your home as a reminder to bless yourself and others. This visual reminder can serve as a symbol of your commitment to living with faith and hope for the next kingdom.

Download more questions and activities for families, Christian initiation groups, and other adult groups at http://www.ltp.org/ahw.

Scripture Insights

Entering the third week of Advent, we remain in expectant preparation for the coming of the messiah. Yet, our focus shifts to joy. Indeed, this is Gaudete Sunday: the Sunday of joy! As John the Baptist continues his ministry of the good news in Luke's Gospel, Paul expounds on his manifesto of rejoicing in the Lord in his letter to the Philippians, and the prophet Zephaniah exhorts all God's people to shout for joy. Today's readings exemplify how looking inside to God for guidance and outside to one another for our mission grounds us in authentic joy in this life.

Writing in the seventh century BC in Jerusalem during the reign of King Josiah, Zephaniah looks ahead to the day of the Lord and living in the kingdom of God. Once God's people are purged of their wrongdoings and shortsighted turning away from God, they will be restored to right relationship with God, who will live in their midst as a mighty savior. Here we can find true joy, relieved of the burdens of this life, living in unmediated relationship with God. Writing to Christians in first-century Philippi, the apostle Paul reinforces "the peace of God that surpasses all understanding" (Philippians 4:7) found in laying ourselves bare before our God in relationship with Christ Jesus. This is how we can live in the joy of our innermost selves.

The missional activity of John the Baptist teaches us to turn this profoundly personal relationship to those we encounter in the world. Giving from our excess and holding ourselves to a strict integrity are required, even if others do not manifest this joy that radiates from our grounded center. Thus, we await in hope and, indeed, bring near the kingdom of God.

◆ How can looking inside for God's guidance ground you to turn outside of yourself in relationship with others?

◆ All are called to some type of ministry. How do you see your mission manifesting itself?

◆ Consider ways to find joy in the mundane, everyday experiences of your life to help you find the surpassing peace of God.

December 19, 2021 FOURTH SUNDAY OF ADVENT

READING I *Micah 5:1-4a*

Thus says the LORD:
You, Bethlehem-Ephrathah,
    too small to be among the clans of Judah,
from you shall come forth for me
    one who is to be ruler in Israel;
whose origin is from of old,
    from ancient times.
Therefore the Lord will give them up,
        until the time
    when she who is to give birth has borne,
and the rest of his kindred shall return
    to the children of Israel.
He shall stand firm and shepherd his flock
    by the strength of the LORD,
    in the majestic name of the LORD, his God;
and they shall remain, for now his greatness
    shall reach to the ends of the earth;
    he shall be peace.

RESPONSORIAL PSALM
Psalm 80:2-3, 15-16, 18-19 (4)

R. Lord, make us turn to you; let us see your face
    and we shall be saved.

O shepherd of Israel, hearken,
    from your throne upon the cherubim,
            shine forth.
Rouse your power,
    and come to save us. R.

Once again, O LORD of hosts,
    look down from heaven, and see;
take care of this vine,
    and protect what your right hand has planted,
    the son of man whom you yourself
            made strong. R.

May your help be with the man of your
            right hand,
    with the son of man whom you yourself
            made strong.
Then we will no more withdraw from you;
    give us new life, and we will call upon
            your name. R.

READING II *Hebrews 10:5-10*

Brothers and sisters:
When Christ came into the world, he said:
    "Sacrifice and offering you did not desire,
    but a body you prepared for me;
    in holocausts and sin offerings you took
            no delight.
    Then I said, 'As is written of me in the scroll,
    behold, I come to do your will, O God.'"

First he says, "Sacrifices and offerings, holocausts and sin offerings, you neither desired nor delighted in." These are offered according to the law. Then he says, "Behold, I come to do your will." He takes away the first to establish the second. By this "will," we have been consecrated through the offering of the body of Jesus Christ once for all.

GOSPEL *Luke 1:39-45*

Mary set out and traveled to the hill country in haste to a town of Judah, where she entered the house of Zechariah and greeted Elizabeth. When Elizabeth heard Mary's greeting, the infant leaped in her womb, and Elizabeth, filled with the Holy Spirit, cried out in a loud voice and said, "Blessed are you among women, and blessed is the fruit of your womb. And how does this happen to me, that the mother of my Lord should come to me? For at the moment the sound of your greeting reached my ears, the infant in my womb leaped for joy. Blessed are you who believed that what was spoken to you by the Lord would be fulfilled."

Practice of Faith

This Gospel, about Mary's visit to Elizabeth, is rich in the reality of Christ's presence and the recognition that he was to be the messiah for all. Even from the early stages of life, John the Baptist "leaped for joy" in recognition of the Savior in his midst. This momentous meeting between the two humble women highlights the power of belief in our Creator's Word. Their courage and witness to the miracles happening in their physical beings are inspiring for us. ◆ Become more aware of women in your parish and workplace who are pregnant and who might be undergoing some hardship. Offer some assistance, supplies, or baby clothes to support their decision to bring life to the world. ◆ Donate your time or financial resources to a local crisis center where women with unplanned pregnancies go for counseling and support. ◆ During the Christmas fund drives, local orphanages also need help; perhaps there, your time and talent would be especially valued.

Download more questions and activities for families, Christian initiation groups, and other adult groups at http://www.ltp.org/ahw.

Scripture Insights

The readings of Advent's Fourth Sunday lead us down the path of messianic expectation to the long-hoped-for arrival. The eighth-century BC prophet Micah speaks God's word of a ruler who is both Shepherd and a majestic Name, bringing peace and greatness. The catch is that he will come forth from tiny Bethlehem, unexpected in every way. In his context, Micah is speaking to the threat of Assyria that will wipe out the Northern Kingdom, from which Judah was spared. In our time, these words translate to an openness to God and how God might work in our world and our lives, counter to society's expectations.

The guiding hand of God, the psalmist proclaims, is always at work for the good of creation, often despite human plans. The New Testament readings further articulate God's will to work in the world, often beyond the ken of human expectation. Hebrews puts forth the atoning sacrifice of "the offering of the body of Jesus Christ" (10:10) in just this manner. Keeping a ritual is not enough if it is empty of heartfelt desire for change and authenticity. This is as true today as it was in the first century. God's gift of Jesus, Christ and Son, to the world in his person and ministry, as well as his atoning sacrifice, was far beyond what the people expected but was precisely what the world so desperately needed.

Luke's Gospel presents the encounter between two faithful women who show themselves open to God working both in the world and in their lives in just such profoundly unexpected ways. As they come together in support of one another, they realize the depth and breadth of God's plan and how they are called beyond both their comfort and society's role for them.

◆ Reflect on your expectations of how God works in the world. How do these expectations both help and hinder true openness in your relationship with God?

◆ How might you ensure an authentic heart during the ritual of the Advent and Christmas seasons?

◆ How can Elizabeth and Mary become universal models in the culmination of this Advent season?

Prayer before Reading the Word

By the light of a star, O God of the universe,
you guided the nations to the Light of the world.

Until this Redeemer comes again in glory,
we, with the Magi, seek the face of the Savior.
Summon us with all those who thirst now
to the banquet of love.
May our hunger be filled and our thirst
              be quenched
with your Word of truth.

Through our Lord Jesus Christ, your Son,
who lives and reigns with you
in the unity of the Holy Spirit,
God, for ever and ever. Amen.

Prayer after Reading the Word

In the beginning, O God, was your Word,
and now in time your Word becomes flesh.
The Light that shines unconquered
through the darkness of the ages,
and has made his dwelling place among us,
transforming earth's gloom into heaven's glory.

As we behold upon the mountains
the messenger who announces your peace,
touch our lips as well that we may lift up
              our voices
as bearers of Good News and heralds
              of salvation.

Through our Lord Jesus Christ,
Emmanuel, God-with-us,
your Son, who lives and reigns with you
in the unity of the Holy Spirit,
God, for ever and ever. Amen.

Weekday Readings

December 27: Feast of St. John, Apostle and Evangelist
  1 John 1:1–4; John 20:1a, 2–8
December 28: Feast of the Holy Innocents
  1 John 1:5—2:2; Matthew 2:13–18
December 29: Fifth Day within the Octave of the Lord
  1 John 2:3–11; Luke 2:22–35
December 30: Sixth Day within the Octave of the Lord
  1 John 2:12–17; Luke 2:36–40
December 31: Seventh Day within the Octave of the Lord
  1 John 2:18–21; John 1:1–18
January 1: Solemnity of Mary, the Holy Mother of God
  Numbers 6:22–27; Galatians 4:4–7; Luke 2:16–21

January 3: *1 John 3:22—4:6; Matthew 4:12–17, 23–25*
January 4: *1 John 4:7–10; Mark 6:34–44*
January 5: *1 John 4:11–18; Mark 6:45–52*
January 6: *1 John 4:19—5:4; Luke 4:14–22*
January 7: *1 John 5:5–13; Luke 5:12–16*
January 8: *1 John 5:14–21; John 3:22–30*

READING I *Isaiah 52:7–10*

How beautiful upon the mountains
　　are the feet of him who brings glad tidings,
announcing peace, bearing good news,
　　announcing salvation, and saying to Zion,
　　"Your God is King!"

Hark! Your sentinels raise a cry,
　　together they shout for joy,
for they see directly, before their eyes,
　　the LORD restoring Zion.
Break out together in song,
　　O ruins of Jerusalem!
For the LORD comforts his people,
　　he redeems Jerusalem.
The LORD has bared his holy arm
　　in the sight of all the nations;
all the ends of the earth will behold
　　the salvation of our God.

RESPONSORIAL PSALM
Psalm 98:1, 2–3, 3–4, 5–6 (3c)

R. All the ends of the earth have seen the saving
　　power of God.

Sing to the LORD a new song,
　　for he has done wondrous deeds;
his right hand has won victory for him,
　　his holy arm.　R.

The LORD has made his salvation known:
　　in the sight of the nations he has revealed
　　　　his justice.
He has remembered his kindness and
　　　　his faithfulness
　　toward the house of Israel.　R.

All the ends of the earth have seen
　　the salvation by our God.
Sing joyfully to the LORD, all you lands;
　　break into song; sing praise.　R.

Sing praise to the Lord with the harp,
　　with the harp and melodious song.
With trumpets and the sound of the horn
　　sing joyfully before the King, the LORD.　R.

READING II *Hebrews 1:1–6*

Brothers and sisters:
In times past, God spoke in partial and various
ways to our ancestors through the prophets; in
these last days, he has spoken to us through the
Son, whom he made heir of all things and through
whom he created the universe, / who is the reful-
gence of his glory, the very imprint of his being, /
and who sustains all things by his mighty word. /
When he had accomplished purification from
sins, / he took his seat at the right hand of the
Majesty on high, / as far superior to the angels / as
the name he has inherited is more excellent
than theirs.
For to which of the angels did God ever say:
　　You are my son; this day I have begotten you?
Or again:
　　*I will be a father to him, and he shall be a son
　　　　to me?*
And again, when he leads the firstborn into the
world, he says:
　　Let all the angels of God worship him.

GOSPEL *John 1:1–18*

Shorter: John 1:1–5, 9–14

In the beginning was the Word, / and the Word
was with God, / and the Word was God. / He was
in the beginning with God. / All things came to
be through him, / and without him nothing came
to be. / What came to be through him was life, /
and this life was the light of the human race; / the
light shines in the darkness, / and the darkness
has not overcome it. / A man named John was sent
from God. He came for testimony, to testify to the
light, so that all might believe through him. He
was not the light, but came to testify to the light.
The true light, which enlightens everyone, was
coming into the world. / He was in the world, /
and the world came to be through him, / but the
world did not know him. / He came to what was
his own, / but his own people did not accept him.

　　But to those who did accept him he gave
power to become children of God, to those who
believe in his name, who were born not by natural
generation nor by human choice nor by a man's

decision but of God. / And the Word became flesh / and made his dwelling among us, / and we saw his glory, / the glory as of the Father's only Son, / full of grace and truth. / John testified to him and cried out, saying, "This was he of whom I said, 'The one who is coming after me ranks ahead of me because he existed before me.'" From his fullness we have all received, grace in place of grace, because while the law was given through Moses, grace and truth came through Jesus Christ. No one has ever seen God. The only Son, God, who is at the Father's side, has revealed him.

Practice of Hope

On this day, we honor a child who came into the world in the midst of chaos. This baby is the One who gives us hope now as we encounter loneliness, despair, or discouragement. We remember our Creator's human gift for us as we gather at the Lord's table in churches around the world. We are humbled both by this gift of life and that we are counted worthy to share at his feast. ◆ Rather than wrapping another physical present for family members, gift them with your presence through an experience that you can do together. Or consider a creative activity you can do as a clan after attending Mass. Your celebration of togetherness will reinforce God's celebration of you. ◆ Be sure to invite or call distant relatives who struggle with the holidays. ◆ Remember those who might be suffering from seasonal depression or who have lost a loved one during the past year.

Download more questions and activities for families, Christian initiation groups, and other adult groups at http://www.ltp.org/ahw.

Scripture Insights

The arrival of the long-awaited messiah comes to pass in today's celebration of the Nativity of the Lord. The prophet Isaiah affirms that this good news, *evangelion*, is the proclamation of a king, avowing this news to be joyous, peaceful, and salvific. The victorious plan of God, the psalmist proclaims, is grounded in merciful faithfulness, manifest in joy, and assessed with justice and fairness.

Hebrews presents the gift of the Son as the gift of the new covenant. The atoning sacrifice of the Son will account for how we have turned away from God. The Son sustains all things in creation through the model of his sacrifice, which presents a path of interrelationship that recognizes the need for mutual indwelling between creation and humankind, a relationship so crucial for our future.

The Prologue to the Gospel of John punctuates these traditional hopes and needs. The profundity of these opening verses cannot be overstated. John begins by reenvisioning the Genesis creation narrative and concludes with an exposition of Jesus, the Christ and Son of God, and his mission to make God known in history. The crux is that the Word of God become flesh in the person of Jesus the Christ and Son is the gift of truth. This gift empowers those who receive and believe in him to become children of God. The mission of the Son of God in the human Christ Jesus is to make this new covenantal relationship possible. This gift to all humankind begins in the Lord's nativity.

◆ Ponder God's plan for covenantal relationship with all humankind through the atoning sacrifice of his Son. What sacrifices might you be called to make?

◆ Consider the interrelationship among God, creation, and humankind. How can you step up your role in this relationship during this new year?

◆ Reflect on the poetic beauty of John's Gospel Prologue. The incarnation of the Word of God has finally come to pass in the nativity.

READING I *1 Samuel 1:20–22, 24–28*

Alternate reading: Sirach 3:2–6, 12–14

In those days Hannah conceived, and at the end of her term bore a son whom she called Samuel, since she had asked the LORD for him. The next time her husband Elkanah was going up with the rest of his household to offer the customary sacrifice to the LORD and to fulfill his vows, Hannah did not go, explaining to her husband, "Once the child is weaned, I will take him to appear before the LORD and to remain there forever; I will offer him as a perpetual nazirite."

Once Samuel was weaned, Hannah brought him up with her, along with a three-year-old bull, an ephah of flour, and a skin of wine, and presented him at the temple of the LORD in Shiloh. After the boy's father had sacrificed the young bull, Hannah, his mother, approached Eli and said: "Pardon, my lord! As you live, my lord, I am the woman who stood near you here, praying to the LORD. I prayed for this child, and the LORD granted my request. Now I, in turn, give him to the LORD; as long as he lives, he shall be dedicated to the LORD." Hannah left Samuel there.

RESPONSORIAL PSALM
Psalm 84:2–3, 5–6, 9–10 (see 5a)

Alternate Psalm: Psalm 128:1–2, 3, 4–5 (see 1)

R. Blessed are they who dwell in your house,
　　O Lord.

How lovely is your dwelling place,
　　O LORD of hosts!
　My soul yearns and pines for the courts
　　　of the LORD.
My heart and my flesh cry out for the
　　living God.　R.

Happy they who dwell in your house!
　　Continually they praise you.
Happy the men whose strength you are!
　　Their hearts are set upon the pilgrimage.　R.

O LORD of hosts, hear our prayer;
　　hearken, O God of Jacob!
O God, behold our shield,
　　and look upon the face of your anointed.　R.

READING II *1 John 3:1–2, 21–24*

Alternate reading: Colossians 3:12–21 or 3:12–17

Beloved: See what love the Father has bestowed on us that we may be called the children of God. And so we are. The reason the world does not know us is that it did not know him. Beloved, we are God's children now; what we shall be has not yet been revealed. We do know that when it is revealed we shall be like him, for we shall see him as he is.

Beloved, if our hearts do not condemn us, we have confidence in God and receive from him whatever we ask, because we keep his commandments and do what pleases him. And his commandment is this: we should believe in the name of his Son, Jesus Christ, and love one another just as he commanded us. Those who keep his commandments remain in him, and he in them, and the way we know that he remains in us is from the Spirit he gave us.

GOSPEL *Luke 2:41–52*

Each year Jesus' parents went to Jerusalem for the feast of Passover, and when he was twelve years old, they went up according to festival custom. After they had completed its days, as they were returning, the boy Jesus remained behind in Jerusalem, but his parents did not know it. Thinking that he was in the caravan, they journeyed for a day and looked for him among their relatives and acquaintances, but not finding him, they returned to Jerusalem to look for him. After three days they found him in the temple, sitting in the midst of the teachers, listening to them and asking them questions, and all who heard him were astounded at his understanding and his answers. When his parents saw him, they were astonished, and his mother said to him, "Son, why have you done this to us? Your father and I have been looking for you with great anxiety." And he said to them, "Why were you looking for me? Did you not know that I must be in my Father's house?" But they did not understand what he said to them. He went down with them and came to Nazareth, and was obedient to them; and his mother kept all these things in her heart. And Jesus advanced in wisdom and age and favor before God and man.

Practice of Charity

Families may be blended, combined, separated, and fractured in our time. Today's Gospel refers to the Holy Family's road trip or pilgrimage to Jerusalem for the Passover, but something goes terribly wrong. There's nothing worse than a lost child; we can feel the parents' anguish. While Mary and Joseph were agonizing over their lost son, Jesus confounded teachers in the temple with his questions and answers. Later, Jesus answered his mother in a manner that perplexed her. ✦ Reflect about times when you have felt lost or confused. How did your life unfold? Pray about those times when God led you through anguish and doubt to a place of safety. Give thanks for any insight that you received. ✦ Do something comforting for someone who feels lost in life. ✦ Consider inviting a struggling friend or parishioner to join your home meal. Talk about memories or topics that bring you both joy.

Download more questions and activities for families, Christian initiation groups, and other adult groups at http://www.ltp.org/ahw.

Scripture Insights

Today's Feast of the Holy Family highlights the importance of family, both in imagery and in history, for understanding God's relationship with humankind. The readings begin in First Samuel with Hannah expressing her thankfulness for God's response to her open petition. She remains faithful to her promise and returns the gift of her child Samuel in consecration to God. Samuel, in turn, becomes one of God's key prophetic spokespeople. Together they present a unique model of family.

The psalmist expounds on this concept of home and family made possible for God's people through the gift of God's anointed one. John's first letter continues this summons to new familial relationships in terms of "the children God" (3:1) by reminding readers of the fourth Gospel's foundational commandments for the new covenant put in place through God's timeless gift. "We," potential children of all time, "should believe in the name of his Son, Jesus Christ, and love one another just as he commanded us" (3:23). This is our gift, our right, and our challenge, now in a world that demands far more structure and compliance than the biblical author envisions.

Luke's Gospel focuses on the one episode Scripture preserves of Jesus' childhood, narrated here in obedience to his calling from his true Father. Jesus was drawn to those from whom he could learn and grow, though it caused concern for his family. Sometimes such hunches take us outside our boxes, as well as those of our family and of our society. This may lead us to the path of finding authentic relationship with God, and thereby broadening our understanding of family and what it means to be a child of God.

✦ How does Hannah's interaction with God, Elkanah, Eli, and, finally, Samuel serve as a model for our relationships?

✦ Consider your family, biological, spiritual, and otherwise chosen. How might you give thanks for them in the coming year?

✦ Reflect on how the dawning Christmas season calls each of us to expand our concept of "family" and challenge the concept of what it means to be "children of God."

READING I *Isaiah 60:1–6*

Rise up in splendor, Jerusalem! Your light
        has come,
    the glory of the Lord shines upon you.
See, darkness covers the earth,
    and thick clouds cover the peoples;
but upon you the LORD shines,
    and over you appears his glory.
Nations shall walk by your light,
    and kings by your shining radiance.
Raise your eyes and look about;
    they all gather and come to you:
your sons come from afar,
    and your daughters in the arms of their nurses.

Then you shall be radiant at what you see,
    your heart shall throb and overflow,
for the riches of the sea shall be emptied out
        before you,
    the wealth of nations shall be brought to you.
Caravans of camels shall fill you,
    dromedaries from Midian and Ephah;
all from Sheba shall come
    bearing gold and frankincense,
    and proclaiming the praises of the LORD.

RESPONSORIAL PSALM *Psalm 72:1–2, 7–8, 10–11, 12–13 (see 11)*

R. Lord, every nation on earth will adore you.

O God, with your judgment endow the king,
    and with your justice the king's son;
he shall govern your people with justice
    and your afflicted ones with judgment. R.

Justice shall flower in his days,
    and profound peace, till the moon be no more.
May he rule from sea to sea,
    and from the River to the ends of
        the earth. R.

The kings of Tarshish and the Isles shall offer gifts;
    the kings of Arabia and Seba shall
        bring tribute.
All kings shall pay him homage,
    all nations shall serve him. R.

For he shall rescue the poor when he cries out,
    and the afflicted when he has no one to
        help him.
He shall have pity for the lowly and the poor;
    the lives of the poor he shall save. R.

READING II *Ephesians 3:2–3a, 5–6*

Brothers and sisters: You have heard of the stewardship of God's grace that was given to me for your benefit, namely, that the mystery was made known to me by revelation. It was not made known to people in other generations as it has now been revealed to his holy apostles and prophets by the Spirit: that the Gentiles are coheirs, members of the same body, and copartners in the promise in Christ Jesus through the gospel.

GOSPEL *Matthew 2:1–12*

When Jesus was born in Bethlehem of Judea, in the days of King Herod, behold, magi from the east arrived in Jerusalem, saying, "Where is the newborn king of the Jews? We saw his star at its rising and have come to do him homage." When King Herod heard this, he was greatly troubled, and all Jerusalem with him. Assembling all the chief priests and the scribes of the people, he inquired of them where the Christ was to be born. They said to him, "In Bethlehem of Judea, for thus it has been written through the prophet:

And you, Bethlehem, land of Judah, / are by no means least among the rulers of Judah; / since from you shall come a ruler, / who is to shepherd my people Israel."

Then Herod called the magi secretly and ascertained from them the time of the star's appearance. He sent them to Bethlehem and said, "Go and search diligently for the child. When you have found him, bring me word, that I too may go and do him homage." After their audience with the king they set out. And behold, the star that they had seen at its rising preceded them, until it came and stopped over the place where the child was. They were overjoyed at seeing the star, and on entering the house they saw the child with Mary his mother. They prostrated themselves and did him homage. Then they opened their treasures and offered him gifts of gold, frankincense, and myrrh. And having been warned in a dream not to return to Herod, they departed for their country by another way.

Practice of Hope

Global positioning systems (GPS) have transformed the way that many people navigate. In today's Gospel, the Magi use the original GPS—God's star—to lead them to the Christ child. In our spiritual life, we can turn to the Word and Eucharist and a deepening prayer practice for the guidance that we need. Our close friends and family also can lead us through instability. ◆ Make a commitment to enhance your prayer life in this new year so that you feel led by God's Spirit rather than the chaos of the times. Perhaps this is the year that you try another prayer discipline, such as lectio divina. ◆ Consider becoming involved in one of your parish's liturgical ministries. ◆ Explore some small groups at your church that study Scripture or spiritual writers in order to meet others who also want to deepen their prayer life.

Download more questions and activities for families, Christian initiation groups, and other adult groups at http://www.ltp.org/ahw.

Scripture Insights

Our study and worship thus far has led us to the Epiphany of the Lord. The Greek *epiphaneia* means "manifestation" or "appearance" and indicates that we now commemorate God's gift of the Christ to all humankind in Jesus of Nazareth. The prophet Isaiah proclaims the light shining in the darkness of the world. Regardless of the dark challenges life in this world present, the radiance of God permeates all corners. The psalmist grounds this symbolic vision in the reality of the just and peaceful rule of God's Anointed One in history.

Paul's Letter to the Ephesians tells of God's stewardship of creation. Gentiles, coheirs of God's plan for the salvation of all humankind alongside their Jewish brethren, fully express the revelation of God through the grace of God's manifold wisdom. The true people of God are made up of all kinds, perfected in the eternal purpose accomplished in Christ Jesus our Lord. God can use any and all possibilities creation offers to reveal himself to those he calls for diverse purposes.

Matthew's Gospel tells of the Christ child, born in Bethlehem in the time of King Herod, who had a death wish for all potential claimants to his status and throne. After the Gentile wise men are profoundly affected by their encounter with the Christ child and his family, they make their own way in the world, defying the powers that be. The magi exemplify how God might call us to live his plan in this world despite our best-laid plans. Further, we all have leading roles in our stories, but we never know when we might be significant supporting actors in the lives of others.

◆ Reflect on the concept of "epiphany" and the multifaceted ways God can manifest in your life.

◆ Considering Paul's summons in his letter, how diverse are the people and purposes in your life? How might you broaden your openness to the wisdom and revelation of God?

◆ In what ways might God be calling you to defy the status quo—your own or society's? How could this benefit you and those around you?

READING I *Isaiah 40:1–5, 9–11*

Alternate reading: Isaiah 42:1–4, 6–7

Comfort, give comfort to my people,
    says your God.
Speak tenderly to Jerusalem, and proclaim
    to her
    that her service is at an end,
    her guilt is expiated;
indeed, she has received from the hand of
    the LORD
    double for all her sins.

A voice cries out:
In the desert prepare the way of the LORD!
    Make straight in the wasteland a highway
    for our God!
Every valley shall be filled in,
    every mountain and hill shall
    be made low;
the rugged land shall be made a plain,
    the rough country, a broad valley.
Then the glory of the LORD shall be revealed,
    and all people shall see it together;
    for the mouth of the LORD has spoken.

Go up onto a high mountain,
    Zion, herald of glad tidings;
cry out at the top of your voice,
    Jerusalem, herald of good news!
Fear not to cry out
    and say to the cities of Judah:
    Here is your God!
Here comes with power
    the Lord GOD,
    who rules by a strong arm;
here is his reward with him,
    his recompense before him.
Like a shepherd he feeds his flock;
    in his arms he gathers the lambs,
carrying them in his bosom,
    and leading the ewes with care.

RESPONSORIAL PSALM *Psalm 104:1b–2, 3–4, 24–25, 27–28, 29–30 (1)*

Alternate Psalm: Psalm 29:1–2, 3–4, 3, 9–10 (11b)

R. O bless the Lord, my soul.

O LORD, my God, you are great indeed!
    You are clothed with majesty and glory,
robed in light as with a cloak.
    You have spread out the heavens like
    a tent-cloth. R.

You have constructed your palace upon the waters.
    You make the clouds your chariot;
you travel on the wings of the wind.
    You make the winds your messengers,
and flaming fire your ministers. R.

How manifold are your works, O LORD!
    In wisdom you have wrought them all—
the earth is full of your creatures;
    the sea also, great and wide,
in which are schools without number
    of living things both small and great. R.

They look to you to give them food in due time.
    When you give it to them, they gather it;
when you open your hand, they are filled with
    good things. R.

If you take away their breath, they perish and
    return to the dust.
    When you send forth your spirit, they
    are created,
and you renew the face of the earth. R.

READING II *Titus 2:11–14; 3:4–7*

Alternate reading: Acts 10:34–38

Beloved: The grace of God has appeared, saving all and training us to reject godless ways and worldly desires and to live temperately, justly, and devoutly in this age, as we await the blessed hope, the appearance of the glory of our great God and savior Jesus Christ, who gave himself for us to deliver us from all lawlessness and to cleanse for himself a people as his own, eager to do what is good.

When the kindness and generous love
of God our savior appeared,
not because of any righteous deeds we had done
but because of his mercy,
he saved us through the bath of rebirth
and renewal by the Holy Spirit,
whom he richly poured out on us
through Jesus Christ our savior,
so that we might be justified by his grace
and become heirs in hope of eternal life.

GOSPEL *Luke 3:15–16, 21–22*

The people were filled with expectation, and all were asking in their hearts whether John might be the Christ. John answered them all, saying, "I am baptizing you with water, but one mightier than I is coming. I am not worthy to loosen the thongs of his sandals. He will baptize you with the Holy Spirit and fire."

After all the people had been baptized and Jesus also had been baptized and was praying, heaven was opened and the Holy Spirit descended upon him in bodily form like a dove. And a voice came from heaven, "You are my beloved Son; with you I am well pleased."

Practice of Hope

At Jesus' baptism, God showed his love in a dramatic way: "heaven was opened and the Holy Spirit descended upon him in bodily form like a dove. And a voice came from heaven, 'You are my beloved Son; with you I am well pleased.'" ◆ Today, we are affirmed as we live our baptismal call at home, community, work, or school. We just need to remind ourselves to look for these signs. ◆ Before going to sleep, gather your memories of the day to appreciate moments of God's presence. Be inspired by how our Creator delights in you. ◆ Send a note to a parent of a recently baptized child or to another adult who made the decision to be baptized. Affirm this person in his or her decision to follow Christ and/or to raise their child in the practice of the faith.

Download more questions and activities for families, Christian initiation groups, and other adult groups at http://www.ltp.org/ahw.

Scripture Insights

Today we celebrate the baptism of Jesus by John the Baptist. Thus far in Luke's Gospel, we have alternated between the births and coming of age of John and Jesus. Here we find that John's ministry has brought many to him and spread an eager hopefulness that he is the long-awaited messiah. John, however, is clear about his role and baptizing ministry as leading people to repentance to prepare the way for the one to come. He presents himself as the Isaian voice crying out in the wilderness proclaiming forgiveness, mercy, and the coming revelation of the glory of God.

In Isaiah's original context, the prophet proclaims the Word of God as the hope for return from exile and restoration of God's people to their land and union with God. The evangelists reenvision this hope in the person of John the Baptist, who prepares the people for restoration and reunion with God through the coming messiah. John's baptism of Jesus inaugurates the revelation of the glory of God as the Holy Spirit descends upon Jesus, who is affirmed as Son.

The letter to Titus characterizes this mission as God's great gift to humankind, given as a loving, Spirit-sharing Savior who leads us into righteousness through his life and sacrifice lived with and for us. Baptism into this mission is just the beginning.

◆ Notice how Scripture can be reinterpreted as new contexts allow for layers of meaning. How has your relationship with Scripture developed and changed over time?

◆ John points people away from himself and toward the one to come. Are you likewise able to check your ego in service to God's plan for you?

◆ Paul teaches that we are justified—put in right relationship with God—through God's grace so that we can live in love and hope. How does baptism reflect the beginning of this life?

Ordinary Time, Winter

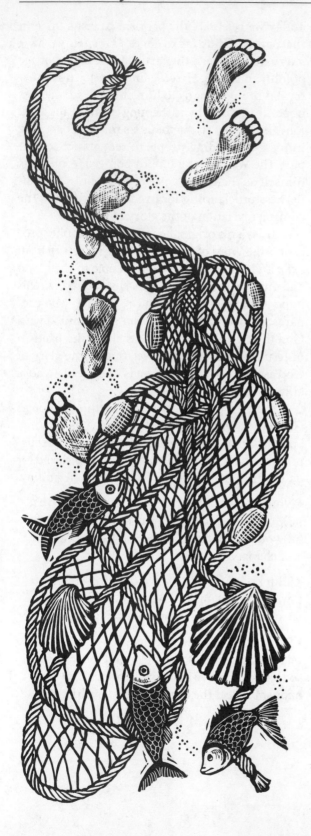

Prayer before Reading the Word

In you, O Lord our God,
we find our joy,
for through your Law and your Prophets
you formed a people in mercy and freedom,
in justice and righteousness.
You call us with your voice of flame.
Give us ears to hear,
lives to respond,
and voices to proclaim the Good News
       of salvation,
which we know in our Savior Jesus Christ,
who lives and reigns with you and the Holy Spirit,
God, now and forever. Amen.

Prayer after Reading the Word

In your Word, Lord God,
you reveal your power to heal and save us.
Let this Good News echo throughout the world,
in every tongue and in every culture,
so that people everywhere may gladly embrace
the salvation and life you offer to all.
Through our Lord Jesus Christ, your Son,
who lives and reigns with you
in the unity of the Holy Spirit,
God, for ever and ever. Amen.

Weekday Readings

January 10: *1 Samuel 1:1–8; Mark 1:14–20*
January 11: *1 Samuel 1:9–20; Mark 1:21–28*
January 12: *1 Samuel 3:1–10, 19–20; Mark 1:29–39*
January 13: *1 Samuel 4:1–11; Mark 1:40–45*
January 14: *1 Samuel 8:4–7, 10–22a; Mark 2:1–12*
January 15: *1 Samuel 9:1–4, 17–19; 10:1a; Murk 2:13–17*

January 17: *1 Samuel 15:16–23; Mark 2:18–22*
January 18: *1 Samuel 16:1–13; Mark 2:23–28*
January 19: *1 Samuel 17:32–33, 37, 40–51; Mark 3:1–6*
January 20: *1 Samuel 18:6–9; 19:1–7; Mark 3:7–12*
January 21: *1 Samuel 24:3–21; Mark 3:13–19*
January 22: *2 Samuel 1:1–4, 11–12, 19, 23–27; Mark 3:20–21*

January 24: *2 Samuel 5:1–7, 10; Mark 3:22–30*
**January 25: Feast of the Conversion
of St. Paul the Apostle
Acts 22:3–16 or Acts 9:1–22; Mark 16:15–18**
January 26: *2 Timothy 1:1–8 or Titus 1:1–5; Mark 4:1–20*
January 27: *2 Samuel 7:18–19, 24–29; Mark 4:21–25*
January 28: *2 Samuel 11:1–4a, 5–10a, 13–17; Mark 4:26–34*
January 29: *2 Samuel 12:1–7a, 10–17; Mark 4:35–41*

January 31: *2 Samuel 15:13–14, 30; 16:5–13; Mark 5:1–20*
February 1: *2 Samuel 18:9–10, 14b, 24–25a, 30—19:3;
Mark 5:21–43*
**February 2: Feast of the Presentation of the Lord
Malachi 3:1–4; Hebrews 2:14–18;
Luke 2:22–40 or 2:22–32**
February 3: *1 Kings 2:1–4, 10–12; Mark 6:7–13*
February 4: *Sirach 47:2–11; Mark 6:14–29*
February 5: *1 Kings 3:4–13; Mark 6:30–34*

February 7: *1 Kings 8:1–7, 9–13; Mark 6:53–56*
February 8: *1 Kings 8:22–23, 27–30; Mark 7:1–13*
February 9: *1 Kings 10:1–10; Mark 7:14–23*
February 10: *1 Kings 11:4–13; Mark 7:24–30*
February 11: *1 Kings 11:29–32; 12:19; Mark 7:31–37*
February 12: *1 Kings 12:26–32; 13:33–34; Mark 8:1–10*

February 14: *James 1:1–11; Mark 8:11–13*
February 15: *James 1:12–18; Mark 8:14–21*
February 16: *James 1:19–27; Mark 8:22–26*
February 17: *James 2:1–9; Mark 8:27–33*
February 18: *James 2:14–24, 26; Mark 8:34—9:1*
February 19: *James 3:1–10; Mark 9:2–13*

February 21: *James 3:13–18; Mark 9:14–29*
**February 22: Feast of the Chair of St. Peter the Apostle
1 Peter 5:1–4; Matthew 16:13–19**
February 23: *James 4:13–17; Mark 9:38–40*
February 24: *James 5:1–6; Mark 9:41–50*
February 25: *James 5:9–12; Mark 10:1–12*
February 26: *James 5:13–20; Mark 10:13–16*

February 28: *1 Peter 1:3–9; Mark 10:17–27*
March 1: *1 Peter 1:10–16; Mark 10:28–31*

Reading I *Isaiah 62:1–5*

For Zion's sake I will not be silent,
  for Jerusalem's sake I will not be quiet,
until her vindication shines forth like the dawn
  and her victory like a burning torch.

Nations shall behold your vindication,
  and all the kings your glory;
you shall be called by a new name
  pronounced by the mouth of the Lord.
You shall be a glorious crown in the hand
    of the Lord,
  a royal diadem held by your God.
No more shall people call you "Forsaken,"
  or your land "Desolate,"
but you shall be called "My Delight,"
  and your land "Espoused."
For the Lord delights in you
  and makes your land his spouse.
As a young man marries a virgin,
  your Builder shall marry you;
and as a bridegroom rejoices in his bride
  so shall your God rejoice in you.

Responsorial Psalm
Psalm 96:1–2, 2–3, 7–8, 9–10 (3)

R. Proclaim his marvelous deeds to all the nations.

Sing to the Lord a new song;
  sing to the Lord, all you lands.
Sing to the Lord; bless his name. R.

Announce his salvation, day after day.
Tell his glory among the nations;
  among all peoples, his wondrous deeds. R.

Give to the Lord, you families of nations,
  give to the Lord glory and praise;
  give to the Lord the glory due his name! R.

Worship the Lord in holy attire.
  Tremble before him, all the earth;
say among the nations: The Lord is king.
  He governs the peoples with equity. R.

Reading II *1 Corinthians 12:4–11*

Brothers and sisters: There are different kinds of spiritual gifts but the same Spirit; there are different forms of service but the same Lord; there are different workings but the same God who produces all of them in everyone. To each individual the manifestation of the Spirit is given for some benefit. To one is given through the Spirit the expression of wisdom; to another, the expression of knowledge according to the same Spirit; to another, faith by the same Spirit; to another, gifts of healing by the one Spirit; to another, mighty deeds; to another, prophecy; to another, discernment of spirits; to another, varieties of tongues; to another, interpretation of tongues. But one and the same Spirit produces all of these, distributing them individually to each person as he wishes.

Gospel *John 2:1–11*

There was a wedding at Cana in Galilee, and the mother of Jesus was there. Jesus and his disciples were also invited to the wedding. When the wine ran short, the mother of Jesus said to him, "They have no wine." And Jesus said to her, "Woman, how does your concern affect me? My hour has not yet come." His mother said to the servers, "Do whatever he tells you." Now there were six stone water jars there for Jewish ceremonial washings, each holding twenty to thirty gallons. Jesus told them, "Fill the jars with water." So they filled them to the brim. Then he told them, "Draw some out now and take it to the headwaiter." So they took it. And when the headwaiter tasted the water that had become wine, without knowing where it came from—although the servers who had drawn the water knew—, the headwaiter called the bridegroom and said to him, "Everyone serves good wine first, and then when people have drunk freely, an inferior one; but you have kept the good wine until now." Jesus did this as the beginning of his signs at Cana in Galilee and so revealed his glory, and his disciples began to believe in him.

Practice of Faith

When we are mindful of what Jesus wants us to do, we may find that miracles occur; we may just need to fill our stone jars with water. God will do the rest. That's our hope as we take steps, one by one, through this life. We need to trust and place ourselves in our Creator's care. The Gospel story about the wedding at Cana is filled with imagery that can enrich us as we place ourselves in that location. ♦ We can be astonished, just like that headwaiter in this Gospel, that God changes us as well when we do what Jesus asks. ♦ Savor this Scripture story and place yourself at the wedding in this time of prayer. Enjoy the abundance of Jesus' love for you. ♦ The next time that you participate at Mass where the Precious Blood is offered, be enriched by the miracle that takes place there as ordinary bread and wine are transformed into the Real Presence.

Download more questions and activities for families, Christian initiation groups, and other adult groups at http://www.ltp.org/ahw.

Scripture Insights

How interesting that the readings integrate Isaiah's marriage imagery with the inauguration of Jesus' ministry at a wedding feast and with Paul's articulation of the gifts of the Spirit. This image of a marriage feast summons further biblical images of the fullness of the messianic era signified by wine and abundance (see Amos 9:13–14; Hosea 2:19–24; 14:7; Isaiah 25:6–8; 54:4–8; 62:4–5; Jeremiah 2:2; 31:12).

The wedding at Cana captures the essence of Jesus' earthly ministry through stark dialogue and vivid imagery that foreshadow the hour of the glory of God. The framework is covenant, the nature of which manifests through believing in the word of Jesus and the revelation of God. The covenantal archetype is presented through the relationship between Jesus and his mother. As woman and mother, she further characterizes both this covenant and the vocation of believers once the hour arrives. She rises to his challenging words and activates them by integrating others.

As his ministry progresses, Jesus upholds the woman as a model (John 16:21). Further, when he approaches and interacts with those he calls "woman," the covenant with this first woman is recalled. When Jesus says to the Samaritan at the well, "Believe me, woman, the hour is coming" (John 4:21), or to Mary of Magdala at the empty tomb, "Woman, why are you weeping? Whom are you looking for?" (John 20:15), we are reminded of the response of the woman who first believed without seeing signs or wonders, who believed foremost in the word of Jesus. Paul articulates this faithful courage as a gift of the Holy Spirit.

♦ Jesus challenges his mother to step up and proclaim her belief in the Word of God. How does Jesus' challenge resonate with you?

♦ How can we fortify our faith through relationship as John teaches in his narrative of Jesus and his mother at the wedding at Cana?

♦ How does the challenge to believe without seeing impact you on a daily basis? How might this be a gift of the Holy Spirit?

READING I *Nehemiah 8:2–4a, 5–6, 8–10*

Ezra the priest brought the law before the assembly, which consisted of men, women, and those children old enough to understand. Standing at one end of the open place that was before the Water Gate, he read out of the book from daybreak till midday, in the presence of the men, the women, and those children old enough to understand; and all the people listened attentively to the book of the law. Ezra the scribe stood on a wooden platform that had been made for the occasion. He opened the scroll so that all the people might see it—for he was standing higher up than any of the people—; and, as he opened it, all the people rose. Ezra blessed the LORD, the great God, and all the people, their hands raised high, answered, "Amen, amen!" Then they bowed down and prostrated themselves before the LORD, their faces to the ground. Ezra read plainly from the book of the law of God, interpreting it so that all could understand what was read. Then Nehemiah, that is, His Excellency, and Ezra the priest-scribe and the Levites who were instructing the people said to all the people: "Today is holy to the LORD your God. Do not be sad, and do not weep"—for all the people were weeping as they heard the words of the law. He said further: "Go, eat rich foods and drink sweet drinks, and allot portions to those who had nothing prepared; for today is holy to our LORD. Do not be saddened this day, for rejoicing in the LORD must be your strength!"

RESPONSORIAL PSALM *Psalm 19:8, 9, 10, 15 (see John 6:63c)*

R. Your words, Lord, are Spirit and life.

The law of the LORD is perfect,
  refreshing the soul;
the decree of the LORD is trustworthy,
  giving wisdom to the simple. R.

The precepts of the LORD are right,
  rejoicing the heart;
the command of the LORD is clear,
  enlightening the eye. R.

The fear of the LORD is pure,
  enduring forever;
the ordinances of the LORD are true,
  all of them just. R.

Let the words of my mouth and the thought
    of my heart
  find favor before you,
O LORD, my rock and my redeemer. R.

READING II *1 Corinthians 12:12–14, 27*

Longer: 1 Corinthians 12:12–30

Brothers and sisters: As a body is one though it has many parts, and all the parts of the body, though many, are one body, so also Christ. For in one Spirit we were all baptized into one body, whether Jews or Greeks, slaves or free persons, and we were all given to drink of one Spirit. Now the body is not a single part, but many. You are Christ's body, and individually parts of it.

GOSPEL *Luke 1:1–4; 4:14–21*

Since many have undertaken to compile a narrative of the events that have been fulfilled among us, just as those who were eyewitnesses from the beginning and ministers of the word have handed them down to us, I too have decided, after investigating everything accurately anew, to write it down in an orderly sequence for you, most excellent Theophilus, so that you may realize the certainty of the teachings you have received.

Jesus returned to Galilee in the power of the Spirit, and news of him spread throughout the whole region. He taught in their synagogues and was praised by all.

He came to Nazareth, where he had grown up, and went according to his custom into the synagogue on the sabbath day. He stood up to read and was handed a scroll of the prophet Isaiah. He unrolled the scroll and found the passage where it was written:

The Spirit of the Lord is upon me, / because he has anointed me / to bring glad tidings to the poor. / He has sent me to proclaim liberty to captives / and recovery of sight to the blind, / to let the oppressed go free, / and to proclaim a year acceptable to the Lord.

Rolling up the scroll, he handed it back to the attendant and sat down, and the eyes of all in the synagogue looked intently at him. He said to them, "Today this Scripture passage is fulfilled in your hearing."

Practice of Hope

When taking in important news today, we trust reliable sources of information. In Jesus' time, we can only imagine the puzzled looks of those in the synagogue as they heard Jesus read from the sacred scroll and say, "Today this Scripture passage is fulfilled in your hearing." As we listen to this Gospel proclaimed at Mass or savor it during our prayer time, we can be assured that God is the source, telling us that Jesus will help us when we feel blind, bound, poor in spirit, or chained to darkness and negativity. We can remember that hope emerged when our Savior was born and that God is with us always through the Spirit. ◆ Although we have stored away Christmas decorations and reminders of the holiday season, we can still marvel at the peace we feel knowing that Jesus was among us on earth to give us a guiding light. ◆ Help someone in your family or parish who might be experiencing depression this winter. Give them care when they feel desperate and alone.

Download more questions and activities for families, Christian initiation groups, and other adult groups at http://www.ltp.org/ahw.

Scripture Insights

The Books of Ezra and Nehemiah recount the end of the Babylonian Exile and the return and restoration of the land following the Edict of Cyrus in 538 BC. Nehemiah 8 records that during the feast of Tabernacles, Ezra read a book of the law (Torah) to all Jerusalem. This could be the first reading of the first five books of the Bible as we now have them. The restoration of the exiled people of Judah to their land culminates in the momentous event of rededicating themselves to the Sinai covenant as the chosen people of God.

Luke's Gospel begins with a dedication. He is following a Greco-Roman convention that places his story to come in the larger context of the tradition and gives its purpose. Luke's "orderly" account narrates the beginning of Jesus' ministry that was full of success and praise, leading to his return to his hometown synagogue in Nazareth. On the sabbath, he reads from the prophet Isaiah about being anointed by God to share good news with the poor. He culminates this passionate intensity with the proclamation that all of this has been fulfilled in him.

The Word of God is timeless. It transcends generations and surpasses attempts to suppress or contain it. Jesus teaches that, as Messiah, he is anointed by God to embody God's Word and bring it into the lived experience of believers. Paul extends this teaching to us, as the Body of Christ. Our task is to find our gifts and vocations in this body. The good news is that there is, indeed, a vocation for each one of us.

◆ The early biblical books, the Torah in Hebrew, present a guide to living in right relationship with God for ancient Jews. What value might this dedication have for Christians today?

◆ Jesus challenges his compatriots to accept God working in him as they have in the past. How do you see Christ working in your world now as he did in the New Testament?

◆ Reflect on your role in the Body of Christ. How might you contribute in your own way?

READING I *Jeremiah 1:4–5, 17–19*

The word of the LORD came to me, saying:
Before I formed you in the womb I knew you,
before you were born I dedicated you,
a prophet to the nations I appointed you.

But do you gird your loins;
stand up and tell them
all that I command you.
Be not crushed on their account,
as though I would leave you crushed
before them;
for it is I this day
who have made you a fortified city,
a pillar of iron, a wall of brass,
against the whole land:
against Judah's kings and princes,
against its priests and people.
They will fight against you but not prevail
over you,
for I am with you to deliver you, says the LORD.

RESPONSORIAL PSALM *Psalm 71:1–2, 3–4, 5–6, 15, 17 (see 15ab)*

R. I will sing of your salvation.

In you, O LORD, I take refuge;
let me never be put to shame.
In your justice rescue me, and deliver me;
incline your ear to me, and save me.   R.

Be my rock of refuge,
a stronghold to give me safety,
for you are my rock and my fortress.
O my God, rescue me from the hand of
the wicked.   R.

For you are my hope, O Lord;
my trust, O God, from my youth.
On you I depend from birth;
from my mother's womb you are
my strength.   R.

My mouth shall declare your justice,
day by day your salvation.
O God, you have taught me from my youth,
and till the present I proclaim your
wondrous deeds.   R.

READING II *1 Corinthians 12:31—13:13*

Shorter: 1 Corinthians 13:4–13

Brothers and sisters: Strive eagerly for the greatest spiritual gifts. But I shall show you a still more excellent way.

If I speak in human and angelic tongues, but do not have love, I am a resounding gong or a clashing cymbal. And if I have the gift of prophecy, and comprehend all mysteries and all knowledge; if I have all faith so as to move mountains, but do not have love, I am nothing. If I give away everything I own, and if I hand my body over so that I may boast, but do not have love, I gain nothing.

Love is patient, love is kind. It is not jealous, it is not pompous, it is not inflated, it is not rude, it does not seek its own interests, it is not quick-tempered, it does not brood over injury, it does not rejoice over wrongdoing but rejoices with the truth. It bears all things, believes all things, hopes all things, endures all things.

Love never fails. If there are prophecies, they will be brought to nothing; if tongues, they will cease; if knowledge, it will be brought to nothing. For we know partially and we prophesy partially, but when the perfect comes, the partial will pass away. When I was a child, I used to talk as a child, think as a child, reason as a child; when I became a man, I put aside childish things. At present we see indistinctly, as in a mirror, but then face to face. At present I know partially; then I shall know fully, as I am fully known. So faith, hope, love remain, these three; but the greatest of these is love.

GOSPEL *Luke 4:21–30*

Jesus began speaking in the synagogue, saying: "Today this Scripture passage is fulfilled in your hearing." And all spoke highly of him and were amazed at the gracious words that came from his mouth. They also asked, "Isn't this the son of Joseph?" He said to them, "Surely you will quote me this proverb, 'Physician, cure yourself,' and say, 'Do here in your native place the things that we heard were done in Capernaum.'" And he said, "Amen, I say to you, no prophet is accepted in his own native place. Indeed, I tell you, there were many widows in Israel in the days of Elijah when the sky was closed for three and a half years and a severe famine spread over the entire land. It was to none of these that Elijah was sent, but only to a widow in Zarephath in the land of Sidon. Again, there were many lepers in Israel during the time of Elisha the prophet; yet not one of them was cleansed, but only Naaman the Syrian." When the people in the synagogue heard this, they were all filled with fury. They rose up, drove him out of the town, and led him to the brow of the hill on which their town had been built, to hurl him down headlong. But Jesus passed through the midst of them and went away.

Practice of Charity

The prophet Jeremiah points out that each of us is precious and that we have a purpose in this world. No matter the obstacle, God will deliver us. Jesus was protected when thrown out of the synagogue. God will be with us too. ◆ Write or call civic leaders if legislation under consideration would be harmful to others. Consider becoming more active about resolving issues that negatively impact the most vulnerable in your community. ◆ Discern how your personal gifts and talents can advance some positive initiatives in your parish, school, workplace, or neighborhood. ◆ Discover how your abilities can inspire others to get involved. Perhaps your parish is championing an effort to assist the homeless or protect the unborn. If there's an initiative that you would like to explore with other parish team members, start gathering information and resources.

Download more questions and activities for families, Christian initiation groups, and other adult groups at http://www.ltp.org/ahw.

Scripture Insights

Today's readings speak to the vocation of the prophet. In contemporary speech, a "prophet" is often identified with a future seer, a "fortune teller." This, however, is not the case in the biblical tradition. The Greek *prophetes* means to "speak for." A true prophet, therefore, is one who speaks for God. Prophets are mediators between God and humankind, a calling that encompasses great glory but also intense suffering.

Jeremiah, our model of the reluctant prophet who suffers for his vocation, is no less staunch in sharing God's Word. He embodies the Lord's strength and fortitude. The apostle Paul characterizes prophecy as a spiritual gift. He grounds every gift of the Holy Spirit in love. Sharpening and implementing such gifts must be, not in pursuit of selfish ambition, but for the good of all. In our time, we often meditate on Paul's hymn to love in the context of romantic engagement, but in his original context, Paul is concerned with the proper foundation of our inspiration and work in the community: faith, hope, and love. If love, steadfast and true, is the crux of our embodiment of the gifts of the Spirit, then they—and we—are properly oriented to the other and the good of all.

Jesus, as he embodies the Word of God professed by Isaiah, becomes a prophet in his own right as he challenges his audience's comfortable notions of being "chosen." He reminds them that God has traditionally looked beyond expectations and the status quo to work his will and implement his plan. Our challenge, likewise, is to be open to the very God in whom we profess to believe, the God who works in anyone, regardless of race, ethnicity, gender, custom, or convention.

◆ Are you open to God's call, no matter the form it might take? What steps could invigorate the openness to which God calls you?

◆ Reflect on the reading from Jeremiah. How has God called you to something more?

◆ How have you considered Paul's hymn to love in 1 Corinthians 13 in the past? How does its integration in today's readings impact your understanding?

READING I *Isaiah 6:1–2a, 3–8*

In the year King Uzziah died, I saw the Lord seated on a high and lofty throne, with the train of his garment filling the temple. Seraphim were stationed above.

They cried one to the other, "Holy, holy, holy is the LORD of hosts! All the earth is filled with his glory!" At the sound of that cry, the frame of the door shook and the house was filled with smoke.

Then I said, "Woe is me, I am doomed! For I am a man of unclean lips, living among a people of unclean lips; yet my eyes have seen the King, the LORD of hosts!" Then one of the seraphim flew to me, holding an ember that he had taken with tongs from the altar.

He touched my mouth with it, and said, "See, now that this has touched your lips, your wickedness is removed, your sin purged."

Then I heard the voice of the Lord saying, "Whom shall I send? Who will go for us?" "Here I am," I said; "send me!"

RESPONSORIAL PSALM
Psalm 138:1–2, 2–3, 4–5, 7–8 (1c)

R. In the sight of the angels I will sing your
       praises, Lord.

I will give thanks to you, O LORD, with all
           my heart,
    for you have heard the words of my mouth;
    in the presence of the angels I will sing
           your praise;
I will worship at your holy temple
    and give thanks to your name. R.

Because of your kindness and your truth;
    for you have made great above all things
    your name and your promise.
When I called, you answered me;
    you built up strength within me. R.

All the kings of the earth shall give thanks to
           you, O LORD,
    when they hear the words of your mouth;
and they shall sing of the ways of the LORD:
    "Great is the glory of the LORD." R.

Your right hand saves me.
    The LORD will complete what he has done
           for me;
your kindness, O LORD, endures forever;
    forsake not the work of your hands. R.

READING II *1 Corinthians 15:1–11*

Shorter: 1 Corinthians 15:3–8, 11

I am reminding you, brothers and sisters, of the gospel I preached to you, which you indeed received and in which you also stand. Through it you are also being saved, if you hold fast to the word I preached to you, unless you believed in vain. For I handed on to you as of first importance what I also received: that Christ died for our sins in accordance with the Scriptures; that he was buried; that he was raised on the third day in accordance with the Scriptures; that he appeared to Cephas, then to the Twelve. After that, he appeared to more than five hundred brothers at once, most of whom are still living, though some have fallen asleep. After that he appeared to James, then to all the apostles. Last of all, as to one born abnormally, he appeared to me. For I am the least of the apostles, not fit to be called an apostle, because I persecuted the church of God. But by the grace of God I am what I am, and his grace to me has not been ineffective. Indeed, I have toiled harder than all of them; not I, however, but the grace of God that is with me. Therefore, whether it be I or they, so we preach and so you believed.

GOSPEL *Luke 5:1–11*

While the crowd was pressing in on Jesus and listening to the word of God, he was standing by the Lake of Gennesaret. He saw two boats there alongside the lake; the fishermen had disembarked and were washing their nets. Getting into one of the boats, the one belonging to Simon, he asked him to put out a short distance from the shore. Then he sat down and taught the crowds from the boat. After he had finished speaking, he said to Simon, "Put out into deep water and lower your nets for a catch." Simon said in reply, "Master, we have worked hard all night and have caught nothing, but at your command I will lower the nets." When they had done this, they caught a great number of fish and their nets were tearing. They signaled to their partners in the other boat to come to help them. They came and filled both boats so that the boats were in danger of sinking. When Simon Peter saw this, he fell at the knees of Jesus and said, "Depart from me, Lord, for I am a sinful man." For astonishment at the catch of fish they had made seized him and all those with him, and likewise James and John, the sons of Zebedee, who were partners of Simon. Jesus said to Simon, "Do not be afraid; from now on you will be catching men." When they brought their boats to the shore, they left everything and followed him.

Practice of Hope

Miracles happen all the time; with the right perspective, miracles are found everywhere. Just think about our human bodies with its myriad cells, ligaments, bones, joints, and organs and how they work independently and in concert with the others. It's amazing that each of us began as two cells colliding, growing, and morphing into the extraordinary wonders that we are. ◆ In today's Gospel, Jesus asks his friends to try a different perspective and to be more persistent. He tells them to fish again and they reluctantly do, but they are astounded when the catch almost tears their nets. This story and the miracles that happen in our midst can inspire us. ◆ Think of a goal or activity with which you struggle, and brainstorm about alternative approaches to ensure its success. Pray about this process for further direction. ◆ Help someone in your family with a new skill or hobby. Encourage them as they try positive activities.

Download more questions and activities for families, Christian initiation groups, and other adult groups at http://www.ltp.org/ahw.

Scripture Insights

Today's readings are crucial for understanding the good news of the Christ event. We begin with Isaiah's vision of God's throne room that results in his call to be God's spokesperson. We move to the psalmist's unwavering faith in God who protects him even when he speaks uncomfortable truth to power. This leads to Luke's narration of the call of the first disciples and Paul's primal creed of the good news.

Unlike our disinclined Jeremiah from last week, Isaiah calls out, "Here I am . . . send me!" He becomes the model for future prophets and disciples. Jesus, in Luke's Gospel, is teaching by the sea and revealing the Word of God. In the midst of manifesting God's prophetic activity, he encounters those who will be his disciples. Simon Peter, James, and John all enter into relationship with Jesus based on his word and deed. They eventually become prophets and apostles in their own rights, but now they are just beginning.

In his First Letter to the Corinthians, Paul recounts the next steps of the revelation of the glory of God. Responding to questions about the reality of the resurrection of the dead with what amounts to the earliest proclamation of the full Gospel, Paul writes to his Corinthian churches in the mid-50s. He affirms the tradition he received and now shares: Jesus, who is God's Anointed One, the Christ, died for the sins of humankind. That this sacrifice atoned for the sins of humankind is manifest through his resurrection and encounters with Peter (Cephas in Aramaic), the inner circle, then James and all commissioned with the Word. Paul recounts this good news in defense of his apostleship so that he can teach further, but his teaching transcends its original context to instruct believers of all times that the good news culminates in eternal union between God and humankind.

◆ In what unexpected ways have you felt called by God to discipleship and/or leadership?

◆ How does Paul's resurrection proclamation affect your understanding of the good news?

◆ Reflect on Luke's Gospel. What has inspired you to follow Christ?

READING I *Jeremiah 17:5–8*

Thus says the LORD:
Cursed is the one who trusts in human beings,
    who seeks his strength in flesh,
    whose heart turns away from the LORD.
He is like a barren bush in the desert
    that enjoys no change of season,
but stands in a lava waste,
    a salt and empty earth.
Blessed is the one who trusts in the LORD,
    whose hope is the LORD.
He is like a tree planted beside the waters
    that stretches out its roots to the stream:
It fears not the heat when it comes;
    its leaves stay green;
in the year of drought it shows no distress,
    but still bears fruit.

RESPONSORIAL PSALM
Psalm 1:1–2, 3, 4, 6 (40:5a)

R. Blessed are they who hope in the Lord.

Blessed the man who follows not
    the counsel of the wicked,
nor walks in the way of sinners,
    nor sits in the company of the insolent,
but delights in the law of the LORD
    and meditates on his law day and night.   R.

He is like a tree
    planted near running water,
that yields its fruit in due season,
    and whose leaves never fade.
Whatever he does, prospers.   R.

Not so the wicked, not so;
    they are like chaff which the wind
        drives away.
For the LORD watches over the way of the just,
    but the way of the wicked vanishes.   R.

READING II *1 Corinthians 15:12, 16–20*

Brothers and sisters: If Christ is preached as raised from the dead, how can some among you say there is no resurrection of the dead? If the dead are not raised, neither has Christ been raised, and if Christ has not been raised, your faith is vain; you are still in your sins. Then those who have fallen asleep in Christ have perished. If for this life only we have hoped in Christ, we are the most pitiable people of all.

But now Christ has been raised from the dead, the firstfruits of those who have fallen asleep.

GOSPEL *Luke 6:17, 20–26*

Jesus came down with the Twelve and stood on a stretch of level ground with a great crowd of his disciples and a large number of the people from all Judea and Jerusalem and the coastal region of Tyre and Sidon. And raising his eyes toward his disciples he said:
    "Blessed are you who are poor,
        for the kingdom of God is yours.
    Blessed are you who are now hungry,
        for you will be satisfied.
    Blessed are you who are now weeping,
        for you will laugh.
    Blessed are you when people hate you,
        and when they exclude and insult you,
        and denounce your name as evil
        on account of the Son of Man.

Rejoice and leap for joy on that day! Behold, your reward will be great in heaven. For their ancestors treated the prophets in the same way.

    But woe to you who are rich,
        for you have received your consolation.
    Woe to you who are filled now,
        for you will be hungry.
    Woe to you who laugh now,
        for you will grieve and weep.
    Woe to you when all speak well of you,
        for their ancestors treated
            the false prophets in this way."

Practice of Faith

In this Gospel's teachable moment, Jesus explains to the gathered that the next life will be a reversal of their suffering. To the poor, he promises abundance and ownership of a kingdom. To those who are hungry, desperate, and filled with sadness, he ensures nourishment and happiness. For people who do good because of their beliefs and suffer persecution, he promises great rewards and satisfaction. We too can remember these proclamations when faced with adversity and long-term suffering. ◆ Read several sections of the encyclical by Pope Francis, *On Care for Our Common Home* (*Laudato Si'*), which reminds us how greed and harmful environmental practices are impacting the world, particularly those of poor nations. ◆ Consider how you can advance Jesus' vision of God's kingdom here and now and how we can help alleviate suffering and the earth's destruction.

Download more questions and activities for families, Christian initiation groups, and other adult groups at http://www.ltp.org/ahw.

Scripture Insights

This Sunday's Old Testament readings present a strong—even harsh—opposition between putting our trust in God and in other people. Neither the prophet nor the psalmist, however, intend that we not seek relationship with those around us. At stake here are how we ground ourselves, understand our value, and find our truth. If we look to God, in whose image and likeness we are made, for our authority and authenticity, we will be able to turn outward in solidarity with others.

Luke's Gospel presents Jesus' teaching on the kingdom of God. What we find across these "blessings" and "woes" are reversals that challenge what society often dictates to be status or success. By contrast, Jesus teaches that those who live in humility and find their authentic selves in this life apart from social conventions—namely, in right relationship with God and others—will know true union with God, both in this life and in the next. The opposite, of course, is also true. If we seek affirmation and authenticity only in fleeting desires and satisfactions, we will have little foundation on which to stand in relationship to God.

Paul takes the next step by teaching that, on our behalf, Christ took on death and beat it. Further, this victory is only the firstfruits. Just as Christ died and was resurrected to eternal union with God, so shall all those who "belong" to Christ. Our hope must lie here. We are to live as if God is our king, and this process of believing and acting will bring about that kingdom. This, in turn, prepares the way for the eternal kingdom and living eternally in union with our Creator.

◆ What does it mean to you to ground your sense of self in God instead of in people or things?

◆ How do the blessings and woes of daily life affect your relationship with God? With others in your life? How might you find the balance to weather such storms more compassionately?

◆ In what ways do our actions, big and small, participate in bringing about the kingdom of God?

READING I
1 SAMUEL 26:2, 7–9, 12–13, 22–23

In those days, Saul went down to the desert of Ziph with three thousand picked men of Israel, to search for David in the desert of Ziph. So David and Abishai went among Saul's soldiers by night and found Saul lying asleep within the barricade, with his spear thrust into the ground at his head and Abner and his men sleeping around him.

Abishai whispered to David: "God has delivered your enemy into your grasp this day. Let me nail him to the ground with one throust on the spear; I will not need a second thrust!" But David said to Abishai, "Do not harm him, for who can lay hands on the LORD's anointed and remain unpunished?" So David took the spear and the water jug from their place at Saul's head, and they got awasy without anyone's seeing or knowing or awakening. All remained asleep, because the LORD had put them into a deep slumber.

Going across to an opposite slope, David stood on a remote hilltop at a great distance from Abner, son of Ner, and the troops.

He said: "Here is the king's spear. Let an attendant come over to get it. The LORD will reward each man for his justice and faithfulneess. Today, though the LORD delivered you into my grasp, I would not harm the LORD's anointed."

RESPONSORIAL PSALM
Psalm 103:1–2, 3–4, 8, 10, 12–13 (8a)

R. The Lord is kind and merciful.

Bless the LORD, O my soul;
   all my being, bless his holy name.
Bless the LORD, O my soul,
   forget not all his benefits. R.

He pardons all your iniquities,
   heals all your ills.
He redeems your life from destruction,
   crowns you with kindness
         and compassion. R.

Merciful and gracious is the LORD,
   slow to anger, and abounding in kindness.
Not according to our sins does he deal with us,
   nor does he requite us according to
         our crimes. R.

As far as the east is from the west,
   so far has he put our transgressions from us.
As a father has compassion on his children,
   so the LORD has compassion on those who
         fear him. R.

READING II *1 Corinthians 15:45–49*

Brothers and sisters: It is written, *The first man, Adam, became a living being*, the last Adam a life-giving spirit. But the spiritual was not first; rather the natural and then the spiritual. The first man was from the earth, earthly; the second man, from heaven. As was the earthly one, so also are the earthly, and as is the heavenly one, so also are the heavenly. Just as we have borne the image of the earthly one, we shall also bear the image of the heavenly one.

GOSPEL *Luke 6:27–38*

Jesus said to his disciples: "To you who hear I say, love your enemies, do good to those who hate you, bless those who curse you, pray for those who mistreat you. To the person who strikes you on one cheek, offer the other one as well, and from the person who takes your cloak, do not withold even your tunic. Give to everyone who asks of you, and from the one who takes what is yours do not demand it back. Do to others as you would have them do to you. For if you love those who love you, what credit is that to you? Even sinners love those who love them. And if you do good to those who do good to you, what credit is that to you? Even sinners do the same. If you lend money to those from whom you expect repayment, what credit is that to you? Even sinners lend to sinners and get back the same amount. But rather, love your enemies and do good to them, and lend expecting nothing back; then your reward will be great and you will be children of the Most High, for he himself is kind to the ungrateful and the wicked. Be merciful, just as your Father is merciful.

"Stop judging and you will not be judged. Stop condemning and you will not be condemned. Forgive and you will be forgiven. Give and gifts will be given to you; a good measure, packed together, shaken down, and overflowing will be poured into your lap. For the measure with which you measure will in return be measured out to you."

Practice of Hope

When we take in the news and see images of greed, illness, crime, and war, it is easy to feel disappointment and perhaps anger and some hopelessness. At times, it can be difficult to avoid discounting people or events that irritate us. Jesus reminds us in this Gospel that good solutions for everyone can begin with one individual. Each of us is responsible for resolving part of a problem. We are called to be countercultural. Jesus guides us to not judge or condemn others because we will be judged and condemned to the same degree. ♦ Pray about a person, event, or issue that oppresses you the most. Allow God to lead you to a different frame of mind or attitude. Perhaps over time, your stance will evolve and you will become more compassionate about the opposite view and the people who hold it. Ask God for solutions that could transform your heart. ♦ How are you challenged by Jesus' question, "If you love those who love you, what credit is that to you?"

Download more questions and activities for families, Christian initiation groups, and other adult groups at http://www.ltp.org/ahw.

Scripture Insights

Today's readings are, on the one hand, about the faithfulness and mercy of God and, on the other, about sin, atonement, and human interactivity. God, the psalmist declares, is "slow to anger, abounding in mercy" (103:8). Throughout history, God has consistently shown compassionate understanding, as a model Father to his children. The key here is the familial relationship that endures highs and lows, rights and wrongs. The biblical writings consistently characterize this relationship as one of covenant, a dynamic commitment of promises and obligations that, if allowed to do so, can grow and develop over time into an eternal union.

David shows his trust in God to thwart his opponents and to invoke justice. This trust brings about God's plan for David and all God's people. Jesus illustrates such trust in God as he summons us to "do to others as you would have them do to you" (Luke 6:31) despite what they may actually do. Jesus is not calling us to be doormats trod upon by all who might take advantage. By contrast, if we find our center and fundamental value in God and our creation in God's image and likeness, such pain can be properly situated. Our true selves will not be altered or hurt by them. We can make decisions, holding ourselves and others accountable and doing the right thing, all while remaining in right relationship with God through Christ and refusing vengeance or petty grievance.

Paul reflects theologically on this call to covenant relationship and just action. He articulates God's plan as it has been from the beginning. Humankind are of both nature and spirit. Paul challenges us to live the natural into the spiritual, to rise above the fray and be who God truly calls us to be.

♦ It can be so difficult to turn the other cheek. How can you find the line to walk between being taken advantage of and being merciful?

♦ In what ways does the psalmist's faith in God's justice inspire you to action?

♦ How can you find comfort in Paul's notion that all of this has been part of God's plan from the beginning?

READING I   *Sirach 27:4–7*

When a sieve is shaken, the husks appear;
    so do one's faults when one speaks.
As the test of what the potter molds is
        in the furnace,
    so in tribulation is the test of the just.
The fruit of a tree shows the care it has had;
    so too does one's speech disclose the bent
        of one's mind.
Praise no one before he speaks,
    for it is then that people are tested.

RESPONSORIAL PSALM
Psalm 92:2–3, 13–14, 15–16 (see 2a)

R. Lord, it is good to give thanks to you.

It is good to give thanks to the LORD,
    to sing praise to your name, Most High,
to proclaim your kindness at dawn
    and your faithfulness throughout
        the night.   R.

The just one shall flourish like the palm tree,
    like a cedar of Lebanon shall he grow.
They that are planted in the house of the LORD
    shall flourish in the courts of our God.   R.

They shall bear fruit even in old age;
    vigorous and sturdy shall they be,
declaring how just is the LORD,
    my rock, in whom there is no wrong.   R.

READING II   *1 Corinthians 15:54–58*

Brothers and sisters: When this which is corruptible clothes itself with incorruptibility and this which is mortal clothes itself with immortality, then the word that is written shall come about:

Death is swallowed up in victory.
Where, O death, is your victory?
Where, O death, is your sting?

The sting of death is sin, and the power of sin is the law. But thanks be to God who gives us the victory through our Lord Jesus Christ.

Therefore, my beloved brothers and sisters, be firm, steadfast, always fully devoted to the work of the Lord, knowing that in the Lord your labor is not in vain.

GOSPEL   *Luke 6:39–45*

Jesus told his disciples a parable, "Can a blind person guide a blind person? Will not both fall into a pit? No disciple is superior to the teacher; but when fully trained, every disciple will be like his teacher. Why do you notice the splinter in your brother's eye, but do not perceive the wooden beam in your own? How can you say to your brother, 'Brother, let me remove that splinter in your eye,' when you do not even notice the wooden beam in your own eye? You hypocrite! Remove the wooden beam from your eye first; then you will see clearly to remove the splinter in your brother's eye.

"A good tree does not bear rotten fruit, nor does a rotten tree bear good fruit. For every tree is known by its own fruit. For people do not pick figs from thornbushes, nor do they gather grapes from brambles. A good person out of the store of goodness in his heart produces good, but an evil person out of a store of evil produces evil; for from the fullness of the heart the mouth speaks."

Practice of Hope

Today's Gospel continues the directives not to judge. Jesus instructs his followers to look inside themselves as he queries, "Why do you notice the splinter in your brother's eye, but do not perceive the wooden beam in your own?" How many times have we been helped or supported by parents, coaches, or mentors who put aside their temptation to be exceedingly critical? And as we get wiser or more experienced, how can we pass along this same understanding, forgiveness, and love? It's tempting to revert to old behaviors when our prayer life lags or we feel disconnected from our spiritual practices. ◆ Make an effort to reach for an inspirational book or another resource when you find yourself judging others. ◆ Kickstart more positive behaviors in yourself or strive for a better attitude when you are feeling spiritually separate from your goal. ◆ As you approach Lent, consider the "wooden beam" in your eye and ask our Creator for help removing it.

Download more questions and activities for families, Christian initiation groups, and other adult groups at http://www.ltp.org/ahw.

Scripture Insights

The passage from Paul's First Letter to the Corinthians contains the heart of today's readings. Across the fifteenth chapter of this letter, Paul teaches the Gospel he has received (1 Corinthians 15:3), which leads him to take on the challenge that death poses to this good news. The one living by faith is invulnerable to the power death. He asks, "Where, O death, is your victory? / Where, O death, is your sting?" (15:55). He answers that it is found only in sin, for which Christ has atoned. Paul is, therefore, uncompromising that, through God's plan, Jesus Christ has taken on death and beat it. Christ's work is not the end of the plan. Paul instructs that we are continuously to take part in the relationship with God, "always fully devoted to the work of the Lord" (15:58).

Today's Gospel reading is from Luke's narration of Jesus' sermon on the plain and reads a lot like Jewish wisdom literature. Jesus presents a series of pithy quips of practical ways to participate in the work of the Lord. From these teachings, we question whether the blind (read: uninformed) can lead others, and we are challenged to self-reflection and discernment before we call out others' weaknesses. Jesus also assures us that fullness of heart must be the locus of our treatment of others.

Jesus calls on his Jewish scriptural tradition for such teachings, and the verses from Sirach punctuate this wisdom. In the biblical tradition, there is no more powerful challenge to think before speaking. Our speech, says Sirach, is the primary testament to our integrity and concern for justice.

◆ Jesus offers practical advice for living in right relationship with God and our fellow humans. How might you carry out his imperatives in your life?

◆ How might you live out Sirach's call to both right speaking and discerning the character of another by their speech on a daily basis?

◆ Paul teaches that we have hope that this life is not the end for the faithful. How might this hope be manifested?

Lent

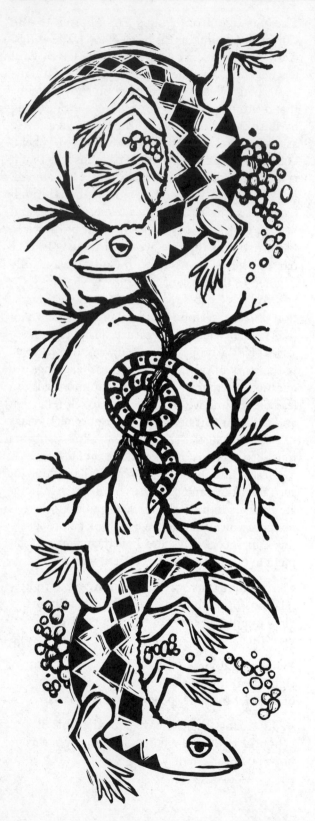

Prayer before Reading the Word

O Lord, great and faithful God,
it is good for us to be here!
Let us listen to your Son, your chosen One.

Shatter the hardness of our hearts
and open our minds to the wisdom of the Gospel,
that we may grasp the lessons you teach us daily
and bring forth the fruit of true
and continual conversion.

We ask this through the One
into whom we have been baptized,
our Lord Jesus Christ, your Son,
who lives and reigns with you
in the unity of the Holy Spirit,
God, for ever and ever. Amen.

Prayer after Reading the Word

Infinite is your compassion, O God,
and gracious the pardon
that Jesus, the Teacher, offers
to every sinner who stands before him.

Gladden our hearts
at the Word that sends us on our way in peace;
and grant that we who have been found
    by your grace
may gladly welcome to the table of your family
all who long to find their way home.

Through Christ,
our peace and reconciliation,
the Lord who lives and reigns with you
in the unity of the Holy Spirit,
God, for ever and ever. Amen.

Weekday Readings

March 2: Ash Wednesday
Joel 2:12–18; 2 Corinthians 5:20—6:2;
Matthew 6:1–6, 16–18
March 3: *Deuteronomy 30:15–20; Luke 9:22–25*
March 4: *Isaiah 58:1–9a; Matthew 9:14–15*
March 5: *Isaiah 58:9b–14; Luke 5:27–32*

March 7: *Leviticus 19:12, 11–18; Matthew 25:31–46*
March 8: *Isaiah 55:10–11; Matthew 6:7–15*
March 9: *Jonah 3:1–10; Luke 11:29–32*
March 10: *Esther C:12, 14–16, 23–25; Matthew 7:7–12*
March 11: *Ezekiel 18:21–28; Matthew 5:20–26*
March 12: *Deuteronomy 26:16–19; Matthew 5:43–48*

March 14: *Daniel 9:4b–10; Luke 6:36–38*
March 15: *Isaiah 1:10, 16–20; Matthew 23:1–12*
March 16: *Jeremiah 18:18–20; Matthew 20:17–28*
March 17: *Jeremiah 17:5–10; Luke 16:19–31*
March 18: *Genesis 37:3–4, 12–13a, 17b–28a;*
Matthew 21:33–43, 45–46
March 19: Solemnity of St. Joseph,
Spouse of the Blessed Virgin Mary
2 Samuel 7:4–5a, 12–14a, 16; Romans 4:13, 16–18, 22;
Matthew 1:16, 18–21, 24a or Luke 2:41–51a

March 21: *2 Kings 5:1–15ab; Luke 4:24–30*
March 22: *Daniel 3:25, 34–43; Matthew 18:21–35*
March 23: *Deuteronomy 4:1, 5–9; Matthew 5:17–19*
March 24: *Jeremiah 7:23–28; Luke 11:14–23*
March 25: Solemnity of the Annunciation of the Lord
Isaiah 7:10–14; 8:10; Hebrews 10:4–10; Luke 1:26–38
March 26: *Hosea 6:1–6; Luke 18:9–14*

March 28: *Isaiah 65:17–21; John 4:43–54*
March 29: *Ezekiel 47:1–9, 12; John 5:1–16*
March 30: *Isaiah 49:8–15; John 5:17–30*
March 31: *Exodus 32:7–14; John 5:31–47*
April 1: *Wisdom 2:1a, 12–22; John 7:1–2, 10, 25–30*
April 2: *Jeremiah 11:18–20; John 7:40–53*

April 4: *Daniel 13:1–9, 15–17, 19–30, 33–62 or 13:41c–62;*
John 8:12–20
April 5: *Numbers 21:4–9; John 8:21–30*
April 6: *Daniel 3:14–20, 91–92, 95; John 8:31–42*
April 7: *Genesis 17:3–9; John 8:51–59*
April 8: *Jeremiah 20:10–13; John 10:31–42*
April 9: *Ezekiel 37:21–28; John 11:45–56*

April 11: *Isaiah 42:1–7; John 12:1–11*
April 12: *Isaiah 49:1–6; John 13:21–33, 36–38*
April 13: *Isaiah 50:4–9a; Matthew 26:14–25*

March 6, 2022 First Sunday of Lent

Reading I *Deuteronomy 26:4–10*

Moses spoke to the people, saying: "The priest shall receive the basket from you and shall set it in front of the altar of the LORD, your God. Then you shall declare before the LORD, your God, 'My father was a wandering Aramean who went down to Egypt with a small household and lived there as an alien. But there he became a nation great, strong, and numerous. When the Egyptians maltreated and oppressed us, imposing hard labor upon us, we cried to the LORD, the God of our fathers, and he heard our cry and saw our affliction, our toil and our oppression. He brought us out of Egypt with his strong hand and outstretched arm, with terrifying power, with signs and wonders; and bringing us into this country, he gave us this land flowing with milk and honey. Therefore, I have now brought you the firstfruits of the products of the soil which you, O LORD, have given me.' And having set them before the LORD, your God, you shall bow down in his presence."

Responsorial Psalm *Psalm 91:1–2, 10–11, 12–13, 14–15 (see 15b)*

R. Be with me, Lord, when I am in trouble.

You who dwell in the shelter of the Most High,
   who abide in the shadow of the Almighty,
say to the LORD, "My refuge and fortress,
   my God, in whom I trust."   R.

No evil shall befall you,
   nor affliction come near your tent,
for to his angels he has given command
      about you,
   that they guard you in all your ways.   R.

Upon their hands they shall bear you up,
   lest you dash your foot against a stone.
You shall tread upon the asp and the viper;
   you shall trample down the lion and
      the dragon.   R.

Because he clings to me, I will deliver him;
   I will set him on high because he
      acknowledges my name.

He shall call upon me, and I will answer him;
   I will be with him in distress;
I will deliver him and glorify him.   R.

Reading II *Romans 10:8–13*

Brothers and sisters: What does Scripture say? / *The word is near you, / in your mouth and in your heart /* —that is, the word of faith that we preach —, for, if you confess with your mouth that Jesus is Lord and believe in your heart that God raised him from the dead, you will be saved. For one believes with the heart and so is justified, and one confesses with the mouth and so is saved. For the Scripture says, *No one who believes in him will be put to shame.* For there is no distinction between Jew and Greek; the same Lord is Lord of all, enriching all who call upon him. For "everyone who calls on the name of the Lord will be saved."

Gospel *Luke 4:1–13*

Filled with the Holy Spirit, Jesus returned from the Jordan and was led by the Spirit into the desert for forty days, to be tempted by the devil. He ate nothing during those days, and when they were over he was hungry. The devil said to him, "If you are the Son of God, command this stone to become bread." Jesus answered him, "It is written, *One does not live on bread alone.*" Then he took him up and showed him all the kingdoms of the world in a single instant. The devil said to him, "I shall give to you all this power and glory; for it has been handed over to me, and I may give it to whomever I wish. All this will be yours, if you worship me." Jesus said to him in reply, "It is written:
   You shall worship the Lord,
      your God,
  and him alone shall you serve."

Then he led him to Jerusalem, made him stand on the parapet of the temple, and said to him, "If you are the Son of God, throw yourself down from here, for it is written:
   He will command his angels concerning you,
      to guard you,
and:

With their hands they will support you,
   lest you dash your foot against a stone."

Jesus said to him in reply, "It also says, *You shall not put the Lord, your God, to the test.*" When the devil had finished every temptation, he departed from him for a time.

Practice of Charity

In today's Gospel, Jesus provides a model of steadfastly turning away from temptation. We can feel driven to pursue careers, achievements, and material things that steer our aim from God. Luke's Gospel shows the devil tempting and harassing Jesus in a number of ways. Jesus' response is simple and focused on God. It is easy to fall for temptations when feeling depressed, hungry, tired, or sick. Even though Jesus was famished, thirsty, weak, and lonely, he focused on his Father. We can do the same. ◆ As you contemplate Jesus' time in the parched desert and his intense discomfort, think about ways you can conserve water and avoid wasting food at home. ◆ With family or friends, make a plan this Lent to use less water and food in solidarity with those who struggle to find clean drinking water and nourishment on a daily basis. ◆ Consider when you have been tempted to do something for power or glory. Pray about that tendency in your life.

Download more questions and activities for families, Christian initiation groups, and other adult groups at http://www.ltp.org/ahw.

Scripture Insights

This week we enter into the season of Lent with calls from the author of Deuteronomy, the psalmist, and Paul in his letter to the Romans to rise to the challenge of our faith and heritage. These readings remind us who we are and whence we came. We are the people of God and we are called always to live as such, even when the evidence from our current social, political, and economic situations would suggest otherwise. God, we are reminded, knows his people, remembers his people, and has a plan for our salvation. Most important, all of this may well be beyond our ken. And that should rather comfort us, not dissuade or create anxiety in us.

Paul teaches that the Word is very near us: in our mouths and in our hearts. We, however, must be still and listen so that we can act accordingly. This is the primary purpose of the season of Lent: to call us to be still and listen. We might be quick to discern what to give up for several weeks, but can we promise to be still and listen? This may be our biggest challenge in the twenty-first century and, therefore, our fundamental challenge during Lent.

Luke's Gospel narrates his understanding of Jesus' temptation prior to his public ministry. Jesus refuses the easy route; rather, he lets go and trusts in God. Notice that he falls back on his traditional grounding in response. This doesn't mean he is unthinking. He reflects, he discerns, and he asks what would God have him do.

◆ Moses asks his people to reflect on their history and how God has formed them. How has God formed you?

◆ Paul teaches, "No one who believes in him will be put to shame." How might this rally you to be open to God in your life?

◆ In Luke's Gospel, Jesus is led by the Spirit but tempted by the devil. How might temptation solidify a person's character and/or vocation?

March 13, 2022 SECOND SUNDAY OF LENT

READING I *Genesis 15:5–12, 17–18*

The Lord God took Abram outside and said, "Look up at the sky and count the stars, if you can. Just so," he added, "shall your descendants be." Abram put his faith in the LORD, who credited it to him as an act of righteousness.

He then said to him, "I am the LORD who brought you from Ur of the Chaldeans to give you this land as a possession." "O Lord GOD," he asked, "how am I to know that I shall possess it?" He answered him, "Bring me a three-year-old heifer, a three-year-old she-goat, a three-year-old ram, a turtledove, and a young pigeon." Abram brought him all these, split them in two, and placed each half opposite the other; but the birds he did not cut up. Birds of prey swooped down on the carcasses, but Abram stayed with them. As the sun was about to set, a trance fell upon Abram, and a deep, terrifying darkness enveloped him.

When the sun had set and it was dark, there appeared a smoking fire pot and a flaming torch, which passed between those pieces. It was on that occasion that the LORD made a covenant with Abram, saying: "To your descendants I give this land, from the Wadi of Egypt to the Great River, the Euphrates."

RESPONSORIAL PSALM
Psalm 27:1, 7–8, 8–9, 13–14 (see 1a)

R. The Lord is my light and my salvation.

The LORD is my light and my salvation;
 whom should I fear?
The LORD is my life's refuge;
 of whom should I be afraid? R.

Hear, O LORD, the sound of my call;
 have pity on me, and answer me.
Of you my heart speaks; you my glance seeks. R.

Your presence, O LORD, I seek.
 Hide not your face from me;
do not in anger repel your servant.
 You are my helper: cast me not off. R.

I believe that I shall see the bounty of the LORD
 in the land of the living.
Wait for the LORD with courage;
 be stouthearted, and wait for the LORD. R.

READING II *Philippians 3:17—4:1*
Shorter: Philippians 3:20—4:1

Join with others in being imitators of me, brothers and sisters, and observe those who thus conduct themselves according to the model you have in us. For many, as I have often told you and now tell you even in tears, conduct themselves as enemies of the cross of Christ. Their end is destruction. Their God is their stomach; their glory is in their "shame." Their minds are occupied with earthly things. But our citizenship is in heaven, and from it we also await a savior, the Lord Jesus Christ. He will change our lowly body to conform with his glorified body by the power that enables him also to bring all things into subjection to himself.

Therefore, my brothers and sisters, whom I love and long for, my joy and crown, in this way stand firm in the Lord.

GOSPEL *Luke 9:28b–36*

Jesus took Peter, John, and James and went up the mountain to pray. While he was praying, his face changed in appearance and his clothing became dazzling white. And behold, two men were conversing with him, Moses and Elijah, who appeared in glory and spoke of his exodus that he was going to accomplish in Jerusalem. Peter and his companions had been overcome by sleep, but becoming fully awake, they saw his glory and the two men standing with him. As they were about to part from him, Peter said to Jesus, "Master, it is good that we are here; let us make three tents, one for you, one for Moses, and one for Elijah." But he did not know what he was saying. While he was still speaking, a cloud came and cast a shadow over them, and they became frightened when they entered the cloud. Then from the cloud came a voice that said, "This is my chosen Son; listen to him." After the voice had spoken, Jesus was found alone. They fell silent and did not at that time tell anyone what they had seen.

Practice of Hope

One can only imagine the looks on the faces of Peter, James, and John, who awoke to see their leader and friend Jesus with a changed appearance and dazzling white clothes. Not only that, Jesus was conversing with Moses and Elijah about the "exodus that he was going to accomplish in Jerusalem." Is it any wonder that Peter, James, and John wanted to celebrate this powerful moment and build tents so that they could revel in the conversation of their spiritual leaders? Soon, however, a cloud and shadow enveloped and frightened them. They fell silent after a voice declared, "This is my chosen Son; listen to him." ◆ Who has provided spiritual leadership to you? In a letter, tell that person how he or she has brought you closer to God. ◆ Consider the work of the parish staff. Tell at least one of them a concrete way they enrich the parish through their ministry. ◆ Examine how your mind is occupied with "earthly things." How can you change that during Lent?

Download more questions and activities for families, Christian initiation groups, and other adult groups at http://www.ltp.org/ahw.

Scripture Insights

This week's readings include Luke's narration of the transfiguration of Jesus into his full glory. As breathtaking as this episode is, the verse that I find most striking in today's readings contains Paul's description of those he calls "enemies of the cross of Christ" (Philippians 3:18). In the Letter to the Philippians, he claims, "Their God is their stomach" (3:19). Is there a more poignant way of illustrating the insatiability of greed in many parts of the Western twenty-first-century world? Paul urges the Philippians and us to seek our identity and destination in Christ. The apostle calls us to live like Jesus, a model of simplicity and generosity (the opposite of greed) for which he himself strives.

Luke's Gospel blesses us with Peter, James, and John's glimpse of the true nature of Jesus, the Christ and Son of God. He clarifies, however, that this is not where we remain. Truth may be revealed to us on the mountain, but we cannot stay there. Our vocation is with our people: humankind who needs us as we need each other. Our call is to "listen to him" (9:36) and bring this revelatory truth into the grassroots. We need the glory of God in Christ, and the Triune God asks that we listen to the One who appeared in glory.

The faithful beauty of this summons is grounded in God's call of Abraham, our father and model of faith, to covenant relationship. We must be open to God's plan for us at every moment of our lives. Abraham was called to leave all he knew to follow God. The generational benefits of that new relationship are only beginning to be manifested.

◆ What does it mean to let your stomach be your god? What alternative does the way of Christ provide?

◆ Reflect on a mountaintop experience. How can it sustain you even through dry times?

◆ When God calls Abraham, he says, "go," and Abraham goes. Could you do likewise?

READING I *Exodus 3:1−8a, 13−15*

Shorter: Exodus 1−3, 7−8, 12−17

Moses was tending the flock of his father-in-law Jethro, the priest of Midian. Leading the flock across the desert, he came to Horeb, the mountain of God. There an angel of the LORD appeared to Moses in fire flaming out of a bush. As he looked on, he was surprised to see that the bush, though on fire, was not consumed. So Moses decided, "I must go over to look at this remarkable sight, and see why the bush is not burned."

When the LORD saw him coming over to look at it more closely, God called out to him from the bush, "Moses! Moses!" He answered, "Here I am." God said, "Come no nearer! Remove the sandals from your feet, for the place where you stand is holy ground. I am the God of your fathers," he continued, "the God of Abraham, the God of Isaac, the God of Jacob." Moses hid his face, for he was afraid to look at God. But the LORD said, "I have witnessed the affliction of my people in Egypt and have heard their cry of complaint against their slave drivers, so I know well what they are suffering. Therefore I have come down to rescue them from the hands of the Egyptians and lead them out of that land into a good and spacious land, a land flowing with milk and honey."

Moses said to God, "But when I go to the Israelites and say to them, 'The God of your fathers has sent me to you,' if they ask me, 'What is his name?' what am I to tell them?" God replied, "I am who am." Then he added, "This is what you shall tell the Israelites: I AM sent me to you."

God spoke further to Moses, "Thus shall you say to the Israelites: The LORD, the God of your fathers, the God of Abraham, the God of Isaac, the God of Jacob, has sent me to you.

"This is my name forever; / thus am I to be remembered through all generations."

RESPONSORIAL PSALM
Psalm 103:1−2, 3−4, 6−7, 8, 11 (8a)

R. The Lord is kind and merciful.

Bless the LORD, O my soul;
   and all my being, bless his holy name.
Bless the LORD, O my soul,
   and forget not all his benefits. R.

He pardons all your iniquities,
   he heals all your ills,
He redeems your life from destruction,
   he crowns you with kindness
      and compassion. R.

The LORD secures justice
   and the rights of all the oppressed.
He has made known his ways to Moses,
   and his deeds to the children of Israel. R.

Merciful and gracious is the LORD,
   slow to anger and abounding in kindness.
For as the heavens are high above the earth,
   so surpassing is his kindness toward those
      who fear him. R.

READING II *1 Corinthians 10:1−6, 10−12*

I do not want you to be unaware, brothers and sisters, that our ancestors were all under the cloud and all passed through the sea, and all of them were baptized into Moses in the cloud and in the sea. All ate the same spiritual food, and all drank the same spiritual drink, for they drank from a spiritual rock that followed them, and the rock was the Christ. Yet God was not pleased with most of them, for they were struck down in the desert.

These things happened as examples for us, so that we might not desire evil things, as they did. Do not grumble as some of them did, and suffered death by the destroyer. These things happened to them as an example, and they have been written down as a warning to us, upon whom the end of the ages has come. Therefore, whoever thinks he is standing secure should take care not to fall.

Some people told Jesus about the Galileans whose blood Pilate had mingled with the blood of their sacrifices. Jesus said to them in reply, "Do you think that because these Galileans suffered in this way they were greater sinners than all other Galileans? By no means! But I tell you, if you do not repent, you will all perish as they did! Or those eighteen people who were killed when the tower at Siloam fell on them—do you think they were more guilty than everyone else who lived in Jerusalem? By no means! But I tell you, if you do not repent, you will all perish as they did!"

And he told them this parable: "There once was a person who had a fig tree planted in his orchard, and when he came in search of fruit on it but found none, he said to the gardener, 'For three years now I have come in search of fruit on this fig tree but have found none. So cut it down. Why should it exhaust the soil?' He said to him in reply, 'Sir, leave it for this year also, and I shall cultivate the ground around it and fertilize it; it may bear fruit in the future. If not you can cut it down.'"

Practice of Faith

In this reading from Exodus, we can only imagine Moses as awestruck as a voice called to him from the burning bush. God called Moses by name, commanding him to remove his sandals, for that area was holy ground. Then we hear the name of all names: the great I AM. How often do we allow ourselves the opportunity to be mystified by the presence of our Lord? Do we stop at the end of each day to reflect on God's presence? ♦ In an extended prayer time, contemplate the moments when you felt God in your midst during the past several years and journal about them. ♦ When you next enter a Catholic church, think about why we genuflect when adoration is taking place or bow when the reserved Eucharist is not exposed. This prayerful action confirms our belief in God's presence in a holy place where our expressions of reverence are most appropriate. ♦ Consider how you honor God's presence during the day.

Download more questions and activities for families, Christian initiation groups, and other adult groups at http://www.ltp.org/ahw.

Scripture Insights

Our Old Testament reading for today is well known to us—likely one we have heard since childhood. Moses, who is tending his father-in-law's flock at the base of Mount Horeb, may be looking for distractions to while away the time when he sees a bush in flames just off the path. What is remarkable is not the burning bush itself but its staying power. The bush is not consumed. As many of us would, Moses decides to check it out.

Moses' openness becomes God's cue to call out to him, indeed, to summon him far beyond what he believes himself capable. Notice that when God calls him by name, Moses responds simply, "Here I am." In Hebrew, this is just one word, *hinneni*. It is how Abraham responded to God at the ultimate test of his faith (Genesis 22) and how many prophets after him also will respond to their call. Once God alerts Moses to the holy ground and identifies himself in the covenantal tradition of Moses' ancestors, Moses lowers his face in fear but remains. Much staying power will be required of him as well in the coming years.

God then reveals his intentions to bring the Israelites out of oppression in Egypt into this very wilderness where they will worship God in freedom. Moses is God's chosen prophet and leader. This scene culminates when, at Moses' request, God further reveals the divine name, YHWH, a form of the verb "to be." God is the essence of being, the "I AM," a name so sacred that it should not be uttered. Our reverence is indicated in the address, "LORD."

♦ Moses is snatched out of his daily routine and called to be a leader and God's spokesperson, or "prophet." Are you open to God calling you in new ways?

♦ Reflect on God as the essence of being. Does this change your concept of God?

♦ How have you been challenged beyond your supposed capabilities in your life? Do you have the staying power to which God calls us? How might you build such endurance?

READING I *Exodus 17:3–7*

In those days, in their thirst for water, the people grumbled against Moses, saying, "Why did you ever make us leave Egypt? Was it just to have us die here of thirst with our children and our livestock?" So Moses cried out to the LORD, "What shall I do with this people? A little more and they will stone me!" The LORD answered Moses, "Go over there in front of the people, along with some of the elders of Israel, holding in your hand, as you go, the staff with which you struck the river. I will be standing there in front of you on the rock in Horeb. Strike the rock, and the water will flow from it for the people to drink." This Moses did, in the presence of the elders of Israel. The place was called Massah and Meribah, because the Israelites quarreled there and tested the LORD, saying, "Is the LORD in our midst or not?"

RESPONSORIAL PSALM
Psalm 95:1–2, 6–7, 8–9 (8)

R. If today you hear his voice, harden not
     your hearts.

Come, let us sing joyfully to the LORD;
    let us acclaim the Rock of our salvation.
Let us come into his presence with thanksgiving;
    let us joyfully sing psalms to him.

Come, let us bow down in worship;
    let us kneel before the LORD who made us.
For he is our God,
    and we are the people he shepherds, the flock
        he guides.

Oh, that today you would hear his voice:
    "Harden not your hearts as at Meribah,
    as in the day of Massah in the desert,
where your fathers tempted me;
    they tested me though they had seen my works."

READING II *Romans 5:1–2, 5–8*

Brothers and sisters: Since we have been justified by faith, we have peace with God through our Lord Jesus Christ, through whom we have gained access by faith to this grace in which we stand, and we boast in hope of the glory of God.

And hope does not disappoint, because the love of God has been poured out into our hearts through the Holy Spirit who has been given to us. For Christ, while we were still helpless, died at the appointed time for the ungodly. Indeed, only with difficulty does one die for a just person, though perhaps for a good person one might even find courage to die. But God proves his love for us in that while we were still sinners Christ died for us.

GOSPEL
John 4:5–15, 19b–26, 39a, 40–42

Longer: John 4:5–42

Jesus came to a town of Samaria called Sychar, near the plot of land that Jacob had given to his son Joseph. Jacob's well was there. Jesus, tired from his journey, sat down there at the well. It was about noon.

A woman of Samaria came to draw water. Jesus said to her, "Give me a drink." His disciples had gone into the town to buy food. The Samaritan woman said to him, "How can you, a Jew, ask me, a Samaritan woman, for a drink?"—For Jews use nothing in common with Samaritans.—Jesus answered and said to her, "If you knew the gift of God and who is saying to you, 'Give me a drink,' you would have asked him and he would have given you living water." The woman said to him, "Sir, you do not even have a bucket and the cistern is deep; where then can you get this living water? Are you greater than our father Jacob, who gave us this cistern and drank from it himself with his children and his flocks?" Jesus answered and said to her, "Everyone who drinks this water will be thirsty again; but whoever drinks the water I shall give will never thirst; the water I shall give will become in him a spring of water welling up to eternal life." The woman said to him, "Sir, give me this water, so that I may not be thirsty or have to keep coming here to draw water.

"I can see that you are a prophet. Our ancestors worshiped on this mountain; but you people say that the place to worship is in Jerusalem." Jesus said to her, "Believe me, woman, the hour is coming when you will worship the Father neither on this mountain nor in Jerusalem. You people worship what you do not understand; we worship what we understand, because salvation is from the Jews. But the hour is coming, and is now here, when true worshipers will worship the Father in Spirit and truth; and indeed the Father seeks such people to worship him. God is Spirit, and those who worship him must worship in Spirit and truth." The woman said to him, "I know that the Messiah is coming, the one called the Christ; when he comes, he will tell us everything." Jesus said to her, "I am he, the one who is speaking with you."

Many of the Samaritans of that town began to believe in him. When the Samaritans came to him, they invited him to stay with them; and he stayed there two days. Many more began to believe in him because of his word, and they said to the woman, "We no longer believe because of your word; for we have heard for ourselves, and we know that this is truly the savior of the world."

Practice of Faith

Jesus promises the Samaritan woman at the well, "Whoever drinks the water I shall give will never thirst." Jesus challenges her (and us) to go to the source of life in him. ◆ When you reach to bless yourself with holy water, recall Jesus' words about eternal life. ◆ Make a conscious effort to think about our belief in the Trinity as you make the sign of the cross. ◆ Pray during Lent for the catechumens who await the life-giving water.

Download more questions and activities for families, Christian initiation groups, and other adult groups at http://www.ltp.org/ahw.

Scripture Insights

At Sychar, the disciples search for food as Jesus rests by Jacob's well. Generally, Samaritans held a Torah-centered faith focusing on the patriarchs, worshiping on Mount Gerazim, and looking for a prophet Moses-like messiah, while Jews held their broader scriptural tradition, including prophets, centered worship in Jerusalem, and hoped for a messiah-king of David. Although sharing the same foundation, the groups shared nothing else: not food, drink, or utensils. When a Samaritan woman comes to the well for her daily water-drawing chore, the scene is set for Jesus to upend conventions and incorporate a woman who is also Samaritan into his own, reconciling long-standing divisions.

Jesus demands a drink. By seeking a drink from the woman's jar, he rejects the religious division between them from the outset, not to mention gender conventions. For her part, the woman boldly queries his behavior. Responding spiritually, Jesus presents the gift of God and living water, referencing their shared Mosaic traditions and today's Old Testament reading.

Jesus challenges her to a new relationship with God through him, hinting at the coming revelation of himself as the "I AM" of God (4:26). She first counters literally but then asks about Jacob "our ancestor" and giver of the well. She is open and, more symbolically, wants to know who Jesus is in relation to their shared history. Jesus responds by challenging her to think further about what he gives: "a spring of water welling up to eternal life" (4:14).

The woman's mission is perfected in the faith of the villagers based on their encounter with Jesus: "we know that this is truly the savior of the world" (4:42). The Samaritan woman becomes both a disciple of Jesus and an apostle to her community.

◆ Are you tied to long-standing practices that may not be life-giving?

◆ In what ways does responding to Christ's call upend today's social conventions?

◆ Reflect on the courage of both Jesus and the Samaritan woman in their openness to one another. How might such openness change your direction for the better?

READING I *Joshua 5:9a, 10–12*

The LORD said to Joshua, "Today I have removed the reproach of Egypt from you."

While the Israelites were encamped at Gilgal on the plains of Jericho, they celebrated the Passover on the evening of the fourteenth of the month. On the day after the Passover, they ate of the produce of the land in the form of unleavened cakes and parched grain. On that same day after the Passover, on which they ate of the produce of the land, the manna ceased. No longer was there manna for the Israelites, who that year ate of the yield of the land of Canaan.

RESPONSORIAL PSALM
Psalm 34:2–3, 4–5, 6–7 (9a)

R. Taste and see the goodness of the Lord.

I will bless the LORD at all times;
   his praise shall be ever in my mouth.
Let my soul glory in the LORD;
   the lowly will hear me and be glad. R.

Glorify the LORD with me,
   let us together extol his name.
I sought the LORD, and he answered me
   and delivered me from all my fears. R.

Look to him that you may be radiant with joy,
   and your faces may not blush with shame.
When the poor one called out, the LORD heard,
   and from all his distress he saved him. R.

READING II *2 Corinthians 5:17–21*

Brothers and sisters: Whoever is in Christ is a new creation: the old things have passed away; behold, new things have come. And all this is from God, who has reconciled us to himself through Christ and given us the ministry of reconciliation, namely, God was reconciling the world to himself in Christ, not counting their trespasses against them and entrusting to us the message of reconciliation. So we are ambassadors for Christ, as if God were appealing through us. We implore you on behalf of Christ, be reconciled to God. For our sake he made him to be sin who did not know sin, so that we might become the righteousness of God in him.

GOSPEL *Luke 15:1–3, 11–32*

Tax collectors and sinners were all drawing near to listen to Jesus, but the Pharisees and scribes began to complain, saying, "This man welcomes sinners and eats with them." So to them Jesus addressed this parable: "A man had two sons, and the younger son said to his father, 'Father give me the share of your estate that should come to me.' So the father divided the property between them. After a few days, the younger son collected all his belongings and set off to a distant country where he squandered his inheritance on a life of dissipation. When he had freely spent everything, a severe famine struck that country, and he found himself in dire need. So he hired himself out to one of the local citizens who sent him to his farm to tend the swine. And he longed to eat his fill of the pods on which the swine fed, but nobody gave him any. Coming to his senses he thought, 'How many of my father's hired workers have more than enough food to eat, but here am I, dying from hunger. I shall get up and go to my father and I shall say to him, "Father, I have sinned against heaven and against you. I no longer deserve to be called your son; treat me as you would treat one of your hired workers."' So he got up and went back to his father. While he was still a long way off, his father caught sight of him, and was filled with compassion. He ran to his son, embraced him and kissed him. His son said to him, 'Father, I have sinned against heaven and against you; I no longer deserve to be called your son.' But his father ordered his servants, 'Quickly bring the finest robe and put it on him; put a ring on his finger and sandals on his feet. Take the fattened calf and slaughter it. Then let us celebrate with a feast, because this son of mine was dead, and has come to life again; he was lost, and has been found.' Then the celebration began. Now the older son had been out in the field and, on his way back, as he neared the house, he heard the sound of music and dancing. He called one of the servants and asked what this might mean. The servant said to him, 'Your brother has returned and your father has slaughtered the fattened calf because he has him back safe and sound.' He became angry, and when he refused to enter the house, his father came out and pleaded with him. He said to his father in reply, 'Look, all these years I served you and not once did I disobey your orders; yet you never gave me even a young goat to feast on with my friends. But when your son returns who swallowed up your property with prostitutes, for him you slaughter the fattened calf.' He said to him, 'My son, you are here with me always; everything I have is yours. But now we must celebrate and rejoice, because your brother was dead and has come to life again; he was lost and has been found.'"

Practice of Hope

People often want their just rewards and so often identify with the older son. Jesus tells this parable, however, to illustrate the depth of his Father's love and forgiveness. When we act like the younger brother and with selfish motives return home, God will run toward us, gushing with love because we headed in the right direction. ◆ Think about times when you were less than sincere in offering an apology. Journal about what happened next: did God or someone good in your life show the depth of forgiveness that exemplifies true love? How can you respond now to someone who needs this kind of mercy? ◆ When have you acted like the older brother and hardened your heart toward someone who sought forgiveness? Pray for a softening of your heart toward that person. ◆ When have you needed mercy and found it? Say a prayer of thanksgiving for that time.

Download more questions and activities for families, Christian initiation groups, and other adult groups at http://www.ltp.org/ahw.

Scripture Insights

Jesus' parable is often called "the prodigal son" but this misses its deeper meaning. If we portray it as the parable of the father with two sons, we see how it challenges us to love without limits.

The father, at his younger son's request, sets him free, so that he can make his own choices and bear their consequences. The son's behest cannot be overstated. He had asked his father if they could pretend he is dead, so that the son could share the wealth. We see that the son quickly dissipates his father's wealth and finds himself in the shocking reality of the unforgiving world. Coming to his senses, he intends to make amends and hope for mercy.

The father awaits his child's return and welcomes him back into the household with great joy and celebration. If we end here, however, we miss the real point. This father risks losing his older son, the one who has remained faithful and true. One was lost and has been found, but as we close, the father is outside, away from the rejoicing, trying to save his second son, to whom he says, "Everything I have is yours" (Luke 15:31). Jesus points to a Father who makes demands of all who follow, but these must be understood in the light of a Father who is found in unexpected places, searching for all his lost children.

What is lost must be found. This message stands, and this is what Paul confirms in his Second Letter to the Corinthians. Jesus reveals a different God expected and invented by the religious culture of his day. It holds power today because we continue to look for God in the wrong places. The God revealed by Jesus is as much a surprise to us as to his listeners. We enthrone God on altars when he is likely to be found out in the dark, trying to save his lost children.

◆ How do you close yourself off from the loving Father that Jesus presents here?

◆ How might you be open to the God Jesus reveals in the parable?

◆ In what ways can you join in seeking out and saving the lost in your daily life?

Reading I
1 Samuel 16:1b, 6–7, 10–13a

The Lord said to Samuel: "Fill your horn with oil, and be on your way. I am sending you to Jesse of Bethlehem, for I have chosen my king from among his sons."

As Jesse and his sons came to the sacrifice, Samuel looked at Eliab and thought, "Surely the Lord's anointed is here before him." But the Lord said to Samuel: "Do not judge from his appearance or from his lofty stature, because I have rejected him. Not as man sees does God see, because man sees the appearance but the Lord looks into the heart." In the same way Jesse presented seven sons before Samuel, but Samuel said to Jesse, "The Lord has not chosen any one of these." Then Samuel asked Jesse, "Are these all the sons you have?" Jesse replied, "There is still the youngest, who is tending the sheep." Samuel said to Jesse, "Send for him; we will not begin the sacrificial banquet until he arrives here." Jesse sent and had the young man brought to them. He was ruddy, a youth handsome to behold and making a splendid appearance. The Lord said, "There—anoint him, for this is the one!" Then Samuel, with the horn of oil in hand, anointed David in the presence of his brothers; and from that day on, the spirit of the Lord rushed upon David.

Reading II Ephesians 5:8–14

Brothers and sisters: You were once darkness, but now you are light in the Lord. Live as children of light, for light produces every kind of goodness and righteousness and truth. Try to learn what is pleasing to the Lord. Take no part in the fruitless works of darkness; rather expose them, for it is shameful even to mention the things done by them in secret; but everything exposed by the light becomes visible, for everything that becomes visible is light. Therefore, it says:

> "Awake, O sleeper,
> and arise from the dead,
> and Christ will give you light."

Gospel John 9:1–41
Shorter: John 9:1, 6–9, 13–17, 34–38

As Jesus passed by he saw a man blind from birth. His disciples asked him, "Rabbi, who sinned, this man or his parents, that he was born blind?" Jesus answered, "Neither he nor his parents sinned; it is so that the works of God might be made visible through him. We have to do the works of the one who sent me while it is day. Night is coming when no one can work. While I am in the world, I am the light of the world." When he had said this, he spat on the ground and made clay with the saliva, and smeared the clay on his eyes, and said to him, "Go wash in the Pool of Siloam"—which means Sent—. So he went and washed, and came back able to see.

His neighbors and those who had seen him earlier as a beggar said, "Isn't this the one who used to sit and beg?" Some said, "It is," but others said, "No, he just looks like him." He said, "I am." So they said to him, "How were your eyes opened?" He replied, "The man called Jesus made clay and anointed my eyes and told me, 'Go to Siloam and wash.' So I went there and washed and was able to see." And they said to him, "Where is he?" He said, "I don't know."

They brought the one who was once blind to the Pharisees. Now Jesus had made clay and opened his eyes on a sabbath. So then the Pharisees also asked him how he was able to see. He said to them, "He put clay on my eyes, and I washed, and now I can see." So some of the Pharisees said, "This man is not from God, because he does not keep the sabbath." But others said, "How can a sinful man do such signs?" And there was a division among them. So they said to the blind man again, "What do you have to say about him, since he opened your eyes?" He said, "He is a prophet."

Now the Jews did not believe that he had been blind and gained his sight until they summoned the parents of the one who had gained his sight. They asked them, "Is this your son, who you say was born blind? How does he now see?" His parents answered and said, "We know that this is our son and that he was born blind. We do not know how he sees now, nor do we know who opened his eyes. Ask him, he is of age; he can speak for himself." His parents said this because they were afraid of the Jews, for the Jews had already agreed that if anyone acknowledged him as the Christ, he would be expelled from the synagogue. For this reason his parents said, "He is of age; question him."

So a second time they called the man who had been blind and said to him, "Give God the praise! We know that this man is a sinner." He replied, "If he is a sinner, I do not know. One thing I do know is that I was blind and now I see." So they said to him, "What did he do to you? How did he open your eyes?" He answered them, "I told you already and you did not listen. Why do you want to hear it again? Do you want to become his disciples, too?" They ridiculed him and said, "You are that man's disciple; we are disciples of Moses! We know that God spoke to Moses, but we do not know where this one is from." The man answered and said to them, "This is what is so amazing, that you do not know where he is from, yet he opened my eyes. We know that God does not listen to sinners, but if one is devout and does his will, he listens to him. It is unheard of that anyone ever opened the eyes of a person born blind. If this man were not from God, he would not be able to do anything." They answered and said to him, "You were born totally in sin, and are you trying to teach us?" Then they threw him out.

When Jesus heard that they had thrown him out, he found him and said, "Do you believe in the Son of Man?" He answered and said, "Who is he, sir, that I may believe in him?" Jesus said to him, "You have seen him, and the one speaking with you is he." He said, "I do believe, Lord," and he worshiped him. Then Jesus said, "I came into this world for judgment, so that those who do not see might see, and those who do see might become blind."

Some of the Pharisees who were with him heard this and said to him, "Surely we are not also blind, are we?" Jesus said to them, "If you were blind, you would have no sin; but now you are saying, 'We see,' so your sin remains."

Scripture Insights

When Jesus and his disciples encounter a man who is blind from birth, the disciples voice an ancient belief that illness and misfortune result from sin. Jesus indicates that the wrong question has been asked. The purpose of this encounter is to further reveal Jesus is the light of the world and life-giving water.

The man obeys Jesus, washes in the Pool of Siloam, and is given sight, but the crowd begins to question the man, eventually bringing him before Pharisees. Only later do we learn that this occurred on a sabbath. John reveals how believing people should respond to this light. Darkness is embodied physically by the blind man but is also embodied spiritually by those more concerned with rules and empty ritual than the potential for new life. Light and sight is openness to God through Christ now.

A trial ensues as the man, then his parents, then the man again are questioned about his background and experience. John teaches not only how Jesus lives out what he claims about himself but also the consequences for those who are open and choose to stand accordingly. Finding meaning in this world may be trying, and we may find ourselves at odds with the system that formed our identity and ritual lives. What happens next, therefore, is crucial.

The account concludes with Jesus supporting the man's stand. Jesus affirms his identity as the Son of Man, one whom the man can see and hear, and the newly sighted man believes and worships Jesus. The man is able to see by the light that comes from God embodied in Jesus Christ. John teaches us how to stand trial for our faith, the realities of blindness and sight, and the ongoing presence of Jesus in our lives. Jesus challenges the closed nature of religious systems that claim knowledge and clarity instead of openness to God.

◆ What rituals are important to you? How do they reveal God's presence to you?

◆ How might you be blind? How might you be open to God's call to you?

◆ In what ways can you challenge closed systems to be open to Jesus' summons?

READING I *Isaiah 43:16–21*

Thus says the LORD,
  who opens a way in the sea
  and a path in the mighty waters,
who leads out chariots and horsemen,
  a powerful army,
till they lie prostrate together, never to rise,
  snuffed out and quenched like a wick.
Remember not the events of the past,
  the things of long ago consider not;
see, I am doing something new!
  Now it springs forth, do you not perceive it?
In the desert I make a way;
  in the wasteland, rivers.
Wild beasts honor me,
  jackals and ostriches,
for I put water in the desert
  and rivers in the wasteland
  for my chosen people to drink,
the people whom I formed for myself,
  that they might announce my praise.

RESPONSORIAL PSALM
Psalm 126:1–2, 2–3, 4–5, 6 (3)

R. The Lord has done great things for us;
      we are filled with joy.

When the LORD brought back the captives
        of Zion,
  we were like men dreaming.
Then our mouth was filled with laughter,
  and our tongue with rejoicing. R.

Then they said among the nations,
  "The LORD has done great things for them."
The LORD has done great things for us;
  we are glad indeed. R.

Restore our fortunes, O LORD,
  like the torrents in the southern desert.
Those that sow in tears
  shall reap rejoicing. R.

Although they go forth weeping,
  carrying the seed to be sown,
they shall come back rejoicing,
  carrying their sheaves. R.

READING II *Philippians 3:8–14*

Brothers and sisters: I consider everything as a loss because of the supreme good of knowing Christ Jesus my Lord. For his sake I have accepted the loss of all things and I consider them so much rubbish, that I may gain Christ and be found in him, not having any righteousness of my own based on the law but that which comes through faith in Christ, the righteousness from God, depending on faith to know him and the power of his resurrection and the sharing of his sufferings by being conformed to his death, if somehow I may attain the resurrection from the dead.

It is not that I have already taken hold of it or have already attained perfect maturity, but I continue my pursuit in hope that I may possess it, since I have indeed been taken possession of by Christ Jesus. Brothers and sisters, I for my part do not consider myself to have taken possession. Just one thing: forgetting what lies behind but straining forward to what lies ahead, I continue my pursuit toward the goal, the prize of God's upward calling, in Christ Jesus.

GOSPEL *John 8:1–11*

Jesus went to the Mount of Olives. But early in the morning he arrived again in the temple area, and all the people started coming to him, and he sat down and taught them. Then the scribes and the Pharisees brought a woman who had been caught in adultery and made her stand in the middle. They said to him, "Teacher, this woman was caught in the very act of committing adultery. Now in the law, Moses commanded us to stone such women. So what do you say?" They said this to test him, so that they could have some charge to bring against him. Jesus bent down and began to write on the ground with his finger. But when they continued asking him, he straightened up and said to them, "Let the one among you who is without sin be the first to throw a stone at her." Again he bent down and wrote on the ground. And in response, they went away one by one, beginning with the elders. So he was left alone with the woman before him. Then Jesus straightened up and said to her,

"Woman, where are they? Has no one condemned you?" She replied, "No one, sir." Then Jesus said, "Neither do I condemn you. Go, and from now on do not sin any more."

Practice of Hope

The account of the woman caught in adultery is as much about the Pharisees and scribes who try to trick Jesus as it is about the woman. The woman may have been caught in the act of adultery, but these religious rulers wanted to persecute Jesus even more, because they were jealous and fearful of his growing influence. ◆ During these final days of Lent, discern what acts of sin or wrongful thinking are standing in the way of your being more open or present to others. How can you lay bare all of the hidden issues that prevent you from living fully with integrity and without regret? ◆ Make an effort to go to your parish's Lenten communal reconciliation service or regularly scheduled confession time. Encourage others in your family or circle of faith-sharing friends to do the same as you prepare for the Paschal Triduum and Easter. ◆ Is there someone who is awaiting your mercy? Seek to reconcile with that person.

Download more questions and activities for families, Christian initiation groups, and other adult groups at http://www.ltp.org/ahw.

Scripture Insights

Isaiah speaks of the power and sovereignty of God, who has a plan for creation and for each of us. The psalmist then promises that sadness will turn to joy and laughter if we stand strong. Paul, in his gentle Letter to the Philippians, further describes our faith lives as journeys pursuing maturity found in hope and satisfaction with God's blessings in whatever form they take.

This teaching culminates in our Gospel: an encounter among Jesus, a woman caught in adultery, and those who test Jesus to her harm. This account is well known, but most early manuscripts do not include it. Remarkably, this powerful vignette was so loved that it nonetheless found a canonical home. Audiences of all time now experience this story of merciful wisdom and compassion.

Scribes and Pharisees bring a woman before Jesus as if to stand trial. They caught her in the very act of adultery, a crime punishable by stoning (Leviticus 20:10; Deuteronomy 22:22–24), and demand Jesus render judgment, but John confirms that Jesus too is on trial. The disinterest in the woman's partner shows that justice is of little concern. Jesus bends and writes in the sand. He whose words have flowed freely now refuses to speak, perhaps indicating they ask the wrong question. Jesus then responds with his encouragement to the one among them without sin to throw the first stone, and then he returns to his writing. One by one, the gathered depart until even the young move away.

The woman stands alone before Jesus. He asserts her autonomy as one who makes her own decisions and has her own relationship with God, then he sends her away with the command to change her ways accordingly.

◆ We are often curious about what Jesus writes, but we cannot know. What do you imagine he might have written?

◆ Jesus does not say words of forgiveness; rather, he agrees that no one remains to condemn the woman and sends her on her way. How might this act of mercy challenge her to live and do better?

◆ How does this Gospel culminate today's teachings?

READING I *Ezekiel 37:12–14*

Thus says the LORD God: O my people, I will open your graves and have you rise from them, and bring you back to the land of Israel. Then you shall know that I am the LORD, when I open your graves and have you rise from them, O my people! I will put my spirit in you that you may live, and I will settle you upon your land; thus you shall know that I am the LORD. I have promised, and I will do it, says the LORD.

RESPONSORIAL PSALM
Psalm 130:1–2, 3–4, 5–6, 7–8 (7)

R. With the Lord there is mercy, and fullness
of redemption.

Out of the depths I cry to you, O LORD;
    LORD, hear my voice!
Let your ears be attentive
    to my voice in supplication. R.

If you, O LORD, mark iniquities,
    LORD, who can stand?
But with you is forgiveness
    that you may be revered. R.

I trust in the LORD;
    my soul trusts in his word.
More than sentinels wait for the dawn,
    let Israel wait for the LORD. R.

For with the LORD is kindness
    and with him is plenteous redemption;
and he will redeem Israel
    from all their iniquities. R.

READING II *Romans 8:8–11*

Brothers and sisters: Those who are in the flesh cannot please God. But you are not in the flesh; on the contrary, you are in the spirit, if only the Spirit of God dwells in you. Whoever does not have the Spirit of Christ does not belong to him. But if Christ is in you, although the body is dead because of sin, the spirit is alive because of righteousness. If the Spirit of the One who raised Jesus from the dead dwells in you, the One who raised Christ from the dead will give life to your mortal bodies also, through his Spirit dwelling in you.

GOSPEL
John 11:3–7, 17, 20–27, 33b–45

Longer: John 11:1–45

The sisters of Lazarus sent word to Jesus, saying, "Master, the one you love is ill." When Jesus heard this he said, "This illness is not to end in death, but is for the glory of God, that the Son of God may be glorified through it." Now Jesus loved Martha and her sister and Lazarus. So when he heard that he was ill, he remained for two days in the place where he was. Then after this he said to his disciples, "Let us go back to Judea."

When Jesus arrived, he found that Lazarus had already been in the tomb for four days. When Martha heard that Jesus was coming, she went to meet him; but Mary sat at home. Martha said to Jesus, "Lord, if you had been here, my brother would not have died. But even now I know that whatever you ask of God, God will give you." Jesus said to her, "Your brother will rise." Martha said, "I know he will rise, in the resurrection on the last day." Jesus told her, "I am the resurrection and the life; whoever believes in me, even if he dies, will live, and everyone who lives and believes in me will never die. Do you believe this?" She said to him, "Yes, Lord. I have come to believe that you are the Christ, the Son of God, the one who is coming into the world."

He became perturbed and deeply troubled, and said, "Where have you laid him?" They said to him, "Sir, come and see." And Jesus wept. So the Jews said, "See how he loved him." But some of them said, "Could not the one who opened the eyes of the blind man have done something so that this man would not have died?"

So Jesus, perturbed again, came to the tomb. It was a cave, and a stone lay across it. Jesus said, "Take away the stone." Martha, the dead man's sister, said to him, "Lord, by now there will be a stench; he has been dead for four days." Jesus said to her, "Did I not tell you that if you believe you will see the glory of God?" So they took away the stone. And Jesus raised his eyes and said, "Father, I thank you for hearing me. I know that you always hear me; but because of the crowd here I have said this, that they may believe that you sent me." And when he had said this, he cried out in a loud voice, "Lazarus, come out!" The dead man came out, tied hand and foot with burial bands, and his face was wrapped in a cloth. So Jesus said to them, "Untie him and let him go."

Now many of the Jews who had come to Mary and seen what he had done began to believe in him.

Practice of Hope

The story of Lazarus is our story too. Lazarus has died and is bound in burial bands, with his hands and feet constricted and his face covered. When Jesus commands, Lazarus leaves the burial place. With another command, the burial cloths are loosened from him. Once Lazarus is freed, many come to believe. We also become bound and closed off from the life Christ offers until we open ourselves to God. ◆ Pray over what keeps you from accepting God's merciful love. Imagine those as cloths that you loosen and hand to Jesus. Thank Jesus for his freeing love. ◆ Invite your friends and family who have been away or distant to join you for a meal or parish event. ◆ Connect with people who have been away from the Christian community so that they know they're missed. Be like Martha and Mary in Bethany who cared for their brother and had enough faith to bring him Jesus.

Download more questions and activities for families, Christian initiation groups, and other adult groups at http://www.ltp.org/ahw.

Scripture Insights

Each reading today speaks of redemption in some form. The reading from Ezekiel looks to the restoration of Israel, a time of resurrection from death. The psalmist sings of the soul awaiting God's mercy, and Paul speaks of the faithful who dwell in the Spirit of God, who has power beyond death.

The Gospel narrates transitions of faith as John leads us from Jesus' public ministry toward his glorifying hour. The longer version of the reading frames the reading with the introduction of Jesus' friends Mary, Martha, and Lazarus (11:1–7) and notes Mary's eventual anointing action. Much occurs in this reading, which climaxes in the spectacular raising of Lazarus from death.

Tensions emerge immediately. Although Jesus loves Lazarus and his sisters, when he hears Lazarus is ill, he stays put for two more days (11:5). Is this what we do when our loved ones ail? So much is said about death in this reading, but ultimately the teaching is about life. The encounters and events show forth God's glory (11:40) and lead to the plot to kill Jesus, but, teaches John, this will not be the end. Through the cross, Jesus will reveal the love of God and return to the glory with the Father that was his before creation. Lazarus comes forth and is freed from the clothes of death, an action that was unnecessary when Peter and the Beloved Disciple find the empty tomb of Jesus (20:4–8). New life abounds.

Across these events many are called to decision: the disciples (11:15–16), Martha (11:25–27), Mary (11:32–34), and "the Jews" (11:45). As we follow this story, we are called to decision by the one who is resurrection and life (11:25–26). Jesus' question to Martha is also directed to us: "Do you believe this?"

◆ The Scriptures challenge us to see what is greater than our understanding. Can you be open to this?

◆ Jesus seems to work counterintuitively to bring us to deeper faith. How does this challenge your sensibilities?

◆ The death of loved ones is difficult to bear. How does Jesus call us to look beyond death?

READING I *Isaiah 50:4–7*

The Lord GOD has given me
 a well-trained tongue,
that I might know how to speak to the weary
 a word that will rouse them.
Morning after morning
 he opens my ear that I may hear;
and I have not rebelled,
 have not turned back.
I gave my back to those who beat me,
 my cheeks to those who plucked my beard;
my face I did not shield
 from buffets and spitting.

The Lord GOD is my help,
 therefore I am not disgraced;
I have set my face like flint,
 knowing that I shall not be put to shame.

READING II *Philippians 2:6–11*

Christ Jesus, though he was in the form of God,
 did not regard equality with God
 something to be grasped.
Rather, he emptied himself,
 taking the form of a slave,
 coming in human likeness;
 and found human in appearance,
 he humbled himself,
 becoming obedient to the point of death,
 even death on a cross.
Because of this, God greatly exalted him
 and bestowed on him the name
 which is above every name,
 that at the name of Jesus
 every knee should bend,
 of those in heaven and on earth and
  under the earth,
 and every tongue confess that
 Jesus Christ is Lord,
 to the glory of God the Father.

GOSPEL *Luke 22:14—23:56*

Shorter: Luke 23:1–49

When the hour came, Jesus took his place at table with the apostles. He said to them, "I have eagerly desired to eat this Passover with you before I suffer, for, I tell you, I shall not eat it again until there is fulfillment in the kingdom of God." Then he took a cup, gave thanks, and said, "Take this and share it among yourselves; for I tell you that from this time on I shall not drink of the fruit of the vine until the kingdom of God comes." Then he took the bread, said the blessing, broke it, and gave it to them, saying, "This is my body, which will be given for you; do this in memory of me." And likewise the cup after they had eaten, saying, "This cup is the new covenant in my blood, which will be shed for you.

"And yet behold, the hand of the one who is to betray me is with me on the table; for the Son of Man indeed goes as it has been determined; but woe to that man by whom he is betrayed." And they began to debate among themselves who among them would do such a deed.

Then an argument broke out among them about which of them should be regarded as the greatest. He said to them, "The kings of the Gentiles lord it over them and those in authority over them are addressed as 'Benefactors'; but among you it shall not be so. Rather, let the greatest among you be as the youngest, and the leader as the servant. For who is greater: the one seated at table or the one who serves? Is it not the one seated at table? I am among you as the one who serves. It is you who have stood by me in my trials; and I confer a kingdom on you, just as my Father has conferred one on me, that you may eat and drink at my table in my kingdom; and you will sit on thrones judging the twelve tribes of Israel.

"Simon, Simon, behold Satan has demanded to sift all of you like wheat, but I have prayed that your own faith may not fail; and once you have turned back, you must strengthen your brothers." He said to him, "Lord, I am prepared to go to prison and to die with you." But he replied, "I tell you, Peter, before the cock crows this day, you will deny three times that you know me."

He said to them, "When I sent you forth without a money bag or a sack or sandals, were you in need of anything?" "No, nothing," they replied. He said to them, "But now one who has a money bag should take it, and likewise a sack, and one who does not have a sword should sell his cloak and buy one. For I tell you that this Scripture must be fulfilled in me, namely, *He was counted among the wicked*; and indeed what is written about me is coming to fulfillment." Then they said, "Lord, look, there are two swords here." But he replied, "It is enough!"

Then going out, he went, as was his custom, to the Mount of Olives, and the disciples followed him. When he arrived at the place he said to them, "Pray that you may not undergo the test." After withdrawing about a stone's throw from them and kneeling, he prayed, saying, "Father, if you are willing, take this cup away from me; still, not my will but yours be done." And to strengthen him an angel from heaven appeared to him. He was in such agony and he prayed so fervently that his sweat became like drops of blood falling on the ground. When he rose from prayer and returned to his disciples, he found them sleeping from grief. He said to them, "Why are you sleeping? Get up and pray that you may not undergo the test."

While he was still speaking, a crowd approached and in front was one of the Twelve, a man named Judas. He went up to Jesus to kiss him. Jesus said to him, "Judas, are you betraying the Son of Man with a kiss?" His disciples realized what was about to happen, and they asked, "Lord, shall we strike with a sword?" And one of them struck the high priest's servant and cut off his right ear. But Jesus said in reply, "Stop, no more of this!" Then he touched the servant's ear and healed him. And Jesus said to the chief priests and temple guards and elders who had come for him, "Have you come out as against a robber, with swords and clubs? Day after day I was with you in the temple area, and you did not seize me; but this is your hour, the time for the power of darkness."

After arresting him they led him away and took him into the house of the high priest; Peter was following at a distance. They lit a fire in the middle of the courtyard and sat around it, and Peter sat down with them. When a maid saw him seated in the light, she looked intently at him and said, "This man too was with him." But he denied it saying, "Woman, I do not know him." A short while later someone else saw him and said, "You too are one of them"; but Peter answered, "My friend, I am not." About an hour later, still another insisted, "Assuredly, this man too was with him, for he also is a Galilean." But Peter said, "My friend, I do not know what you are talking about." Just as he was saying this, the cock crowed, and the Lord turned and looked at Peter; and Peter remembered the word of the Lord, how he had said to him, "Before the cock crows today, you will deny me three times." He went out and began to weep bitterly. The men who held Jesus in custody were ridiculing and beating him. They blindfolded him and questioned him, saying, "Prophesy! Who is it that struck you?" And they reviled him in saying many other things against him.

When day came the council of elders of the people met, both chief priests and scribes, and they brought him before their Sanhedrin. They said, "If you are the Christ, tell us," but he replied to them, "If I tell you, you will not believe, and if I question, you will not respond. But from this time on the Son of Man will be seated at the right hand of the power of God." They all asked, "Are you then the Son of God?" He replied to them, "You say that I am." Then they said, "What further need have we for testimony? We have heard it from his own mouth."

Then the whole assembly of them arose and brought him before Pilate. They brought charges against him, saying, "We found this man misleading our people; he opposes the payment of taxes to Caesar and maintains that he is the Christ, a king." Pilate asked him, "Are you the king of the Jews?" He said to him in reply, "You say so." Pilate then addressed the chief priests and the crowds, "I find this man not guilty." But they were adamant and said, "He is inciting the people with his teaching throughout all Judea, from Galilee where he began even to here."

On hearing this Pilate asked if the man was a Galilean; and upon learning that he was under Herod's jurisdiction, he sent him to Herod, who was in Jerusalem at that time. Herod was very glad to see Jesus; he had been wanting to see him for a long time, for he had heard about him and had been hoping to see him perform some sign. He questioned him at length, but he gave him no answer. The chief priests and scribes, meanwhile, stood by accusing him harshly. Herod and his soldiers treated him contemptuously and mocked him, and after clothing him in resplendent garb, he sent him back to Pilate. Herod and Pilate became friends that very day, even though they had been enemies formerly. Pilate then summoned the chief priests, the rulers, and the people and said to them, "You brought this man to me and accused him of inciting the people to revolt. I have conducted my investigation in your presence and have not found this man guilty of the charges you have brought against him, nor did Herod, for he sent him back to us. So no capital crime has been committed by him. Therefore I shall have him flogged and then release him."

But all together they shouted out, "Away with this man! Release Barabbas to us." — Now Barabbas had been imprisoned for a rebellion that had taken place in the city and for murder.—Again Pilate addressed them, still wishing to release Jesus, but they continued their shouting, "Crucify him! Crucify him!" Pilate addressed them a third time, "What evil has this man done? I found him guilty of no capital crime. Therefore I shall have him flogged and then release him." With loud shouts, however, they persisted in calling for his crucifixion, and their voices prevailed. The verdict of Pilate was that their demand should be granted. So he released the man who had been imprisoned for rebellion and murder, for whom they asked, and he handed Jesus over to them to deal with as they wished.

As they led him away they took hold of a certain Simon, a Cyrenian, who was coming in from the country; and after laying the cross on him, they made him carry it behind Jesus. A large crowd of people followed Jesus, including many women who mourned and lamented him. Jesus turned to them and said, "Daughters of Jerusalem, do not weep for me; weep instead for yourselves and for your children for indeed, the days are coming when people will say, 'Blessed are the bar-

ren, the wombs that never bore and the breasts that never nursed.' At that time people will say to the mountains, 'Fall upon us!' and to the hills, 'Cover us!' for if these things are done when the wood is green what will happen when it is dry?" Now two others, both criminals, were led away with him to be executed.

When they came to the place called the Skull, they crucified him and the criminals there, one on his right, the other on his left. Then Jesus said, "Father, forgive them, they know not what they do." They divided his garments by casting lots. The people stood by and watched; the rulers, meanwhile, sneered at him and said, "He saved others, let him save himself if he is the chosen one, the Christ of God." Even the soldiers jeered at him. As they approached to offer him wine they called out, "If you are King of the Jews, save yourself." Above him there was an inscription that read, "This is the King of the Jews."

Now one of the criminals hanging there reviled Jesus, saying, "Are you not the Christ? Save yourself and us." The other, however, rebuking him, said in reply, "Have you no fear of God, for you are subject to the same condemnation? And indeed, we have been condemned justly, for the sentence we received corresponds to our crimes, but this man has done nothing criminal." Then he said, "Jesus, remember me when you come into your kingdom." He replied to him, "Amen, I say to you, today you will be with me in Paradise."

It was now about noon and darkness came over the whole land until three in the afternoon because of an eclipse of the sun. Then the veil of the temple was torn down the middle. Jesus cried out in a loud voice, "Father, into your hands I commend my spirit"; and when he had said this he breathed his last.

[Here all kneel and pause for a short time.]

The centurion who witnessed what had happened glorified God and said, "This man was innocent beyond doubt." When all the people who had gathered for this spectacle saw what had happened, they returned home beating their breasts; but all his acquaintances stood at a distance, including the women who had followed him from Galilee and saw these events.

Now there was a virtuous and righteous man named Joseph, who, though he was a member of the council, had not consented to their plan of action. He came from the Jewish town of Arimathea and was awaiting the kingdom of God. He went to Pilate and asked for the body of Jesus. After he had taken the body down, he wrapped it in a linen cloth and laid him in a rock-hewn tomb in which no one had yet been buried. It was the day of preparation, and the sabbath was about to begin. The women who had come from Galilee with him followed behind, and when they had seen the tomb and the way in which his body was laid in it, they returned and prepared spices and perfumed oils. Then they rested on the sabbath according to the commandment.

Practice of Charity

In the first part of the passion Gospel from Luke, Jesus gives another perspective to leadership when he tells his closest friends, "let the greatest among you be as the youngest, and the leader as the servant." Continuing his teaching on leadership, Jesus says, "I am among you as the one who serves." ◆ Consider any leadership role you have, whether in your family, at work, or among friends. How does this Gospel change your perspective on leadership? How can your leadership conform to the Gospel? Make concrete steps to change your leadership style. ◆ Consider workers in the service industry whom you encounter. How do you show appreciation? ◆ During this Holy Week, write a note to someone who has served you, perhaps a maintenance person at work or in the parish, a sales clerk, or a hostess at a restaurant and express your appreciation for their service.

Download more questions and activities for families, Christian initiation groups, and other adult groups at http://www.ltp.org/ahw.

Scripture Insights

Paul's Letter to the Philippians gave homage in the early Church to the Christ event. Paul describes Jesus as one in the form of God who humbled himself by taking on our form and going to a sacrificial death to exemplify the love God has for us. This early hymn shows how we recognize Jesus as Christ and Lord who brings God's glory into our world.

Luke's passion is shaped by tradition. The Passover preparations and meal are unique as Jesus instructs the disciples on the importance of service for the future mission. At the Mount of Olives, Jesus' prayer is framed by warnings against temptation, and his arrest in betrayal and violence, even as Jesus heals the high priest's injured slave. Peter's later denials, where he fails to identify with Jesus when challenged, are told before the account of Jesus' suffering. The assault during the arrest is met with healing, and Peter's betrayal is met with forgiveness and repentance.

At the trial before the Sanhedrin, Jesus accepts that he is the Christ, the Son of Man who will come as the final judge, and the Son of God. The Roman trial follows, set around a visit to Herod. Jesus emerges as king and is eventually handed over to death by Pilate, who, nonetheless, declares him innocent. Finally, with words of compassion and warning, Luke describes Jesus' road to the cross.

Jesus is crucified between criminals; he forgives his crucifiers, and he welcomes repentant sinners. While he commends his spirit into the Father's hands, the Roman centurion announces what many have known all along: "This man was innocent beyond doubt." All return home, beating their breasts in grief and ripe for repentance.

◆ What does Paul's hymn reveal about Jesus' suffering and death?

◆ How does Luke's passion narrative show Jesus as both prophet and savior?

◆ As Jesus ends his earthly mission in forgiveness, Luke sends us out in repentance and mission. What is your mission during this Holy Week?

Holy Thursday brings to an end the forty days of Lent, which make up the season of anticipation of the great Three Days. Composed of prayer, almsgiving, fasting, and the preparation of the catechumens for baptism, the season of Lent is now brought to a close, and the Three Days begin as we approach the liturgy of Holy Thursday evening. As those to be initiated into the Church have prepared themselves for their entrance into the fullness of life, so have we been awakening in our hearts, minds, and bodies our own entrances into the life of Christ, experienced in the life of the Church.

The Sacred Paschal Triduum (Latin for "three days") is the center, the core, of the entire year for Christians. These Three Days mark the mystery around which our entire lives are played out. Adults in the community are invited to plan ahead so that the whole time from Thursday night until Easter Sunday is free of social engagements, free of entertainment, and free of meals except for the most basic nourishment. We measure these days—indeed, our very salvation in the life of God—in step with the catechumens themselves; we are revitalized as we support them along the way and participate in their initiation rites.

We are asked to fast on Good Friday and to continue fasting, if possible, all through Holy Saturday as strictly as we can so that we come to the Easter Vigil hungry and full of excitement, parched and longing to feel the sacred water of the font on our skin. We pare down distractions on Good Friday and Holy Saturday so that we may be free for prayer and anticipation, for reflection, preparation, and silence. The Church is getting ready for the great night of the Easter Vigil.

As one who has been initiated into the Church, as one whose life has been wedded to this community gathered at the table, you should anticipate the Triduum with concentration and vigor. With you, the whole Church knows that our presence for the liturgies of the Triduum is not just an invitation. Everyone is needed. We pull out all the stops for these days. As humans, wedded to humanity by the joys and travails of life and grafted onto the body of the Church by the sanctifying waters of Baptism, we lead the new members into new life in this community of faith.

To this end, the Three Days are seen not as three distinct liturgies, but as one movement. These days have been connected liturgically from the early days of the Christian Church. As members of this community, we should be personally committed to preparing for and attending the Triduum and its culmination in the Easter Vigil of Holy Saturday.

The Church proclaims the direction of the Triduum with the opening antiphon of Holy Thursday, which comes from Paul's Letter to the Galatians (6:14). With this verse the Church sets a spiritual environment into which we as committed Christians enter the Triduum:

> *We should glory in the Cross*
>   *of our Lord Jesus Christ,*
> *in whom is our salvation, life and resurrection,*
> *through whom we are saved and delivered.*

HOLY THURSDAY

On Thursday evening we enter into this Triduum together. Whether presider, lector, preacher, greeter, altar server, minister of the Eucharist, decorator, or person in the remote corner in the last pew of the church, we begin, as always, by hearkening to the Word of God. These are the Scriptures for the liturgy of Holy Thursday:

Exodus 12:1–8, 11–14
Ancient instructions for the meal of the Passover.

1 Corinthians 11:23–26
Eat the bread and drink the cup until the return of the Lord.

John 13:1–15
Jesus washes the feet of the disciples.

Then the priest, like Jesus, does something strange: he washes feet. Jesus gave us this image of what the Church is supposed to look like, feel like, act like. Our position—whether as observer, washer or washed, servant or served—may be difficult. Yet we learn from the discomfort, from the awkwardness.

Then we celebrate the Eucharist. Because it is connected to the other liturgies of the Triduum on Good Friday and Holy Saturday night, the evening liturgy of Holy Thursday has no ending. Whether we stay to pray awhile or leave, we are now in the quiet, peace, and glory of the Triduum.

GOOD FRIDAY

We gather quietly in community on Friday and again listen to the Word of God:

Isaiah 52:13—53:12
The servant of the Lord was crushed for our sins.

Hebrews 4:14–16; 5:7–9
The Son of God learned obedience through his suffering.

John 18:1—19:42
The passion of Jesus Christ.

After the homily, we pray at length for all the world's needs: for the Church; for the pope, the clergy and all the baptized; for those preparing for initiation; for the unity of Christians; for Jews; for non-Christians; for atheists; for all in public office; and for those in special need.

Then there is another once-a-year event: the holy cross is held up in our midst, and we come forward one by one to do reverence with a kiss, bow, or genuflection. This communal reverence of an instrument of torture recalls the painful price, in the past and today, of salvation, the way in which our redemption is wrought, the scourging and humiliation of Jesus Christ that bring direction and life back to a humanity that is lost and dead. During the adoration of the cross, we sing not only of the sorrow, but of the glory of the cross by which we have been saved.

Again, we bring to mind the words of Paul (Galatians 6:14), on which last night's entrance antiphon is loosely based: "May I never boast except in the cross of our Lord Jesus Christ, through which the world has been crucified to me, and I to the world."

We continue in fasting and prayer and vigil, in rest and quiet, through Saturday. This Saturday for us is God's rest at the end of creation. It is Christ's repose in the tomb. It is Christ's visit with the dead.

EASTER VIGIL

Hungry now, pared down to basics, lightheaded from vigilance and full of excitement, we, the already baptized, gather in darkness and light a new fire. From this blaze we light a great candle that will make this night bright for us and will burn throughout Easter Time.

We hearken again to the Word of God with some of the most powerful narratives and proclamations of our tradition:

Genesis 1:1—2:2
The creation of the world.

Genesis 22:1–18
The sacrifice of Isaac.

Exodus 14:15—15:1
The crossing of the Red Sea.

Isaiah 54:5–14
You will not be afraid.

Isaiah 55:1–11
Come, come to the water.

Baruch 3:9–15, 32—4:4
Walk by the light of wisdom.

Ezekiel 36:16–17a, 18–28
The Lord says: I will sprinkle water.

Romans 6:3–11
United with him in death.

Year A: Matthew 28:1–10, Year B: Mark 16:1–7, Year C: Luke 24:1–12
Jesus has been raised.

After the readings, we call on our saints to stand with us as we go to the font and the priest celebrant blesses the waters. The chosen of all times and all places attend to what is about to take place. The elect renounce evil, profess the faith of the Church, and are baptized and anointed.

All of us renew our baptism. These are the moments when death and life meet, when we reject evil and make our promises to God. All of this is in the communion of the Church. So together we go to the table and celebrate the Easter Eucharist.

Prayer before Reading the Word

God of our ancestors,
you have raised up Jesus
and exalted him at your right hand
as Leader and Savior.

Open our minds to understand the Scriptures,
and, as with great joy we bless you in your temple,
make us witnesses who can proclaim
the repentance and forgiveness
you extend to all the nations
in the name of Jesus,
the Messiah, our great high priest,
who intercedes before you on our behalf,
living and reigning with you
in the unity of the Holy Spirit,
God, for ever and ever. Amen.

Prayer after Reading the Word

O God, the fountain of joy and of peace,
into the hands of your risen Son
you have entrusted the destinies
of peoples and of nations.

Keep us safe in those arms
from which no one can snatch us,
that we may proclaim your Word
in peace and in persecution,
until at last we stand before the Lamb
with songs of praise on our lips.

We ask this through the Lord Jesus,
our Passover and our Peace,
who lives and reigns with you
in the unity of the Holy Spirit,
God, for ever and ever. Amen.

Weekday Readings

April 18: Monday within the Octave of Easter
Acts 2:14, 22–33; Matthew 28:8–15
April 19: Tuesday within the Octave of Easter
Acts 2:36–41; John 20:11–18
April 20: Wednesday within the Octave of Easter
Acts 3:1–10; Luke 24:13–35
April 21: Thursday within the Octave of Easter
Acts 3:11–26; Luke 24:35–48
April 22: Friday within the Octave of Easter
Acts 4:1–12; John 21:1–14
April 23: Saturday within the Octave of Easter
Acts 4:13–21; Mark 16:9–15

April 25: Feast of St. Mark, Evangelist
1 Peter 5:5b–14; Mark 16:15–20
April 26: *Acts 4:32–37; John 3:7b–15*
April 27: *Acts 5:17–26; John 3:16–21*
April 28: *Acts 5:27–33; John 3:31–36*
April 29: *Acts 5:34–42; John 6:1–15*
April 30: *Acts 6:1–7; John 6:16–21*

May 2: *Acts 6:8–15; John 6:22–29*
May 3: Feast of Sts. Philip and James, Apostles
1 Corinthians 15:1–8; John 14:6–14
May 4: *Acts 8:1b–8; John 6:35–40*
May 5: *Acts 8:26–40; John 6:44–51*
May 6: *Acts 9:1–20; John 6:52–59*
May 7: *Acts 9:31–42; John 6:60–69*

May 9: *Acts 11:1–18; John 10:1–10*
May 10: *Acts 11:19–26; John 10:22–30*
May 11: *Acts 12:24—13:5a; John 12:44–50*
May 12: *Acts 13:13–25; John 13:16–20*
May 13: *Acts 13:26–33; John 14:1–6*
May 14: Feast of St. Matthias, Apostle
Acts 1:15–17, 20–26; John 15:9–17

May 16: *Acts 14:5–18; John 14:21–26*
May 17: *Acts 14:19–28; John 14:27–31a*
May 18: *Acts 15:1–6; John 15:1–8*
May 19: *Acts 15:7–21; John 15:9–11*
May 20: *Acts 15:22–31; John 15:12–17*
May 21: *Acts 16:1–10; John 15:18–21*

May 23: *Acts 16:11–15; John 15:26—16:4a*
May 24: *Acts 16:22–34; John 16:5–11*
May 25: *Acts 17:15, 22—18:1; John 16:12–15*
May 26: Solemnity of the Ascension of the Lord
[Ecclesiastical Provinces of Boston, Hartford,
New York, Newark, Omaha, and Philadelphia]
Acts 1:1–11; Ephesians 1:17–23 or Hebrews 9:24–28;
10:19–23; Luke 24:46–53
May 26: *Acts 18:1–8; John 16:16–20*
May 27: *Acts 18:9–18; John 16:20–23*
May 28: *Acts 18:23–28; John 16:23b–28*

May 30: *Acts 19:1–8; John 16:29–33*
**May 31: Feast of the Visitation of
the Blessed Virgin Mary**
Zephaniah 3:14–18a or Romans 12:9–16;
Luke 1:39–56
June 1: *Acts 20:28–38; John 17:11b–19*
June 2: *Acts 22:30; 23:6–11; John 17:20–26*
June 3: *Acts 25:13b–21; John 21:15–19*
June 4: *Acts 28:16–20, 30–31; John 21:20–25*

READING I *Acts 10:34a; 37–43*

Peter proceeded to speak and said: "You know what has happened all over Judea, beginning in Galilee after the baptism that John preached, how God anointed Jesus of Nazareth with the Holy Spirit and power. He went about doing good and healing all those oppressed by the devil, for God was with him. We are witnesses of all that he did both in the country of the Jews and in Jerusalem. They put him to death by hanging him on a tree. This man God raised on the third day and granted that he be visible, not to all the people, but to us, the witnesses chosen by God in advance, who ate and drank with him after he rose from the dead. He commissioned us to preach to the people and testify that he is the one appointed by God as judge of the living and the dead. To him all the prophets bear witness, that everyone who believes in him will receive forgiveness of sins through his name."

RESPONSORIAL PSALM
Psalm 118:1–2, 16–17, 22–23 (24)

R. This is the day the Lord has made; let us
      rejoice and be glad.
or: Alleluia.

Give thanks to the LORD, for he is good,
  for his mercy endures forever.
Let the house of Israel say,
  "His mercy endures forever." R.

"The right hand of the LORD has struck
      with power;
  the right hand of the LORD is exalted.
I shall not die, but live,
  and declare the works of the LORD." R.

The stone which the builders rejected
  has become the cornerstone.
By the LORD has this been done;
  it is wonderful in our eyes. R.

READING II *Colossians 3:1–4*

Alternate: 1 Corinthians 5:6b–8

Brothers and sisters: If then you were raised with Christ, seek what is above, where Christ is seated at the right hand of God. Think of what is above, not of what is on earth. For you have died, and your life is hidden with Christ in God. When Christ your life appears, then you too will appear with him in glory.

GOSPEL *John 20:1–9*

Alternate readings: Luke 24:1–12; or at an afternoon or evening Mass: Luke 24:13–35

On the first day of the week, Mary of Magdala came to the tomb early in the morning, while it was still dark, and saw the stone removed from the tomb. So she ran and went to Simon Peter and to the other disciple whom Jesus loved, and told them, "They have taken the Lord from the tomb, and we don't know where they put him." So Peter and the other disciple went out and came to the tomb. They both ran, but the other disciple ran faster than Peter and arrived at the tomb first; he bent down and saw the burial cloths there, but did not go in. When Simon Peter arrived after him, he went into the tomb and saw the burial cloths there, and the cloth that had covered his head, not with the burial cloths but rolled up in a separate place. Then the other disciple also went in, the one who had arrived at the tomb first, and he saw and believed. For they did not yet understand the Scripture that he had to rise from the dead.

Practice of Hope

What a privilege for Mary of Magdala to be at the tomb of Jesus and to be among the first to begin a journey from darkness to light, a journey to faith. Christ's rising from the dead, conquering death, gave Mary hope and gives us hope today. ◆ Take time this week to observe the signs of new life around you. Be aware of budding trees, of young birds, of growth in your relationships. How can you care for any of the new life that surrounds you? ◆ Nurture new life at your parish by greeting people, especially those whom you do not know. Consider being a greeter for the parish. ◆ Do flower beds on your parish grounds need to be tended? Is there a community garden in your neighborhood at which you could volunteer? Think of other ways you can care for new life.

Download more questions and activities for families, Christian initiation groups, and other adult groups at http://www.ltp.org/ahw.

Scripture Insights

John narrates Mary of Magdala's coming to Jesus' tomb on the week's first day. Mary is alone and "it was still dark." For John, darkness can indicate lack of faith, and that is the case with Mary. She will come into the light but has a journey to travel. Seeing the stone removed, she rushes to Simon Peter and the Beloved Disciple to report the tomb emptied. Where is the executed Jesus? We know that God is the one involved, but they must still catch on.

Peter and the Beloved Disciple run to the tomb. Peter leads, but the other disciple passes him, sees that the signs of death are absent, but relinquishes first entry. Peter has emerged as the leader, while the Beloved is the model disciple who both gives access and defers to his leader. We see the burial cloths rolled to one side, contrasting Jesus' raising of Lazarus, who was still bound. This is distinctive. Following into the empty tomb, the Beloved Disciple sees further evidence of death overcome by God. The burial cloths are folded and lain at opposite ends of the tomb. He believes (John 20:8). Peter's and Mary's responses are not recorded; their faith journeys need more time.

The disciples return home, as yet unaware of the Scripture of Jesus' resurrection. The Scripture is John's Gospel, and we eventually learn that we are blessed to have it (20:30–31). They witnessed, but we are summoned to believe because of that witness, to believe without seeing. Paul summons us likewise in his letter to the Colossians, as does Luke in the Acts of the Apostles. To find our place, we must "seek what is above" (Colossians 3:1).

◆ John claims that, despite our fears, death is not the end of Jesus' story. How does this offer you hope?

◆ Reflect on Jesus' summons to believe without seeing. How does this climax in the Easter story?

◆ In Acts, Peter comes to believe that all are accepted in the new covenant. How might Christ appear in your life, even unexpectedly?

READING I *Acts 5:12–16*

Many signs and wonders were done among the people at the hands of the apostles. They were all together in Solomon's portico. None of the others dared to join them, but the people esteemed them. Yet more than ever, believers in the Lord, great numbers of men and women, were added to them. Thus they even carried the sick out into the streets and laid them on cots and mats so that when Peter came by, at least his shadow might fall on one or another of them. A large number of people from the towns in the vicinity of Jerusalem also gathered, bringing the sick and those disturbed by unclean spirits, and they were all cured.

RESPONSORIAL PSALM
Psalm 118:2–4, 13–15, 22–24 (1)

R. Give thanks to the Lord, for he is good, his
       love is everlasting.
or: Alleluia.

Let the house of Israel say,
   "His mercy endures forever."
Let the house of Aaron say,
   "His mercy endures forever."
Let those who fear the LORD say,
   "His mercy endures forever." R.

I was hard pressed and was falling,
   but the LORD helped me.
My strength and my courage is the LORD,
   and he has been my savior.
The joyful shout of victory
   in the tents of the just. R.

The stone which the builders rejected
   has become the cornerstone.
By the LORD has this been done;
   it is wonderful in our eyes.
This is the day the LORD has made;
   let us be glad and rejoice in it. R.

READING II
Revelation 1:9–11a, 12–13, 17–19

I, John, your brother, who share with you the distress, the kingdom, and the endurance we have in Jesus, found myself on the island called Patmos because I proclaimed God's word and gave testimony to Jesus. I was caught up in spirit on the Lord's day and heard behind me a voice as loud as a trumpet, which said, "Write on a scroll what you see." Then I turned to see whose voice it was that spoke to me, and when I turned, I saw seven gold lampstands and in the midst of the lampstands one like a son of man, wearing an ankle-length robe, with a gold sash around his chest.

When I caught sight of him, I fell down at his feet as though dead. He touched me with his right hand and said, "Do not be afraid. I am the first and the last, the one who lives. Once I was dead, but now I am alive forever and ever. I hold the keys to death and the netherworld. Write down, therefore, what you have seen, and what is happening, and what will happen afterwards."

GOSPEL *John 20:19–31*

On the evening of that first day of the week, when the doors were locked, where the disciples were, for fear of the Jews, Jesus came and stood in their midst and said to them, "Peace be with you." When he had said this, he showed them his hands and his side. The disciples rejoiced when they saw the Lord. Jesus said to them again, "Peace be with you. As the Father has sent me, so I send you." And when he had said this, he breathed on them and said to them, "Receive the Holy Spirit. Whose sins you forgive are forgiven them, and whose sins you retain are retained."

Thomas, called Didymus, one of the Twelve, was not with them when Jesus came. So the other disciples said to him, "We have seen the Lord." But he said to them, "Unless I see the mark of the nails in his hands and put my finger into the nailmarks and put my hand into his side, I will not believe."

Now a week later his disciples were again inside and Thomas was with them. Jesus came, although the doors were locked, and stood in their midst and said, "Peace be with you." Then he said to Thomas, "Put your finger here and see my hands, and bring your hand and put it into my side, and do not be unbelieving, but believe." Thomas answered and said to him, "My Lord and my God!" Jesus said to him, "Have you come to believe because you have seen me? Blessed are those who have not seen and have believed."

Now Jesus did many other signs in the presence of his disciples that are not written in this book. But these are written that you may come to believe that Jesus is the Christ, the Son of God, and that through this belief you may have life in his name.

Practice of Faith

The account of Thomas' doubting assures us that even Jesus' followers, even those who had seen with their eyes, could struggle with belief. Thomas' story can help us during the times that we face doubt. ◆ Continue to grow your faith in Jesus through Scripture and tradition. Enrich your spiritual life through reading. Consider asking a parish staff member to suggest an author or look for suggestions in the local Catholic newspaper or magazine. ◆ Through your actions, help others who struggle with their faith. Perhaps a friend or family member isn't convinced that going to church is worth their time. Tell him or her about how your belief in Jesus affects your decisions, outlook on life, and hope for eternal life. ◆ Accompany a person who is struggling with faith. Spend time just listening to the person. Remember, as Pope Francis states in *The Joy of the Gospel*, the Church "is a place for everyone, with all their problems."

Download more questions and activities for families, Christian initiation groups, and other adult groups at http://www.ltp.org/ahw.

Scripture Insights

As we enter this week's readings from John's Gospel, Mary of Magdala has encountered the risen Christ, who sent her on a mission to prepare the other disciples for post-resurrection encounters (20:10–18). On the evening of the same day, Jesus comes to his frightened disciples with his greeting of peace (20:19).

Jesus shows his piercings and the disciples rejoice to see him. They see their Lord, yet there is something unworldly. The risen Jesus is the same—but different! He then associates them with his God-directed mission. Jesus is the sent one of God, and he now formally sends them as promised (13:20). Their commission is guaranteed by a creative act: Jesus breathes the Holy Spirit upon them, just as the Spirit hovered over creation (Genesis 1:2). They now have two tasks: forgive the sins of any who seek and bring the ongoing presence of Christ into the world.

Then we learn Thomas was not with the disciples for this encounter, and he will not accept the believing community unless he physically encounters the risen Jesus. Again on a Sunday, they encounter Jesus' peace, but now Thomas is there. Jesus challenges Thomas to place his finger into his wounds, asking him to stop his unbelief and become a believer. In response, Thomas makes a confession that summarizes all that faith requires. Jesus, as risen Lord, is the revelation of the presence of God among humankind. Jesus further asserts that those who believe without seeing such signs are blessed, thereby summoning us all to faith.

John preliminarily concludes in hope that the signs and wonders he shared has affirmed our belief in Jesus as Christ and Son of God. This is how we will find true life in this world. The Acts reading shows the firstfruits of this new life.

◆ Mary of Magdala is called the "Apostle to the Apostles." How does she inspire you to tell others about Christ?

◆ Thomas gives voice to all our doubts, fears, and need for proof. How does the risen Christ come to him? How do you notice the risen Christ?

◆ What do you think it means for you to have life in Jesus' name?

READING I *Acts 5:27–32, 40b–41*

When the captain and the court officers had brought the apostles in and made them stand before the Sanhedrin, the high priest questioned them, "We gave you strict orders, did we not, to stop teaching in that name? Yet you have filled Jerusalem with your teaching and want to bring this man's blood upon us." But Peter and the apostles said in reply, "We must obey God rather than men. The God of our ancestors raised Jesus, though you had him killed by hanging him on a tree. God exalted him at his right hand as leader and savior to grant Israel repentance and forgiveness of sins. We are witnesses of these things, as is the Holy Spirit whom God has given to those who obey him."

The Sanhedrin ordered the apostles to stop speaking in the name of Jesus, and dismissed them. So they left the presence of the Sanhedrin, rejoicing that they had been found worthy to suffer dishonor for the sake of the name.

RESPONSORIAL PSALM
Psalm 30:2, 4, 5–6, 11–12, 13 (2a)

R. I will praise you, Lord, for you have rescued me.
or: Alleluia.

I will extol you, O LORD, for you drew me clear
   and did not let my enemies rejoice over me.
O LORD, you brought me up from the
      netherworld;
   you preserved me from among those going
      down into the pit. R.

Sing praise to the LORD, you his faithful ones,
   and give thanks to his holy name.
For his anger lasts but a moment;
   a lifetime, his good will.
At nightfall, weeping enters in,
   but with the dawn, rejoicing. R.

Hear, O LORD, and have pity on me;
   O LORD, be my helper.
You changed my mourning into dancing;
   O LORD, my God, forever will I give
      you thanks. R.

READING II *Revelation 5:11–14*

I, John, looked and heard the voices of many angels who surrounded the throne and the living creatures and the elders. They were countless in number, and they cried out in a loud voice:
  "Worthy is the Lamb that was slain
    to receive power and riches, wisdom
       and strength,
    honor and glory and blessing."
Then I heard every creature in heaven and on earth and under the earth and in the sea, everything in the universe, cry out:
  "To the one who sits on the
       throne and to the Lamb
    be blessing and honor, glory and might,
    forever and ever."
The four living creatures answered, "Amen," and the elders fell down and worshiped.

GOSPEL *John 21:1–19*

Shorter: John 21:1–14

At that time, Jesus revealed himself again to his disciples at the Sea of Tiberias. He revealed himself in this way. Together were Simon Peter, Thomas called Didymus, Nathanael from Cana in Galilee, Zebedee's sons, and two others of his disciples. Simon Peter said to them, "I am going fishing." They said to him, "We also will come with you." So they went out and got into the boat, but that night they caught nothing. When it was already dawn, Jesus was standing on the shore; but the disciples did not realize that it was Jesus. Jesus said to them, "Children, have you caught anything to eat?" They answered him, "No." So he said to them, "Cast the net over the right side of the boat and you will find something." So they cast it, and were not able to pull it in because of the number of fish. So the disciple whom Jesus loved said to Peter, "It is the Lord." When Simon Peter heard that it was the Lord, he tucked in his garment, for he was lightly clad, and jumped into the sea. The other disciples came in the boat, for they were not far from shore, only about a hundred yards, dragging the net with the fish. When they climbed out on shore, they saw a charcoal fire with fish on it and bread. Jesus said to them, "Bring some of the fish you just caught." So Simon Peter went over and dragged the net ashore full of one hundred fifty-three large fish. Even though there were so many, the net was not torn. Jesus said to them, "Come, have breakfast." And none of the disciples dared to ask him, "Who are you?" because they realized it was the Lord. Jesus came over and took the bread and gave it to them, and in like manner the fish. This was now the third time Jesus was revealed to his disciples after being raised from the dead.

When they had finished breakfast, Jesus said to Simon Peter, "Simon, son of John, do you love me more than these?" Simon Peter answered him, "Yes, Lord, you know that I love you." Jesus said to him, "Feed my lambs." He then said to Simon Peter a second time, "Simon, son of John, do you love me?" Simon Peter answered him, "Yes, Lord, you know that I love you." Jesus said to him, "Tend my sheep." Jesus said to him the third time, "Simon, son of John, do you love me?" Peter was distressed that Jesus had said to him a third time, "Do you love me?" and he said to him, "Lord, you know everything; you know that I love you." Jesus said to him, "Feed my sheep. Amen, amen, I say to you, when you were younger, you used to dress yourself and go where you wanted; but when you grow old, you will stretch out your hands, and someone else will dress you and lead you where you do not want to go." He said this signifying by what kind of death he would glorify God. And when he had said this, he said to him, "Follow me."

Practice of Charity

John's Gospel shows the Lord feeding, forgiving, and inspiring his disciples to move on. Just as God does this for us, we are to do it for others. ♦ Invite someone who is struggling to a meal in your home. Offer your hospitality with no expectations and appreciate their presence. ♦ Journal about times when you have felt forgiveness as well as times in which you have forgiven others.

Download more questions and activities for families, Christian initiation groups, and other adult groups at http://www.ltp.org/ahw.

Scripture Insights

John 21 reintroduces the Gospel through an epilogue. This later time and place by the Galilean sea alerts us that the story is not ended. Indeed, the journey of believing may never end as such. We follow Peter's lead, who last spoke thrice denying Jesus while warming himself by a charcoal fire with Jesus' enemies in the high priest's court. He had sworn to lay down his life for Jesus, but his defense was prevented in the garden. The earnest leader denied all relationship with Jesus. Now, he says, "I'm going fishing." Peter was to lead others to new life in community but has returned to his old life.

After a dark night, morning breaks to reveal Jesus ashore, guiding even actively failing disciples. The Beloved Disciple continues to witness and give access by recognizing the Lord. Peter, in keeping with his zealous character, jumps into the sea to get to Jesus. Reaching land, he returns on Jesus' command to haul the catch ashore in the unbroken net. The abundance echoes the wine and food Jesus provided (2:1–12; 6:1–14), representing the inclusivity of the Church.

Jesus meets the disciples around a new charcoal fire and meal. Reconciling Peter's relationship with Jesus takes center stage as Jesus confronts Peter repeatedly, upsetting his equilibrium and challenging him to decision and new action. Thrice inquiring about Peter's love, Jesus brings him into a binding relationship with missional consequences. Peter's leadership is clarified pastorally as he is mandated the new shepherd of the flock of the children of God, his journey culminating in the story even as it begins anew beyond the story's boundaries as Jesus commands, "Follow me."

♦ Peter was going to take up his former life of fishing. When have you been tempted to return to a previous way of living?

♦ Jesus ultimately meets Peter where he is, in his imperfection. How is this a powerful lesson of hope for struggling believers of all time?

♦ John characterizes Peter as the leader and the Beloved Disciple as the model believer. How might we discern our gifts if the best leader may not be the best disciple, and vice versa?

READING I *Acts 13:14, 43–52*

Paul and Barnabas continued on from Perga and reached Antioch in Pisidia. On the sabbath they entered the synagogue and took their seats. Many Jews and worshipers who were converts to Judaism followed Paul and Barnabas, who spoke to them and urged them to remain faithful to the grace of God.

On the following sabbath almost the whole city gathered to hear the word of the Lord. When the Jews saw the crowds, they were filled with jealousy and with violent abuse contradicted what Paul said. Both Paul and Barnabas spoke out boldly and said, "It was necessary that the word of God be spoken to you first, but since you reject it and condemn yourselves as unworthy of eternal life, we now turn to the Gentiles. For so the Lord has commanded us, *I have made you a light to the Gentiles, that you may be an instrument of salvation to the ends of the earth.*"

The Gentiles were delighted when they heard this and glorified the word of the Lord. All who were destined for eternal life came to believe, and the word of the Lord continued to spread through the whole region. The Jews, however, incited the women of prominence who were worshipers and the leading men of the city, stirred up a persecution against Paul and Barnabas, and expelled them from their territory. So they shook the dust from their feet in protest against them, and went to Iconium. The disciples were filled with joy and the Holy Spirit.

RESPONSORIAL PSALM
Psalm 100:1–2, 3, 5 (3c)

R. We are his people, the sheep of his flock.
or: Alleluia.

Sing joyfully to the LORD, all you lands;
    serve the LORD with gladness;
    come before him with joyful song.   R.

Know that the LORD is God;
    he made us, his we are,
    his people, the flock he tends.   R.

The LORD is good:
    his kindness endures forever,
    and his faithfulness, to all generations.   R.

READING II *Revelation 7:9, 14b–17*

I, John, had a vision of a great multitude, which no one could count, from every nation, race, people, and tongue. They stood before the throne and before the Lamb, wearing white robes and holding palm branches in their hands.

Then one of the elders said to me, "These are the ones who have survived the time of great distress; they have washed their robes and made them white in the blood of the Lamb.

"For this reason they stand before God's throne
    and worship him day and night in
        his temple.
The one who sits on the throne
    will shelter them.
They will not hunger or thirst anymore,
    nor will the sun or any heat strike them.
For the Lamb who is in the center of the throne
    will shepherd them
    and lead them to springs
        of life-giving water,
    and God will wipe away every tear from
        their eyes."

GOSPEL *John 10:27–30*

Jesus said: "My sheep hear my voice; I know them, and they follow me. I give them eternal life, and they shall never perish. No one can take them out of my hand. My Father, who has given them to me, is greater than all, and no one can take them out of the Father's hand. The Father and I are one."

Practice of Hope

In the first reading from the Acts of the Apostles, Paul and Barnabas allow God's Spirit to work through them as they preach to Jews and Gentiles in distant regions. Some Jewish leaders are jealous, however, and speak against the apostles. Paul and Barnabas remain true to their calling in the face of harassment. With perseverance, they spread the Lord's Word throughout the region. ◆ Take stock of your personal skills and talents and examine how you use them for God's glory. How can you seek to be a light to others? ◆ Consider embarking on a new hobby, activity, or endeavor that brings you enjoyment. Most likely, you are being inspired by our Creator to enhance the world with more of your gifts and energy. ◆ Meditate on the image of the Good Shepherd. Listen for God's voice.

Download more questions and activities for families, Christian initiation groups, and other adult groups at http://www.ltp.org/ahw.

Scripture Insights

Today's Gospel passage is situated within an event occurring in John 10:22–42. The verses just prior to today's Gospel note that the account occurs in the temple area on the Portico of Solomon in winter during the feast of Dedication (John 10:22–23), known today as Hanukkah. Jesus focuses first on his role as the messiah then climaxes in his self-revelation as the Son of God. In this brief discourse, we learn it is not sufficient to hear the shepherd's voice; true disciples follow it. The reward is life in union in this relationship. We can never be snatched from God's hands. This life, however, begins with belonging to God here and now. It continues even as we pass from this world into God's eternal presence.

Solomon's portico, on the eastern face of the temple, is a fitting backdrop for this discourse occurring during the festival commemorating Judaism's resistance to blasphemy, idolatry, and apostasy. Speculation about Jesus' messiahship has been in the air for some time. Jesus intensifies the imagery of his relationship with God as Son to the Father. He draws his sheep to him and, in so doing, presses far beyond both his interrogators' messianic expectations and comfort level by presenting his oneness with God.

"The Father and I are one" (10:30) articulates a familiar truth for us, but first-century Jewish people found it difficult. One teaching they understood unambiguously was that God is one (Deuteronomy 6:4). When Jesus spoke of "the Father and I," it seemed like two, but this is the stunning beauty of God's gift of Jesus to the world. The Son is indeed one with the Father in love and pastoral care for all who are open to their one voice.

◆ How do you see Jesus as caring for you in union with the Father and the Holy Spirit?

◆ In Acts, the apostles stand up to the powerful. How might you rise to such a challenge?

◆ John follows the psalmist in speaking of God's enduring mercy and faithfulness. Do you envision God and/or Christ as Shepherd? If so, how does this help? If not, how might it?

READING I Acts 14:21–27

After Paul and Barnabas had proclaimed the good news to that city and made a considerable number of disciples, they returned to Lystra and to Iconium and to Antioch. They strengthened the spirits of the disciples and exhorted them to persevere in the faith, saying, "It is necessary for us to undergo many hardships to enter the kingdom of God." They appointed elders for them in each church and, with prayer and fasting, commended them to the Lord in whom they had put their faith. Then they traveled through Pisidia and reached Pamphylia. After proclaiming the word at Perga they went down to Attalia. From there they sailed to Antioch, where they had been commended to the grace of God for the work they had now accomplished. And when they arrived, they called the church together and reported what God had done with them and how he had opened the door of faith to the Gentiles.

RESPONSORIAL PSALM
Psalm 145:8–9, 10–11, 12–13 (see 1)

R. I will praise your name for ever, my king and
        my God.
or: Alleluia.

The LORD is gracious and merciful,
    slow to anger and of great kindness.
The LORD is good to all
    and compassionate toward all his works. R.

Let all your works give you thanks, O LORD,
    and let your faithful ones bless you.
Let them discourse of the glory of your kingdom
    and speak of your might. R.

Let them make known your might to the
        children of Adam,
    and the glorious splendor of your kingdom.
Your kingdom is a kingdom for all ages,
    and your dominion endures through
        all generations. R.

READING II Revelation 21:1–5a

Then I, John, saw a new heaven and a new earth. The former heaven and the former earth had passed away, and the sea was no more. I also saw the holy city, a new Jerusalem, coming down out of heaven from God, prepared as a bride adorned for her husband. I heard a loud voice from the throne saying, "Behold, God's dwelling is with the human race. He will dwell with them and they will be his people and God himself will always be with them as their God. He will wipe every tear from their eyes, and there shall be no more death or mourning, wailing or pain, for the old order has passed away."

The One who sat on the throne said, "Behold, I make all things new."

GOSPEL John 13:31–33a, 34–35

When Judas had left them, Jesus said, "Now is the Son of Man glorified, and God is glorified in him. If God is glorified in him, God will also glorify him in himself, and God will glorify him at once. My children, I will be with you only a little while longer. I give you a new commandment: love one another. As I have loved you, so you also should love one another. This is how all will know that you are my disciples, if you have love for one another."

Practice of Charity

Our readings invite us to imagine and strive for a world utterly transformed by God's love. When have you experienced God's love through someone else? In what concrete way have you loved others? Is there a person or group of people from whom you are deliberately withholding your love? Talk with Jesus about this situation. ◆ List all of the countries of the world that you can think of. Pray for God's love to fill every person in every nation. Conclude your prayer with today's psalm. ◆ Talk with someone who is mourning the death of a loved one. Pray for that person, or pray with him or her if you can. Ask God to "wipe every tear from their eyes."

Download more questions and activities for families, Christian initiation groups, and other adult groups at http://www.ltp.org/ahw.

Scripture Insights

The first reading for this Fifth Sunday of Easter reminds us of the energy of a young and enthusiastic community of faith. While this passage from Acts brings to conclusion the first missionary journey of Paul and Barnabas, it also provides us with insight as to how the members of the early Church needed to support and encourage one another to remain faithful, particularly in times of hardship.

In our text from the Book of Revelation, reminiscent of the concluding chapters of Isaiah, we hear of a time to come when all will be well, when the world as we know it will be no more. The picture is one of restoration and consolation. God will "make all things new" (21:5a).

The setting of today's Gospel passage is the Last Supper. Our lectionary reading has selected certain verses from John 13 in a manner that does not necessarily help us understand what has transpired and what will happen. In the opening verses of this chapter, Jesus washes the feet of his disciples; in the closing verses (three verses after today's reading), Peter asks Jesus where he is going and wants to know why he cannot go with him. Jesus responds by telling Peter that he will deny Jesus three times. Thus, while our reading for today most definitely refers to and emphasizes a new commandment of love, the depth of Jesus' love seems to be undercut by the removal of several verses of this pericope. Jesus commands us "to love one another" (13:35). Even when we fail to love as Jesus loves, his love will embrace us when we return.

◆ On a map in your Bible, find the cities where Paul and Barnabas traveled. Reflect on their passion as they spread the good news over such a vast region, approximately 1,200 miles.

◆ Read today's responsorial psalm reflectively. How have you experienced God's mercy and kindness? Identify one or more events when you have known the compassion of God.

◆ Read John 13:1–35 and reflect on the depth of Jesus' love.

READING I *Acts 15:1–2, 22–29*

Some who had come down from Judea were instructing the brothers, "Unless you are circumcised according to the Mosaic practice, you cannot be saved." Because there arose no little dissension and debate by Paul and Barnabas with them, it was decided that Paul, Barnabas, and some of the others should go up to Jerusalem to the apostles and elders about this question.

The apostles and elders, in agreement with the whole church, decided to choose representatives and to send them to Antioch with Paul and Barnabas. The ones chosen were Judas, who was called Barsabbas, and Silas, leaders among the brothers. This is the letter delivered by them:

"The apostles and the elders, your brothers, to the brothers in Antioch, Syria, and Cilicia of Gentile origin: greetings. Since we have heard that some of our number who went out without any mandate from us have upset you with their teachings and disturbed your peace of mind, we have with one accord decided to choose representatives and to send them to you along with our beloved Barnabas and Paul, who have dedicated their lives to the name of our Lord Jesus Christ. So we are sending Judas and Silas who will also convey this same message by word of mouth: 'It is the decision of the Holy Spirit and of us not to place on you any burden beyond these necessities, namely, to abstain from meat sacrificed to idols, from blood, from meats of strangled animals, and from unlawful marriage. If you keep free of these, you will be doing what is right. Farewell.'"

RESPONSORIAL PSALM
Psalm 67:2–3, 5, 6, 8 (4)

R. O God, let all the nations praise you!
or: Alleluia.

May God have pity on us and bless us;
   may he let his face shine upon us.
So may your way be known upon earth;
   among all nations, your salvation. R.

May the nations be glad and exult
   because you rule the peoples in equity;
   the nations on the earth you guide. R.

May the peoples praise you, O God;
   may all the peoples praise you!
May God bless us,
   and may all the ends of the earth
      fear him! R.

READING II *Revelation 21:10–14, 22–23*

The angel took me in spirit to a great, high mountain and showed me the holy city Jerusalem coming down out of heaven from God. It gleamed with the splendor of God. Its radiance was like that of a precious stone, like jasper, clear as crystal. It had a massive, high wall, with twelve gates where twelve angels were stationed and on which names were inscribed, the names of the twelve tribes of the Israelites. There were three gates facing east, three north, three south, and three west. The wall of the city had twelve courses of stones as its foundation, on which were inscribed the twelve names of the twelve apostles of the Lamb.

I saw no temple in the city for its temple is the Lord God almighty and the Lamb. The city had no need of sun or moon to shine on it, for the glory of God gave it light, and its lamp was the Lamb.

GOSPEL *John 14:23–29*

Jesus said to his disciples: "Whoever loves me will keep my word, and my Father will love him, and we will come to him and make our dwelling with him. Whoever does not love me does not keep my words; yet the word you hear is not mine but that of the Father who sent me.

"I have told you this while I am with you. The Advocate, the Holy Spirit, whom the Father will send in my name, will teach you everything and remind you of all that I told you. Peace I leave with you; my peace I give to you. Not as the world gives do I give it to you. Do not let your hearts be troubled or afraid. You heard me tell you, 'I am going away and I will come back to you.' If you loved me, you would rejoice that I am going to the Father;

for the Father is greater than I. And now I have told you this before it happens, so that when it happens you may believe."

Practice of Faith

Our faith in Christ is grounded on the teaching of the apostles, who were filled with and guided by the Holy Spirit. The same Spirit that continues to guide the Church today also dwells within each of us and leads us to true and lasting peace. ◆ What keeps you from resting in God's peace right now? Share your deepest fears with God. Ponder the fears that his Son may have felt too. ◆ Spend time in Eucharistic adoration this week. Reflect on the ways God has drawn close to you in Christ. Ask God to help you bear Christ's light to places and situations that remain in darkness. ◆ Learn more about the foundations of our faith, our creeds, by reading the *Catechism of the Catholic Church*, 185–195. (The catechism can be found on the internet.) As you recite the Nicene or Apostles' Creed at Mass, pay close attention to the meaning of each line.

Download more questions and activities for families, Christian initiation groups, and other adult groups at http://www.ltp.org/ahw.

Scripture Insights

The reading from Acts alerts us to the intense controversy between Jewish and Gentile followers of Jesus. While the first two verses of the reading make it clear that circumcision was the primary issue, twenty verses that detail whether this and other Jewish customs were to be practiced by Gentile converts are not part of the reading in the lectionary. In essence, those verses show the significance of these Jewish practices in the early Church. The text goes on to state that the decision not to place any undue burden on the Gentiles came from the Holy Spirit.

The responsorial psalm refrain, "O God, let all the nations praise you," seems to reinforce the notion of inclusivity that Acts expresses. Our gracious God invites all peoples into a loving relationship. No one from any land is excluded.

The Gospel reading for today is from a section of John known as the "last discourse," Jesus' final words to his disciples during the Last Supper. Within these chapters (14—17), we hear Jesus giving instructions to his disciples. Today's portion of this material focuses on the coming of the Holy Spirit, the gift of peace, and Jesus' return to his Father. The tender words in verse 27, "Do not let your hearts be troubled," were also spoken at the very beginning of this discourse (14:1). Jesus' return to the Father, after his passion, will bring about a new relationship and a new era, that of the Holy Spirit.

◆ Conflict within Christian communities is not unusual. When have you experienced such tension, and how was it resolved?

◆ Recognizing the many lands that are in a state of war, pray today's responsorial psalm and ask God for guidance as to how you can help bring peace to our troubled world.

◆ Reflect on the words "do not let your hearts be troubled." Imagine that Jesus is speaking these words to you today.

READING I *Acts 1:1–11*

In the first book, Theophilus, I dealt with all that Jesus did and taught until the day he was taken up, after giving instructions through the Holy Spirit to the apostles whom he had chosen. He presented himself alive to them by many proofs after he had suffered, appearing to them during forty days and speaking about the kingdom of God. While meeting with them, he enjoined them not to depart from Jerusalem, but to wait for "the promise of the Father about which you have heard me speak; for John baptized with water, but in a few days you will be baptized with the Holy Spirit."

When they had gathered together they asked him, "Lord, are you at this time going to restore the kingdom to Israel?" He answered them, "It is not for you to know the times or seasons that the Father has established by his own authority. But you will receive power when the Holy Spirit comes upon you, and you will be my witnesses in Jerusalem, throughout Judea and Samaria, and to the ends of the earth." When he had said this, as they were looking on, he was lifted up, and a cloud took him from their sight. While they were looking intently at the sky as he was going, suddenly two men dressed in white garments stood beside them. They said, "Men of Galilee, why are you standing there looking at the sky? This Jesus who has been taken up from you into heaven will return in the same way as you have seen him going into heaven."

RESPONSORIAL PSALM
Psalm 47:2–3, 6–7, 8–9 (6)

R. God mounts his throne to shouts of joy:
 a blare of trumpets for the Lord.
or: Alleluia.

All you peoples, clap your hands,
 shout to God with cries of gladness,
for the LORD, the Most High, the awesome,
 is the great king over all the earth. R.

God mounts his throne amid shouts of joy;
 the LORD, amid trumpet blasts.
Sing praise to God, sing praise;
 sing praise to our king, sing praise. R.

For king of all the earth is God;
 sing hymns of praise.
God reigns over the nations,
 God sits upon his holy throne. R.

READING II
Hebrews 9:24–28; 10:19–23

Alternate reading: Ephesians 1:17–23

Christ did not enter into a sanctuary made by hands, a copy of the true one, but heaven itself, that he might now appear before God on our behalf. Not that he might offer himself repeatedly, as the high priest enters each year into the sanctuary with blood that is not his own; if that were so, he would have had to suffer repeatedly from the foundation of the world. But now once for all he has appeared at the end of the ages to take away sin by his sacrifice. Just as it is appointed that men and women die once, and after this the judgment, so also Christ, offered once to take away the sins of many, will appear a second time, not to take away sin but to bring salvation to those who eagerly await him.

Therefore, brothers and sisters, since through the blood of Jesus we have confidence of entrance into the sanctuary by the new and living way he opened for us through the veil, that is, his flesh, and since we have "a great priest over the house of God," let us approach with a sincere heart and in absolute trust, with our hearts sprinkled clean from an evil conscience and our bodies washed in pure water. Let us hold unwaveringly to our confession that gives us hope, for he who made the promise is trustworthy.

GOSPEL *Luke 24:46–53*

Jesus said to his disciples: "Thus it is written that the Christ would suffer and rise from the dead on the third day and that repentance, for the forgiveness of sins, would be preached in his name to all the nations, beginning from Jerusalem. You are witnesses of these things. And behold I am sending the promise of my Father upon you; but stay in the city until you are clothed with power from on high."

Then he led them out as far as Bethany, raised his hands, and blessed them. As he blessed them he parted from them and was taken up to heaven. They did him homage and then returned to Jerusalem with great joy, and they were continually in the temple praising God.

Practice of Hope

Each reading refers to God's *promise*. The promises to offer salvation to all and to share the Holy Spirit are fulfilled. Other promises, such as the fulfillment of God's kingdom, we await in hope. ♦ How well do you keep your promises? Ask God to help you make and keep promises that are life-giving and holy. ♦ Study an image of the Ascension that you especially like. What do you feel as you look at the image? What does this image reveal about what God has promised us in Christ? ♦ Invite a few friends to share their hopes with you. What are their short-term hopes? What are their long-term ones? Could they be more open to the guidance of the Holy Spirit? Could you?

Download more questions and activities for families, Christian initiation groups, and other adult groups at http://www.ltp.org/ahw.

Scripture Insights

On the Solemnity of the Ascension of the Lord, we hear different accounts of this event from the evangelist Luke. The earlier depiction appears at the end of Luke's Gospel, while the latter account, our first reading, is from the opening verses of the Acts of the Apostles. Both readings instruct Jesus' followers to remain in Jerusalem until they receive the "promise of the Father" (Luke 24:49 and Acts 1:4), that is, the Holy Spirit. Similarly, both texts refer to these individuals as "witnesses" (Luke 24:48 and Acts 1:8). The Greek word that is translated *witnesses* actually means "martyrs." Thus, we can conclude that some followers of Jesus will be martyred for testifying to the words and works of the Lord. Despite this implication, the Gospel of Luke concludes that these witnesses of Jesus "returned to Jerusalem with great joy" (24:52).

Our selection from Hebrews presents us with some challenges. With eighteen verses of the text not included in the lectionary, we do not hear a portion of Hebrews that elaborates on Jesus' mission. Within today's selection, we are told that Jesus, the Christ, has entered into the heavenly sanctuary. While the sanctuary of the temple was indeed a holy place, the earthly sacrifices that take place there cannot be compared to the "once for all" (9:26) sacrifice of Jesus. On this Solemnity of the Ascension, we celebrate Jesus' return to the Father. We celebrate that we too will be welcomed into our heavenly home at the appointed time. Having been baptized into Christ, we recall the final words of today's selection from Hebrews: "Let us hold unwaveringly to our confession that gives us hope, for he who made the promise is trustworthy" (10:23).

♦ When you reflect on "the promise of the Father" in today's readings, how do you envision yourself as being a recipient of the Holy Spirit?

♦ How do you witness to the words and works of Jesus?

♦ Reread today's responsorial psalm and reflect on how you experience God within this vast universe.

READING I *Acts 7:55–60*

Stephen, filled with the Holy Spirit, looked up intently to heaven and saw the glory of God and Jesus standing at the right hand of God, and Stephen said, "Behold, I see the heavens opened and the Son of Man standing at the right hand of God." But they cried out in a loud voice, covered their ears, and rushed upon him together. They threw him out of the city, and began to stone him. The witnesses laid down their cloaks at the feet of a young man named Saul. As they were stoning Stephen, he called out, "Lord Jesus, receive my spirit." Then he fell to his knees and cried out in a loud voice, "Lord, do not hold this sin against them"; and when he said this, he fell asleep.

RESPONSORIAL PSALM
Psalm 97:1–2, 6–7, 9 (1a, 9a)

R. The Lord is king, the most high over all
   the earth.
or: Alleluia.

The LORD is king; let the earth rejoice;
   let the many islands be glad.
Justice and judgment are the foundation
      of his throne. R.

The heavens proclaim his justice,
   and all peoples see his glory.
All gods are prostrate before him. R.

You, O LORD, are the Most High over all
      the earth,
   exalted far above all gods. R.

READING II
Revelation 22:12–14, 16–17, 20

I, John, heard a voice saying to me: "Behold, I am coming soon. I bring with me the recompense I will give to each according to his deeds. I am the Alpha and the Omega, the first and the last, the beginning and the end."

Blessed are they who wash their robes so as to have the right to the tree of life and enter the city through its gates.

"I, Jesus, sent my angel to give you this testimony for the churches. I am the root and offspring of David, the bright morning star."

The Spirit and the bride say, "Come." Let the hearer say, "Come." Let the one who thirsts come forward, and the one who wants it receive the gift of life-giving water.

The one who gives this testimony says, "Yes, I am coming soon." Amen! Come, Lord Jesus!

GOSPEL *John 17:20–26*

Lifting up his eyes to heaven, Jesus prayed, saying: "Holy Father, I pray not only for them, but also for those who will believe in me through their word, so that they may all be one, as you, Father, are in me and I in you, that they also may be in us, that the world may believe that you sent me. And I have given them the glory you gave me, so that they may be one, as we are one, I in them and you in me, that they may be brought to perfection as one, that the world may know that you sent me, and that you loved them even as you loved me. Father, they are your gift to me. I wish that where I am they also may be with me, that they may see my glory that you gave me, because you loved me before the foundation of the world. Righteous Father, the world also does not know you, but I know you, and they know that you sent me. I made known to them your name and I will make it known, that the love with which you loved me may be in them and I in them."

Practice of Charity

Jesus gave his life to gather people and bring them into eternal union with God and each other. Stephen imitated the Lord, following him even into death. ◆ Will you let love lead you that far? How do you limit your love for others, for God, and for yourself? ◆ Slowly reread the Gospel passage. What obstacles to unity do you see in your family? What obstacles to unity do you see in your community? How do you contribute to disunity and division? Take ownership of that failure, and apologize to someone you may have harmed because of it. ◆ Make a list of all the martyrs you can think of. Choose one and learn more about that person. How did that person imitate Christ?

Download more questions and activities for families, Christian initiation groups, and other adult groups at http://www.ltp.org/ahw.

Scripture Insights

On this Seventh Sunday of Easter, we find ourselves between two solemnities, the Ascension and Pentecost. Today's first reading from Acts recounts the martyrdom of Stephen and introduces Saul, later to be named Paul. Paul will become a key figure in the latter portion of this book. In today's selection, it would be difficult to miss the echoes of words heard previously, words that had been spoken by Jesus. Stephen, like Jesus, prays that his executioners may be forgiven.

The Gospel from John begins very much in the same way as today's reading from Acts. The text begins, "Lifting up his eyes to heaven, Jesus prayed." At the hour of Stephen's death, he "looked up intently to heaven and saw the glory of God and Jesus standing at the right hand of God." The Gospel continues with Jesus' prayer to his Father. Immediately after this prayer, John's Gospel tells us of Jesus' betrayal and arrest.

Today's responsorial psalm is identified as a psalm of God's kingship. It is one of a small collection of psalms that extol God's reign throughout the known cosmos. In Psalm 97, we hear that justice is foundational to God's reign. This text provides us with an interesting contrast with the ways of human justice depicted in Acts, where Stephen, innocent of any crime, is stoned to death.

◆ As you reflect on today's readings, consider how followers of Jesus are invited to live as Jesus lived. More specifically, consider the importance of prayer and forgiveness in the Christian life.

◆ Reflect on Saul/Paul's conversion. He is introduced in today's first reading at the stoning of Stephen, where his presence affirmed the stoning. Try to imagine the depth of his encounter with God that would cause his change of heart. Where do you need a change of heart? Will you allow God to work this conversion in you?

◆ What does today's Gospel reveal about the relationship of Jesus to the Father? How can you have a more intimate relationship with God?

READING I Acts 2:1–11

When the time for Pentecost was fulfilled, they were all in one place together. And suddenly there came from the sky a noise like a strong driving wind, and it filled the entire house in which they were. Then there appeared to them tongues as of fire, which parted and came to rest on each one of them. And they were all filled with the Holy Spirit and began to speak in different tongues, as the Spirit enabled them to proclaim.

Now there were devout Jews from every nation under heaven staying in Jerusalem. At this sound, they gathered in a large crowd, but they were confused because each one heard them speaking in his own language. They were astounded, and in amazement they asked, "Are not all these people who are speaking Galileans? Then how does each of us hear them in his native language? We are Parthians, Medes, and Elamites, inhabitants of Mesopotamia, Judea and Cappadocia, Pontus and Asia, Phrygia and Pamphylia, Egypt and the districts of Libya near Cyrene, as well as travelers from Rome, both Jews and converts to Judaism, Cretans and Arabs, yet we hear them speaking in our own tongues of the mighty acts of God."

RESPONSORIAL PSALM Psalm 104:1, 24, 29–30, 31, 34 (see 30)

R. Lord, send out your Spirit, and renew the face
      of the earth.
or: Alleluia.

Bless the LORD, O my soul!
  O LORD, my God, you are great indeed!
How manifold are your works, O LORD!
  The earth is full of your creatures. R.

If you take away their breath, they perish
  and return to their dust.
When you send forth your spirit,
      they are created,
  and you renew the face of the earth. R.

May the glory of the LORD endure forever;
  may the LORD be glad in his works!
Pleasing to him be my theme;
  I will be glad in the LORD. R.

READING II Romans 8:8–17

Alternate reading: 1 Corinthians 12:3b–7, 12–13

Brothers and sisters: Those who are in the flesh cannot please God. But you are not in the flesh; on the contrary, you are in the spirit, if only the Spirit of God dwells in you. Whoever does not have the Spirit of Christ does not belong to him. But if Christ is in you, although the body is dead because of sin, the spirit is alive because of righteousness. If the Spirit of the one who raised Jesus from the dead dwells in you, the one who raised Christ from the dead will give life to your mortal bodies also, through his Spirit that dwells in you. Consequently, brothers and sisters, we are not debtors to the flesh, to live according to the flesh. For if you live according to the flesh, you will die, but if by the Spirit you put to death the deeds of the body, you will live.

For those who are led by the Spirit of God are sons of God. For you did not receive a spirit of slavery to fall back into fear, but you received a spirit of adoption, through whom we cry, "Abba, Father!" The Spirit himself bears witness with our spirit that we are children of God, and if children, then heirs, heirs of God and joint heirs with Christ, if only we suffer with him so that we may also be glorified with him.

GOSPEL John 14:15–16, 23b–26

Alternate reading: John 20:19–23

Jesus said to his disciples: "If you love me, you will keep my commandments. And I will ask the Father, and he will give you another Advocate to be with you always.

"Whoever loves me will keep my word, and my Father will love him, and we will come to him and make our dwelling with him. Those who do not love me do not keep my words; yet the word you hear is not mine but that of the Father who sent me.

"I have told you this while I am with you. The Advocate, the Holy Spirit whom the Father will send in my name, will teach you everything and remind you of all that I told you."

Practice of Hope

Today we celebrate the birth of the Church. God fills us with the Holy Spirit so that we will participate in his Son's mission to bring everyone into his kingdom. ◆ Offer this prayer throughout the week: Come Holy Spirit, / fill the hearts of your faithful and kindle in them the fire of your love. / Send forth your Spirit and they shall be created. / And you shall renew the face of the earth. / O God, who by the light of the Holy Spirit, / did instruct the hearts of the faithful, / grant that by the same Spirit / we may be truly wise and ever rejoice in his consolation, / through Christ our Lord. Amen. ◆ Consider becoming part of a liturgical ministry, or reflect on how you have grown through the ministry you already do. ◆ Enkindle hope in God's kingdom by volunteering in some way in your local community.

Download more questions and activities for families, Christian initiation groups, and other adult groups at http://www.ltp.org/ahw.

Scripture Insights

This joyous Solemnity of Pentecost brings the Easter season to a conclusion. In today's Gospel, Jesus tells his disciples that his Father will send them the Holy Spirit, and we witness this promise brought to fulfillment in the reading from Acts. How is this Spirit manifested in Acts? It is noisy, powerful, fiery, and enabling. Those who received the Spirit were able to speak in different languages. Thus, "devout Jews from every nation under heaven" (2:5) who were staying in Jerusalem were able to understand what was proclaimed to them. This event has sometimes been understood as a reversal of the event of the Tower of Babel, a time when people challenged God through their desire for power. As a result, God confused their language and scattered them over the earth.

The power of the first reading is reinforced in the refrain from the responsorial psalm: "Lord, send out your Spirit, and renew the face of the earth." This hymn of praise recognizes God as creator of all and understands that without God's breath of life, we perish.

Paul's text from the Letter to the Romans also recognizes the power of God's life-giving Spirit. Paul reminds us that if we embrace this Spirit, if the Spirit dwells within us, we are children of God and heirs with Christ. Accepting such a gift has consequences. Like Christ, we will suffer, but we also will be glorified with him.

◆ Spend time in quiet with the words, "The Spirit himself bears witness with our spirit that we are children of God, and if children, then heirs." Let the words speak to you. Respond to God in prayer.

◆ Some patristic authors identified seven gifts of the Holy Spirit: wisdom, understanding, counsel, fortitude, knowledge, piety, and fear of the Lord. Which of these gifts would you like to pray for today? How would this gift help you to be a better disciple?

◆ Pray the response from today's responsorial psalm. How do you envision God renewing the face of the earth?

Ordinary Time, Summer

Prayer before Reading the Word

Wise and merciful God,
grant us a heart
thirsting for your truth,
longing for your presence,
and ready to hear you in the word of your Son.
Grant us the wisdom of your Spirit,
the understanding bestowed on
          the true disciples,
that we may carry the cross each day
and follow after your Son, our Lord Jesus Christ,
who lives and reigns with you
in the unity of the Holy Spirit,
God, for ever and ever. Amen.

Prayer after Reading the Word

Your word resounds in your Church, O God,
as a fountain of wisdom and a rule of life;
make us, O God, faithful disciples of
          that wisdom,
whose Teacher and Master is Christ
and whose chair of learning is the cross.
Schooled in this unique wisdom,
may we be prepared to conquer our fears
          and temptations,
to take up our cross daily
and to follow Jesus toward true life.
Through our Lord Jesus Christ, your Son,
who lives and reigns with you
in the unity of the Holy Spirit,
God, for ever and ever. Amen.

Weekday Readings

June 6: *Genesis 3:9–15, 20 or Acts 1:12–14; John 19:25–34*
June 7: *1 Kings 17:7–16; Matthew 5:13–16*
June 8: *1 Kings 18:20–39; Matthew 5:17–19*
June 9: *1 Kings 18:41–46; Matthew 5:20–26*
June 10: *1 Kings 19:9a, 11–16; Matthew 5:27–32*
June 11: *Acts 11:21b–26; 13:1–3; Matthew 5:33–37*

June 13: *1 Kings 21:1–16; Matthew 5:38–42*
June 14: *1 Kings 21:17–29; Matthew 5:43–48*
June 15: *2 Kings 2:1, 6–14; Matthew 6:1–6, 16–18*
June 16: *Sirach 48:1–14; Matthew 6:7–15*
June 17: *2 Kings 11:1–4, 9–18, 20; Matthew 6:19–23*
June 18: *2 Chronicles 24:17–25; Matthew 6:24–34*

June 20: *2 Kings 17:5–8, 13–15a, 18; Matthew 7:1–5*
June 21: *2 Kings 19:9b–11, 14–21, 31–35a, 36;*
 Matthew 7:6, 12–14
June 22: *2 Kings 22:8–13; 23:1–3; Matthew 7:15–20*
June 23 Solemnity of the Nativity of St. John the Baptist
 Vigil: Jeremiah 1:4–10; 1 Peter 1:8–12; Luke 1:5–17
 Day: Isaiah 49:1–6; Acts 13:22–26; Luke 1:57–66, 80
June 24: Solemnity of the Most Sacred Heart of Jesus
 Ezekiel 34:11–16; Romans 5:5b–11; Luke 15:3–7
June 25: *Lamentations 2:2, 10–14, 18–19; Luke 2:41–51*

June 27: *Amos 2:6–10, 13–16; Matthew 8:18–22*
June 28: *Amos 3:1–8; 4:11–12; Matthew 8:23–27*
June 29: Solemnity of Sts. Peter and Paul, Apostles
 Vigil: Acts 3:1–10; Galatians 1:11–20; John 21:15–19
 Day: Acts 12:1–11; 2 Timothy 4:6–8, 17–18;
 Matthew 16:13–19
June 30: *Amos 7:10–17; Matthew 9:1–8*
July 1: *Amos 8:4–6, 9–12; Matthew 9:9–13*
July 2: *Amos 9:11–15; Matthew 9:14–17*

July 4: *Hosea 2:16, 17c–18, 21–22; Matthew 9:18–26*
July 5: *Hosea 8:4–7, 11–13; Matthew 9:32–38*
July 6: *Hosea 10:1–3, 7–8, 12; Matthew 10:1–7*
July 7: *Hosea 11:1–4, 8e–9; Matthew 10:7–15*
July 8: *Hosea 14:2–10; Matthew 10:16–23*
July 9: *Isaiah 6:1–8; Matthew 10:24–33*

July 11: *Isaiah 1:10–17; Matthew 10:34—11:1*
July 12: *Isaiah 7:1–9; Matthew 11:20–24*
July 13: *Isaiah 10:5–7, 13b–16; Matthew 11:25–27*
July 14: *Isaiah 26:7–9, 12, 16–19; Matthew 11:28–30*
July 15: *Isaiah 38:1–6, 21–22, 7–8; Matthew 12:1–8*
July 16: *Micah 2:1–5; Matthew 12:14–21*

July 18: *Micah 6:1–4, 6–8; Matthew 12:38–42*
July 19: *Micah 7:14–15, 18–20; Matthew 12:46–50*
July 20: *Jeremiah 1:1, 4–10; Matthew 13:1–9*
July 21: *Jeremiah 2:1–3, 7–8, 12–13; Matthew 13:10–17*

July 22: Feast of St. Mary Magdalene
 Song of Songs 3:1–4b or 2 Corinthians 5:14–17;
 John 20:1–2, 11–18
July 23: *Jeremiah 7:1–11; Matthew 13:24–30*

July 25: Feast of St. James, Apostle
 2 Corinthians 4:7–15; Matthew 20:20–28
July 26: *Jeremiah 14:17–22; Matthew 13:36–43*
July 27: *Jeremiah 15:10, 16–21; Matthew 13:44–46*
July 28: *Jeremiah 18:1–6; Matthew 13:47–53*
July 29: *Jeremiah 26:1–9; John 11:19–27 or Luke 10:38–42*
July 30: *Jeremiah 26:11–16, 24; Matthew 14:1–12*

August 1: *Jeremiah 28:1–17; Matthew 14:13–21*
August 2: *Jeremiah 30:1–2, 12–15, 18–22; Matthew 14:22–36*
 or Matthew 15:1–2, 10–14
August 3: *Jeremiah 31:1–7; Matthew 15:21–28*
August 4: *Jeremiah 31:31–34; Matthew 16:13–23*
August 5: *Nahum 2:1, 3; 3:1–3, 6–7; Matthew 16:24–28*
August 6: Feast of the Transfiguration of the Lord
 Daniel 7:9–10, 13–14; 2 Peter 1:16–19; Luke 9:28b–36

August 8: *Ezekiel 1:2–5, 24–28c; Matthew 17:22–27*
August 9: *Ezekiel 2:8—3:4; Matthew 18:1–5, 10, 12–14*
August 10: Feast of St. Lawrence, Deacon and Martyr
 2 Corinthians 9:6–10; John 12:24–26
August 11: *Ezekiel 12:1–12; Matthew 18:21—19:1*
August 12: *Ezekiel 16:1–15, 60, 63 or 16:59–63;*
 Matthew 19:3–12
August 13: *Ezekiel 18:1–10, 13b, 30–32; Matthew 19:13–15*

August 15: Solemnity of the Assumption
 of the Blessed Virgin Mary
 Revelation 11:19a; 12:1–6a, 10ab;
 1 Corinthians 15:20–27; Luke 1:39–56
August 16: *Ezekiel 28:1–10; Matthew 19:23–30*
August 17: *Ezekiel 34:1–11; Matthew 20:1–16*
August 18: *Ezekiel 36:23–28; Matthew 22:1–14*
August 19: *Ezekiel 37:1–14; Matthew 22:34–40*
August 20: *Ezekiel 43:1–7ab; Matthew 23:1–12*

August 22: *2 Thessalonians 1:1–5, 11–12; Matthew 23:13–22*
August 23: *2 Thessalonians 2:1–3a, 14–17;*
 Matthew 23:23–26
August 24: Feast of St. Bartholomew, Apostle
 Revelation 21:9b–14; John 1:45–51
August 25: *1 Corinthians 1:1–9; Matthew 24:42–51*
August 26: *1 Corinthians 1:17–25; Matthew 25:1–13*
August 27: *1 Corinthians 1:26–31; Matthew 25:14–30*

READING I　*Proverbs 8:22–31*

Thus says the wisdom of God:
"The LORD possessed me, the beginning
　　of his ways,
　　the forerunner of his prodigies of long ago;
from of old I was poured forth,
　　at the first, before the earth.
When there were no depths I was
　　brought forth,
　　when there were no fountains or springs
　　of water;
before the mountains were settled into place,
　　before the hills, I was brought forth;
while as yet the earth and fields were not made,
　　nor the first clods of the world.

"When the Lord established the heavens
　　I was there,
　　when he marked out the vault over the face
　　of the deep;
when he made firm the skies above,
　　when he fixed fast the foundations of
　　the earth;
when he set for the sea its limit,
　　so that the waters should not transgress
　　his command;
then was I beside him as his craftsman,
　　and I was his delight day by day,
playing before him all the while,
　　playing on the surface of his earth;
　　and I found delight in the human race."

RESPONSORIAL PSALM
Psalm 8:4–5, 6–7, 8–9 (2a)

R. O Lord, our God, how wonderful your name
　　in all the earth!

When I behold your heavens, the work of
　　your fingers,
　　the moon and the stars which you set
　　in place—
what is man that you should be mindful of him,
　　or the son of man that you should care
　　for him?　R.

You have made him little less than the angels,
　　and crowned him with glory and honor.
You have given him rule over the works of
　　your hands,
　　putting all things under his feet.　R.

All sheep and oxen,
　　yes, and the beasts of the field,
the birds of the air, the fishes of the sea,
　　and whatever swims the paths
　　of the seas.　R.

READING II　*Romans 5:1–5*

Brothers and sisters: Therefore, since we have been justified by faith, we have peace with God through our Lord Jesus Christ, through whom we have gained access by faith to this grace in which we stand, and we boast in hope of the glory of God. Not only that, but we even boast of our afflictions, knowing that affliction produces endurance, and endurance, proven character, and proven character, hope, and hope does not disappoint, because the love of God has been poured out into our hearts through the Holy Spirit that has been given to us.

GOSPEL　*John 16:12–15*

Jesus said to his disciples: "I have much more to tell you, but you cannot bear it now. But when he comes, the Spirit of truth, he will guide you to all truth. He will not speak on his own, but he will speak what he hears, and will declare to you the things that are coming. He will glorify me, because he will take from what is mine and declare it to you. Everything that the Father has is mine; for this reason I told you that he will take from what is mine and declare it to you."

Practice of Faith

God has expressed himself to us through creation, in history, by the words of prophets, and, most fully, in the person of Jesus. Through Christ and the gift of the Holy Spirit, we have come to know God as a communion of three divine Persons, yet our understanding of and relationship with God continues to deepen. ◆ What do you believe about God? How have your beliefs changed over the years? Are there ways of thinking about or praying to God that you have resisted? Think of your closest family members and friends. How well do you know them? How well do they know you? How could you deepen these relationships? ◆ Spend some time outdoors in a park or other natural setting. What do you see, hear, smell, and feel? Thank God for the gift of our natural world. ◆ What concrete steps can you take to help protect our environment?

Download more questions and activities for families, Christian initiation groups, and other adult groups at http://www.ltp.org/ahw.

Scripture Insights

The readings selected for today's Solemnity of the Most Holy Trinity and next week's Solemnity of the Most Holy Body and Blood of Christ highlight these celebrations. Each of today's readings invites us to ponder the mystery of the Trinity.

Today's reading from the Book of Proverbs is a beautiful and somewhat mysterious passage in which we hear Wisdom speak of being with God at the beginning of creation. The passage is one of several texts from the Old Testament that personifies "wisdom." Interestingly, the gender of wisdom is feminine. While a significant number of studies assert that wisdom may have represented a goddess in an early period, we know that in the Wisdom tradition of the Old Testament, "wisdom" and "folly" are often depicted as feminine figures. Since a portion of the Book of Proverbs is recognized as instruction for young men, these texts are often understood as representing the choice that must be made in life, a choice between wisdom or folly. In light of the New Testament, wisdom is associated with the *Logos*, the Word, who was with God in the beginning. Such an understanding is expressed most clearly in the Prologue of John's Gospel.

Our responsorial psalm continues the focus on the marvels of creation. Who among us can look at the heavenly skies on a clear evening and not be wrapped in wonder?

While the selection from Romans emphasizes the gift of peace we have received through Jesus, the Gospel informs us that Jesus did not bring his disciples to full knowledge of who he was while he was among them. He did, however, tell them of the coming of the Spirit, a Spirit who would guide them in truth. It is the mystery of the Trinity that we ponder today.

◆ Take a few minutes to consider what it means to be baptized in the name of each Person of the Trinity—the Father, the Son, and the Holy Spirit.

◆ Is there one Person of the Trinity whom you pray to most often? Ponder who that is and reflect on why you are drawn to this Person.

◆ How has an affliction that you endured resulted in hope?

READING I *Genesis 14:18–20*

In those days, Melchizedek, king of Salem, brought out bread and wine, and being a priest of God Most High, he blessed Abram with these words: / "Blessed be Abram by God Most High, / the creator of heaven and earth; / and blessed be God Most High, / who delivered your foes into your hand." / Then Abram gave him a tenth of everything.

RESPONSORIAL PSALM
Psalm 110:1, 2, 3, 4 (4b)

R. You are a priest for ever, in the line
      of Melchizedek.

The LORD said to my Lord: "Sit at my right hand
    till I make your enemies your footstool." R.

The scepter of your power the LORD will stretch
      forth from Zion:
    "Rule in the midst of your enemies." R.

"Yours is princely power in the day of your birth,
      in holy splendor;
before the daystar, like the dew,
      I have begotten you." R.

The LORD has sworn, and he will not repent:
    "You are a priest forever, according to the
        order of Melchizedek." R.

READING II *1 Corinthians 11:23–26*

Brothers and sisters: I received from the Lord what I also handed on to you, that the Lord Jesus, on the night he was handed over, took bread, and, after he had given thanks, broke it and said, "This is my body that is for you. Do this in remembrance of me." In the same way also the cup, after supper, saying, "This cup is the new covenant in my blood. Do this, as often as you drink it, in remembrance of me." For as often as you eat this bread and drink the cup, you proclaim the death of the Lord until he comes.

GOSPEL *Luke 9:11b–17*

Jesus spoke to the crowds about the kingdom of God, and he healed those who needed to be cured. As the day was drawing to a close, the Twelve approached him and said, "Dismiss the crowd so that they can go to the surrounding villages and farms and find lodging and provisions; for we are in a deserted place here." He said to them, "Give them some food yourselves." They replied, "Five loaves and two fish are all we have, unless we ourselves go and buy food for all these people." Now the men there numbered about five thousand. Then he said to his disciples, "Have them sit down in groups of about fifty." They did so and made them all sit down. Then taking the five loaves and the two fish, and looking up to heaven, he said the blessing over them, broke them, and gave them to the disciples to set before the crowd. They all ate and were satisfied. And when the left-over fragments were picked up, they filled twelve wicker baskets.

Practice of Hope

Today we celebrate all of the ways that God nourishes us in Christ. We also look ahead in hope to the fullness of God's kingdom when all people will have enough to eat and will sit together in eternal fellowship. ◆ Fast one day this week. Notice your hunger. What are all the ways God feeds you? For what are you still hungry? Do you fill yourself with the right food—spiritual as well as physical? ◆ Share a meal with your family and/or friends. Turn off the TV, your phone, etc. Try to keep the conversation on meaningful, enriching topics. Listen to how everyone is doing. ◆ Volunteer at a soup kitchen. Join some guests during the meal and listen to their stories.

Download more questions and activities for families, Christian initiation groups, and other adult groups at http://www.ltp.org/ahw.

Scripture Insights

Our readings for this Solemnity of the Most Holy Body and Blood of Christ, also known as Corpus Christi, invite us to reflect on the many ways that God nourishes us, especially how he feeds us in the Eucharist.

The first reading from the Book of Genesis presents us with the mysterious king and priest, Melchizedek, king of Salem. While much has been written about this figure, scholars continue to study his origins and his significance. Melchizedek, who offers bread and wine to Abram and then blesses him in the name of God Most High, has come to be recognized as one who prefigures Christ.

In our responsorial psalm, we find the second of three occurrences of Melchizedek in the Scriptures. Psalm 110, possibly composed for the coronation of the Davidic king, shows the giving of power from God and the granting of the status of the priest Melchizedek. (The third and final appearance of this figure is in chapters 5—7 of Hebrews.)

While First Corinthians offers a succinct account of the celebration of the Eucharist in the early Church, the Gospel from Luke focuses attention on the multiplication of the five loaves and two fish. The Twelve are more than ready to dismiss the five thousand men (and most likely a great number of women and children) so that they and Jesus might have something to eat. After the Twelve follow Jesus' orders to have the people sit in groups of fifty, Jesus takes the loaves and fish, looks heavenward, blesses the food, and has the disciples distribute the food. The entire crowd was satisfied, and an abundance of leftover food was collected. This Gospel reminds us that God nourishes us abundantly.

◆ Reflect on how the Eucharist nourishes you. How do you feed people who are hungry, both physically and spiritually?

◆ How does your local parish reach out to assist those who hunger and thirst?

◆ As you reread today's Gospel, reflect on the abundance that was collected from the crowd. What does this abundance suggest to you?

READING I   *1 Kings 19:16b, 19–21*

The LORD said to Elijah: "You shall anoint Elisha, son of Shaphat of Abel-meholah, as prophet to succeed you."

Elijah set out and came upon Elisha, son of Shaphat, as he was plowing with twelve yoke of oxen; he was following the twelfth. Elijah went over to him and threw his cloak over him. Elisha left the oxen, ran after Elijah, and said, "Please, let me kiss my father and mother goodbye, and I will follow you." Elijah answered, "Go back! Have I done anything to you?" Elisha left him, and taking the yoke of oxen, slaughtered them; he used the plowing equipment for fuel to boil their flesh, and gave it to his people to eat. Then Elisha left and followed Elijah as his attendant.

RESPONSORIAL PSALM   *Psalm 16:1–2, 5, 7–8, 9–10, 11 (see 5a)*

R. You are my inheritance, O Lord.

Keep me, O God, for in you I take refuge;
    I say to the LORD, "My Lord are you."
O LORD, my allotted portion and my cup,
    you it is who hold fast my lot.   R.

I bless the LORD who counsels me;
    even in the night my heart exhorts me.
I set the LORD ever before me;
    with him at my right hand, I shall not
       be disturbed.   R.

Therefore my heart is glad and my soul rejoices;
    my body, too, abides in confidence,
because you will not abandon my soul to
       the netherworld,
    nor will you suffer your faithful one to
       undergo corruption.   R.

You will show me the path to life,
    fullness of joys in your presence,
    the delights at your right hand forever.   R.

READING II   *Galatians 5:1, 13–18*

Brothers and sisters: For freedom Christ set us free; so stand firm and do not submit again to the yoke of slavery.

For you were called for freedom, brothers and sisters. But do not use this freedom as an opportunity for the flesh; rather, serve one another through love. For the whole law is fulfilled in one statement, namely, *You shall love your neighbor as yourself.* But if you go on biting and devouring one another, beware that you are not consumed by one another.

I say, then: live by the Spirit and you will certainly not gratify the desire of the flesh. For the flesh has desires against the Spirit, and the Spirit against the flesh; these are opposed to each other, so that you may not do what you want. But if you are guided by the Spirit, you are not under the law.

GOSPEL   *Luke 9:51–62*

When the days for Jesus' being taken up were fulfilled, he resolutely determined to journey to Jerusalem, and he sent messengers ahead of him. On the way they entered a Samaritan village to prepare for his reception there, but they would not welcome him because the destination of his journey was Jerusalem. When the disciples James and John saw this they asked, "Lord, do you want us to call down fire from heaven to consume them?" Jesus turned and rebuked them, and they journeyed to another village.

As they were proceeding on their journey someone said to him, "I will follow you wherever you go." Jesus answered him, "Foxes have dens and birds of the sky have nests, but the Son of Man has nowhere to rest his head."

And to another he said, "Follow me." But he replied, "Lord, let me go first and bury my father." But he answered him, "Let the dead bury their dead. But you, go and proclaim the kingdom of God." And another said, "I will follow you, Lord, but first let me say farewell to my family at home." To him Jesus said, "No one who sets a hand to the plow and looks to what was left behind is fit for the kingdom of God."

Practice of Charity

Following Christ requires total commitment. The longer the commitment is delayed, the harder it becomes to learn how to be a good disciple and the less likely the individual is to follow Jesus at all. James and John certainly had much to learn about discipleship! ◆ Whom do you find difficult to love? Imagine Jesus sitting beside you. How would you talk to each other about this difficulty? ◆ Do you know someone who is in the seminary or entering religious life? Send that person a note of support and pray for him or her throughout the week. ◆ Reflect on Galatians 5:13–26 (an extension of the second reading). In what ways have you welcomed the Spirit into your life? In what ways are you still enslaved to things that are harmful or even evil?

Download more questions and activities for families, Christian initiation groups, and other adult groups at http://www.ltp.org/ahw.

Scripture Insights

Today's reading from the First Book of Kings is a small portion of one of the best-known chapters of this book. Today's selection, however, is better understood within its context. Several verses earlier, Elijah, fearful for his life, takes refuge in a cave of Mount Horeb (another name for Sinai). Immediately prior to this, the notorious Queen Jezebel had threatened to have Elijah killed because he was responsible for the death of the prophets of the foreign god, Baal, whom Jezebel worshiped (1 Kings 19:2). According to 1 Kings 18:22, these prophets numbered 450. In that verse, Elijah claims himself as "the only remaining prophet of the LORD." Thus, in today's reading, we find Elijah throwing his cloak over Elisha, who will eventually succeed Elijah. By slaughtering the oxen that he had used for plowing, Elisha confirms that he is changing the direction of his life. Elisha will attend to Elijah until the time that Elisha succeeds the prophet. The passage in 2 Kings 2:9–12 recounts the succession event.

The Gospel from Luke begins the story of Jesus' journey to Jerusalem, which concludes in chapter 19. Today's twelve verses are quite packed. The first portion of the text makes it clear that Jesus and his disciples were not welcome in the Samaritan village where they had stopped. Hostility between the Jews and Samaritans was long-standing and had existed for hundreds of years. In the second portion of the Gospel are three brief encounters. In the first encounter, an individual offers to follow Jesus anywhere; in the second and third encounters, Jesus invites people to follow him. In each case, the individual is unable to accept the demands of discipleship.

◆ Reread today's passage from First Kings and reflect on how Elisha received his call to be a prophet.

◆ In today's Gospel, what kinds of demands does discipleship make?

◆ What similarities do you find between the reading from First Kings and the Gospel? What is the cost of responding to God's invitation?

READING I *Isaiah 66:10–14c*

Thus says the LORD:
Rejoice with Jerusalem and be glad because
    of her,
  all you who love her;
exult, exult with her,
  all you who were mourning over her!
Oh, that you may suck fully
  of the milk of her comfort,
that you may nurse with delight
  at her abundant breasts!
For thus says the LORD:
Lo, I will spread prosperity over Jerusalem
    like a river,
  and the wealth of the nations
    like an overflowing torrent.
As nurslings, you shall be carried in her arms,
  and fondled in her lap;
as a mother comforts her child,
  so will I comfort you;
  in Jerusalem you shall find your comfort.

When you see this, your heart shall rejoice
  and your bodies flourish like the grass;
the LORD's power shall be known to
    his servants.

RESPONSORIAL PSALM
Psalm 66:1–3, 4–5, 6–7, 16, 20 (1)

R. Let all the earth cry out to God with joy.

Shout joyfully to God, all the earth;
  sing praise to the glory of his name;
  proclaim his glorious praise.
Say to God, "How tremendous are
    your deeds!" R.

"Let all on earth worship and sing praise to you,
  sing praise to your name!"
Come and see the works of God,
  his tremendous deeds among the children
    of Adam. R.

He changed the sea into dry land;
  through the river they passed on foot;
  therefore let us rejoice in him.
He rules by his might forever. R.

Hear now, all you who fear God,
  while I declare what he has done for me.
Blessed be God, who refused me not
  my prayer or his kindness! R.

READING II *Galatians 6:14–18*

Brothers and sisters: May I never boast except in the cross of our Lord Jesus Christ, through which the world has been crucified to me, and I to the world. For neither does circumcision mean anything, nor does uncircumcision, but only a new creation. Peace and mercy be to all who follow this rule and to the Israel of God.

From now on, let no one make troubles for me; for I bear the marks of Jesus on my body.

The grace of our Lord Jesus Christ be with your spirit, brothers and sisters. Amen.

GOSPEL *Luke 10:1–12, 17–20*

Shorter: Luke 10:1–9

At that time the Lord appointed seventy-two others whom he sent ahead of him in pairs to every town and place he intended to visit. He said to them, "The harvest is abundant but the laborers are few; so ask the master of the harvest to send out laborers for his harvest. Go on your way; behold, I am sending you like lambs among wolves. Carry no money bag, no sack, no sandals; and greet no one along the way. Into whatever house you enter, first say, 'Peace to this household.' If a peaceful person lives there, your peace will rest on him; but if not, it will return to you. Stay in the same house and eat and drink what is offered to you, for the laborer deserves his payment. Do not move about from one house to another. Whatever town you enter and they welcome you, eat what is set before you, cure the sick in it and say to them, 'The kingdom of God is at hand for you.' Whatever town you enter and they do not receive you, go out into the streets and say, 'The dust of your town that clings to our feet, even that we shake off against you.' Yet know this: the kingdom of God is at hand. I tell you, it will be more tolerable for Sodom on that day than for that town."

The seventy-two returned rejoicing, and said, "Lord, even the demons are subject to us because of your name." Jesus said, "I have observed Satan fall like lightning from the sky. Behold, I have given you the power to 'tread upon serpents' and scorpions and upon the full force of the enemy and nothing will harm you. Nevertheless, do not rejoice because the spirits are subject to you, but rejoice because your names are written in heaven."

Practice of Hope

These readings fill us with hope. Jesus shares his power to cast out evil in all its forms. St. Paul participates in this life-saving power and bravely overcomes the hardship it brings. Isaiah's prophecy inspires us to strive for that kingdom in which God's love consoles, nurtures, and protects us forever. ◆ Imagine that you are one of the disciples Jesus sent out. What do you say and do? What challenges do you meet? What further help do you need from the Lord? ◆ Missionary work is often called the propagation of the faith. Learn more about how your local parish or diocese supports the propagation of the faith. How can you also support this work? ◆ Read about St. Francis Xavier, the patron saint of missionaries. Ask for his intercession on behalf of those striving throughout the world to share Christ's love with new people.

Download more questions and activities for families, Christian initiation groups, and other adult groups at http://www.ltp.org/ahw.

Scripture Insights

Today's reading from Isaiah is from the very last chapter of this monumental prophetic book. In some respects, the last two chapters of Isaiah might be considered a grand finale to a work that spans an extensive period of Israel's relationship with God. This passage, addressed to the postexilic community, offers hope to the people who did not see God's promises made to the exiles as coming to fulfillment. The message to this community is: "Rejoice!" God will comfort you, and you will know the Lord's saving power.

The responsorial psalm reinforces the message in Isaiah, as the psalmist invites the assembly to sing God's praises. The psalm moves between worshiping God and recalling the saving deeds that God has performed on behalf of his people.

In the concluding verses of Paul's Letter to the Galatians, we hear that Paul takes pride in his commitment to the cross of the Lord Jesus Christ. Paul, who had been a persecutor of the followers of Jesus, now proclaims that the only important thing in life is to become a new creation in Christ.

The Gospel passage from Luke provides us with some idea of the urgency of the disciples' mission. Nowhere else in the Gospels do we hear of this group of seventy-two followers of Jesus. Elsewhere, the Scriptures identify the twelve. This increase in the number of those preaching the news of the kingdom might be understood as a foreshadowing of what will take place in the years to come.

In some way, all of today's readings speak of a people who know that they are of God. While the cost of discipleship is high, the people of God can only rejoice in what the Lord has done for them.

◆ Reread the text from Isaiah. Where in your life do you need comfort? Quietly stay with an image of God consoling you.

◆ St. Paul speaks boldly about his commitment to the good news of Jesus Christ. How do you live your commitment to the Gospel?

◆ In today's Gospel, the disciples of Jesus are given their instructions for ministry. What directives do you think Jesus would give to you today?

READING I *Deuteronomy 30:10–14*

Moses said to the people: "If only you would heed the voice of the LORD, your God, and keep his commandments and statutes that are written in this book of the law, when you return to the LORD, your God, with all your heart and all your soul.

"For this command that I enjoin on you today is not too mysterious and remote for you. It is not up in the sky, that you should say, 'Who will go up in the sky to get it for us and tell us of it, that we may carry it out?' Nor is it across the sea, that you should say, 'Who will cross the sea to get it for us and tell us of it, that we may carry it out?' No, it is something very near to you, already in your mouths and in your hearts; you have only to carry it out."

RESPONSORIAL PSALM *Psalm 69:14, 17, 30–31, 33–34, 36, 37 (see 33)*

Alternate reading: Psalm 19:8, 9, 10, 11 (9a)

R. Turn to the Lord in your need, and you
      will live.

I pray to you, O LORD,
    for the time of your favor, O God!
In your great kindness answer me
    with your constant help.
Answer me, O LORD, for bounteous is
      your kindness;
    in your great mercy turn toward me. R.

I am afflicted and in pain;
    let your saving help, O God, protect me.
I will praise the name of God in song,
    and I will glorify him
      with thanksgiving. R.

"See, you lowly ones, and be glad;
    you who seek God, may your hearts revive!
For the LORD hears the poor,
    and his own who are in bonds
      he spurns not." R.

For God will save Zion
    and rebuild the cities of Judah.
The descendants of his servants shall inherit it,
    and those who love his name shall inhabit it.

READING II *Colossians 1:15–20*

Christ Jesus is the image of the invisible God,
    the firstborn of all creation.
For in him were created all things
      in heaven and on earth,
    the visible and the invisible,
    whether thrones or dominions or
      principalities or powers;
    all things were created through him and
      for him.
He is before all things,
    and in him all things hold together.
He is the head of the body, the church.
He is the beginning, the firstborn from the dead,
    that in all things he himself might
      be preeminent.
For in him all the fullness was pleased to dwell,
    and through him to reconcile
      all things for him,
    making peace by the blood of his cross
    through him, whether those on earth or
      those in heaven.

GOSPEL *Luke 10:25–37*

There was a scholar of the law who stood up to test him and said, "Teacher, what must I do to inherit eternal life?" Jesus said to him, "What is written in the law? How do you read it?" He said in reply,
    "You shall love the Lord, your God,
    with all your heart,
    with all your being,
    with all your strength,
    and with all your mind,
    and your neighbor as yourself."
He replied to him, "You have answered correctly; do this and you will live."

But because he wished to justify himself, he said to Jesus, "And who is my neighbor?" Jesus replied, "A man fell victim to robbers as he went down from Jerusalem to Jericho. They stripped and beat him and went off leaving him half-dead. A priest happened to be going down that road, but when he saw him, he passed by on the opposite side. Likewise a Levite came to the place, and when he saw him, he passed by on the opposite side. But a Samaritan traveler who came upon him was moved with compassion at the sight. He approached the victim, poured oil and wine over his wounds and bandaged them. Then he lifted him up on his own animal, took him to an inn, and cared for him. The next day he took out two silver coins and gave them to the innkeeper with the instruction, 'Take care of him. If you spend more than what I have given you, I shall repay you on my way back.' Which of these three, in your opinion, was neighbor to the robbers' victim?" He answered, "The one who treated him with mercy." Jesus said to him, "Go and do likewise."

Practice of Charity

Jesus urges us to treat everyone as our neighbor, whether we know them or not. As we hear in the hymn from Colossians, all are connected to one another and to creation itself through Christ, in whom "all things hold together." ◆ Imagine traveling that road to Jericho. What would have kept you from helping the person who had been attacked? What would have motivated you to help? ◆ Sponsor an evening of dialogue about racism. If possible, invite people of different backgrounds to share their stories. A helpful guide is the US Conference of Catholic Bishops' pastoral letter *Open Wide Our Hearts: The Enduring Call to Love*. The bishops have provided extensive study questions at http://www.usccb.org/issues-and-action/human-life-and-dignity/racism/index.cfm. ◆ Consider new ways to care for God's creation. Find guidance at Catholic Climate Covenant (https://catholicclimatecovenant.org).

Download more questions and activities for families, Christian initiation groups, and other adult groups at http://www.ltp.org/ahw.

Scripture Insights

In the reading from the Book of Deuteronomy, Moses instructs the people about the law. The law that is referred to is far from what most people would consider upon hearing the word *law*. In the Old Testament, the word *law*, which appears most often in the Book of Psalms and the Book of Deuteronomy, is understood as "instruction" or "teaching" and was intended to be a guide for living life well. Thus, we hear the psalmist extol the blessings of the law throughout Psalm 119, the lengthiest of all psalms. Moses wants the people to understand that God's law is within them and that they need only to recognize it and live it.

Luke's Gospel also turns our attention to the law when the so-called "scholar of the law" asks Jesus about inheriting eternal life. When Jesus questions him about what is written in the law, the scholar refers to teachings found in Deuteronomy (see 6:5) and Leviticus (see 19:9–18). When the scholar questions Jesus further, "And who is my neighbor?" Jesus tells the parable of the Good Samaritan, a story that exemplifies the selfless love of a true neighbor. In today's Gospel, it can be noted readily that knowing the "right answer" does not equate with understanding the Scriptures.

◆ When have you put yourself at risk to help someone, as does the Good Samaritan? If there were repercussions, were you still glad that you showed mercy?

◆ The reading from Deuteronomy concludes with Moses stating that God's law is "something very near to you, already in your mouths and in your hearts; you have only to carry it out." Jesus' response to the scholar is "You have answered correctly; do this and you will live." How are these statements similar? What do these words tell you about a life that is faithful to God?

◆ The author of the Letter to the Colossians extols Christ Jesus as "the image of the invisible God, the firstborn of all creation." Is it difficult for you to understand that Jesus is both human and divine?

July 17, 2022 SIXTEENTH SUNDAY IN ORDINARY TIME

READING I *Genesis 18:1–10a*

The LORD appeared to Abraham by the terebinth of Mamre, as he sat in the entrance of his tent, while the day was growing hot. Looking up, Abraham saw three men standing nearby. When he saw them, he ran from the entrance of the tent to greet them; and bowing to the ground, he said: "Sir, if I may ask you this favor, please do not go on past your servant. Let some water be brought, that you may bathe your feet, and then rest yourselves under the tree. Now that you have come this close to your servant, let me bring you a little food, that you may refresh yourselves; and afterward you may go on your way." The men replied, "Very well, do as you have said."

Abraham hastened into the tent and told Sarah, "Quick, three measures of fine flour! Knead it and make rolls." He ran to the herd, picked out a tender, choice steer, and gave it to a servant, who quickly prepared it. Then Abraham got some curds and milk, as well as the steer that had been prepared, and set these before the three men; and he waited on them under the tree while they ate.

They asked Abraham, "Where is your wife Sarah?" He replied, "There in the tent." One of them said, "I will surely return to you about this time next year, and Sarah will then have a son."

RESPONSORIAL PSALM
Psalm 15:2–3, 3–4, 5 (1a)

R. He who does justice will live in the presence
      of the Lord.

One who walks blamelessly and does justice;
   who thinks the truth in his heart
   and slanders not with his tongue.   R.

Who harms not his fellow man,
   nor takes up a reproach against his neighbor;
by whom the reprobate is despised,
   while he honors those who fear the LORD.   R.

Who lends not his money at usury
   and accepts no bribe against the innocent.
One who does these things
   shall never be disturbed.   R.

READING II *Colossians 1:24–28*

Brothers and sisters: Now I rejoice in my sufferings for your sake, and in my flesh I am filling up what is lacking in the afflictions of Christ on behalf of his body, which is the church, of which I am a minister in accordance with God's stewardship given to me to bring to completion for you the word of God, the mystery hidden from ages and from generations past. But now it has been manifested to his holy ones, to whom God chose to make known the riches of the glory of this mystery among the Gentiles; it is Christ in you, the hope for glory. It is he whom we proclaim, admonishing everyone and teaching everyone with all wisdom, that we may present everyone perfect in Christ.

GOSPEL *Luke 10:38–42*

Jesus entered a village where a woman whose name was Martha welcomed him. She had a sister named Mary who sat beside the Lord at his feet listening to him speak. Martha, burdened with much serving, came to him and said, "Lord, do you not care that my sister has left me by myself to do the serving? Tell her to help me." The Lord said to her in reply, "Martha, Martha, you are anxious and worried about many things. There is need of only one thing. Mary has chosen the better part and it will not be taken from her."

Practice of Faith

Both Abraham and Mary are fully attentive to the needs of their guests. Their guests, in turn, offer something to their hosts that is far greater than the hospitality shown to them. Martha almost lost out on what Jesus offered. ◆ If your life is especially busy right now and you are losing your regular prayer time, look for ways to offer a simple prayer while dressing, driving, or walking, or even while going from one room to the next. Pray short prayers such as, "Jesus, be with me." ◆ Spend thirty minutes this week reading Scripture. Choose a psalm or read Paul's letter to the Colossians. ◆ Offer to help set up for and/or clean up after an event in your parish. By helping you might lighten the load of those who are in charge of the event.

Download more questions and activities for families, Christian initiation groups, and other adult groups at http://www.ltp.org/ahw.

Scripture Insights

In the reading from Genesis, Abraham has some unusual guests. The story continues in the Bible for nearly another five verses after today's passage. Those verses include Abraham's wife, Sarah, overhearing and laughing at the announcement that she would have a son within the year. Only we, the readers, know from the opening verse that "the LORD appeared to Abraham" in this sequence (although verse 13 makes this clear, stating, "But the LORD said to Abraham"). Three chapters later, in Genesis 21, Isaac is born to Sarah and Abraham.

The Gospel passage is both familiar and challenging. While the Gospel of John recounts two stories involving the sisters Martha and Mary (see John 11, "the raising of Lazarus," and John 12, "the anointing at Bethany"), only Luke tells of this particular incident. The event recorded here, as in our first reading, is about hospitality. It is Martha's home, and it is she who welcomes Jesus. Mary sits at his feet.

The insightful commentary of Fred B. Craddock suggests that we not trivialize this scene. As Craddock states, "There is a time to go and do; there is a time to listen and reflect. Knowing which and when is a matter of spiritual discernment."

◆ Many North Americans associate hospitality with entertaining friends, not with serving strangers. How has our culture shaped how we act toward strangers?

◆ As early as Genesis 12, God promises Abraham that he will have many descendants. The intervening stories between that text and the birth of Isaac might prompt the question of whether that promise will be fulfilled. How have you experienced God's faithfulness?

◆ At the time of Jesus, women were not allowed to "sit at the feet" (receive instruction) of rabbis. In today's Gospel, Jesus not only allows Mary to sit at his feet but also states that she has chosen wisely. In what other ways does Jesus act unconventionally?

READING I   *Genesis 18:20–32*

In those days, the LORD said: "The outcry against Sodom and Gomorrah is so great, and their sin so grave, that I must go down and see whether or not their actions fully correspond to the cry against them that comes to me. I mean to find out."

While Abraham's visitors walked on farther toward Sodom, the LORD remained standing before Abraham. Then Abraham drew nearer and said: "Will you sweep away the innocent with the guilty? Suppose there were fifty innocent people in the city; would you wipe out the place, rather than spare it for the sake of the fifty innocent people within it? Far be it from you to do such a thing, to make the innocent die with the guilty so that the innocent and the guilty would be treated alike! Should not the judge of all the world act with justice?" The LORD replied, "If I find fifty innocent people in the city of Sodom, I will spare the whole place for their sake." Abraham spoke up again: "See how I am presuming to speak to my LORD, though I am but dust and ashes! What if there are five less than fifty innocent people? Will you destroy the whole city because of those five?" He answered, "I will not destroy it, if I find forty-five there." But Abraham persisted, saying "What if only forty are found there?" He replied, "I will forbear doing it for the sake of the forty." Then Abraham said, "Let not my Lord grow impatient if I go on. What if only thirty are found there?" He replied, "I will forbear doing it if I can find but thirty there." Still Abraham went on, "Since I have thus dared to speak to my Lord, what if there are no more than twenty?" The LORD answered, "I will not destroy it, for the sake of the twenty." But he still persisted: "Please, let not my Lord grow angry if I speak up this last time. What if there are at least ten there?" He replied, "For the sake of those ten, I will not destroy it."

RESPONSORIAL PSALM
Psalm 138:1–2, 2–3, 6–7, 7–8 (3a)

R. Lord, on the day I called for help, you answered me.

I will give thanks to you, O LORD, with all my heart,
    for you have heard the words of my mouth;
    in the presence of the angels
       I will sing your praise;
I will worship at your holy temple
    and give thanks to your name.   R.

Because of your kindness and your truth;
    for you have made great above all things
    your name and your promise.
When I called you answered me;
    you built up strength within me.   R.

The LORD is exalted, yet the lowly he sees,
    and the proud he knows from afar.
Though I walk amid distress, you preserve me;
    against the anger of my enemies you raise
       your hand.   R.

Your right hand saves me.
    The LORD will complete what he has done
       for me;
your kindness, O LORD, endures forever;
    forsake not the work of your hands.

READING II   *Colossians 2:12–14*

Brothers and sisters: You were buried with him in baptism, in which you were also raised with him through faith in the power of God, who raised him from the dead. And even when you were dead in transgressions and the uncircumcision of your flesh, he brought you to life along with him, having forgiven us all our transgressions; obliterating the bond against us, with its legal claims, which was opposed to us, he also removed it from our midst, nailing it to the cross.

GOSPEL   *Luke 11:1–13*

Jesus was praying in a certain place, and when he had finished, one of his disciples said to him, "Lord, teach us to pray just as John taught his disciples." He said to them, "When you pray, say:

Father, hallowed be your name,
　your kingdom come.
　　Give us each day our daily bread
　　and forgive us our sins
　for we ourselves forgive everyone in debt to us,
　and do not subject us to the final test."

And he said to them, "Suppose one of you has a friend to whom he goes at midnight and says, 'Friend, lend me three loaves of bread, for a friend of mine has arrived at my house from a journey and I have nothing to offer him,' and he says in reply from within, 'Do not bother me; the door has already been locked and my children and I are already in bed. I cannot get up to give you anything.' I tell you, if he does not get up to give the visitor the loaves because of their friendship, he will get up to give him whatever he needs because of his persistence.

"And I tell you, ask and you will receive; seek and you will find; knock and the door will be opened to you. For everyone who asks, receives; and the one who seeks, finds; and to the one who knocks, the door will be opened. What father among you would hand his son a snake when he asks for a fish? Or hand him a scorpion when he asks for an egg? If you then, who are wicked, know how to give good gifts to your children, how much more will the Father in heaven give the Holy Spirit to those who ask him?"

Practice of Faith

God does not want merely to be believed in but to be in relationship with us. God wants to console and uplift us, to guide and challenge us. God reveals himself to us and awaits our response. ◆ There are countless ways we can accept God's invitation and strengthen our relationship with him. Consider learning a new way to pray. Try praying with your body by lifting up your hands, bowing, or kneeling. ◆ Read more about the Lord's Prayer. A discussion of the prayer begins with number 2759 of the *Catechism of the Catholic Church.* ◆ Participate in an opportunity for communal prayer such as the Rosary or Morning Prayer from the Liturgy of the Hours. If there is a convent or monastery near you, find a time to visit and pray with the members of that community.

Download more questions and activities for families, Christian initiation groups, and other adult groups at http://www.ltp.org/ahw.

Scripture Insights

The reading from Genesis is a continuation of last week's first reading, with fewer than ten verses omitted from the story. Because of the missing verses, we do not hear that while Abraham accompanied his visitors on their way toward Sodom, God was deliberating whether to inform Abraham of the plan to destroy that city. Once the Lord has spoken to Abraham about this, Abraham engages the Lord in a conversation about the justice of the plan. God had heard the pleas of innocent people who had been oppressed by the Sodomites and had determined to destroy the city. It was Abraham who spoke up on behalf of the innocent and questioned God's design to kill them along with the guilty. Abraham reveals himself to be a just man who calls God's ways into question.

The responsorial refrain from Psalm 138 is a lovely expression of gratitude. The psalmist recalls praying to God when in a situation of need and God's response. As a result of God's compassion, the psalmist expresses gratitude and praise, a fitting response to the gift of God's love.

Today's Gospel on prayer contains material for a great deal of reflection. It begins with Luke's version of the Our Father, which is slightly different from the better-known prayer in Matthew. Two examples follow the prayer; one represents the importance of persistence in prayer and the other that God hears our prayer.

◆ In the Gospel, a disciple requests that Jesus teach the disciples how to pray. Have you ever asked a spiritual mentor to help you pray?

◆ Consider how the readings from Genesis and the Gospel both depict individuals who freely approach God. Abraham reasons with God because he does not think that the decision to kill all the people of Sodom is just, while the disciple approaches Jesus because he wants to learn from Jesus.

◆ Can you speak freely to God when you are in need?

READING I *Ecclesiastes 1:2; 2:21–23*

Vanity of vanities, says Qoheleth,
   vanity of vanities! All things are vanity!
   Here is one who has labored with wisdom and knowledge and skill, and yet to another who has not labored over it, he must leave property. This also is vanity and a great misfortune. For what profit comes to man from all the toil and anxiety of heart with which he has labored under the sun? All his days sorrow and grief are his occupation; even at night his mind is not at rest. This also is vanity.

RESPONSORIAL PSALM *Psalm 90:3–4, 5–6, 12–13, 14 and 17 (8)*

R. If today you hear his voice, harden not
      your hearts.

You turn man back to dust,
   saying, "Return, O children of men."
For a thousand years in your sight
   are as yesterday, now that it is past,
   or as a watch of the night. R.

You make an end of them in their sleep;
   the next morning they are like
      the changing grass,
which at dawn springs up anew,
   but by evening wilts and fades. R.

Teach us to number our days aright,
   that we may gain wisdom of heart.
Return, O LORD! How long?
   Have pity on your servants! R.

Fill us at daybreak with your kindness,
   that we may shout for joy
      and gladness all our days.
And may the gracious care of the LORD our God
      be ours;
   prosper the work of our hands for us!
   Prosper the work of our hands! R.

READING II *Colossians 3:1–5, 9–11*

Brothers and sisters: If you were raised with Christ, seek what is above, where Christ is seated at the right hand of God. Think of what is above, not of what is on earth. For you have died, and your life is hidden with Christ in God. When Christ your life appears, then you too will appear with him in glory.

Put to death, then, the parts of you that are earthly: immorality, impurity, passion, evil desire, and the greed that is idolatry. Stop lying to one another, since you have taken off the old self with its practices and have put on the new self, which is being renewed, for knowledge, in the image of its creator. Here there is not Greek and Jew, circumcision and uncircumcision, barbarian, Scythian, slave, free; but Christ is all and in all.

GOSPEL *Luke 12:13–21*

Someone in the crowd said to Jesus, "Teacher, tell my brother to share the inheritance with me." He replied to him, "Friend, who appointed me as your judge and arbitrator?" Then he said to the crowd, "Take care to guard against all greed, for though one may be rich, one's life does not consist of possessions."

Then he told them a parable. "There was a rich man whose land produced a bountiful harvest. He asked himself, 'What shall I do, for I do not have space to store my harvest?' And he said, 'This is what I shall do: I shall tear down my barns and build larger ones. There I shall store all my grain and other goods and I shall say to myself, "Now as for you, you have so many good things stored up for many years, rest, eat, drink, be merry!"' But God said to him, 'You fool, this night your life will be demanded of you; and the things you have prepared, to whom will they belong?' Thus will it be for all who store up treasure for themselves but are not rich in what matters to God."

Practice of Charity

The rich man in the Gospel failed to share his abundance with others. Instead, he looked after only himself, thereby revealing that he was poor in what matters to God. God is rich in love, for God is love itself. The more that God's love fills us, the more we will want to share what we have with others. ◆ Evaluate your financial situation. Could you afford to be more financially supportive of those in need? ◆ On a normal day, track how you spend each fifteen to thirty minutes. What does your time log reveal about what is truly important to you? Should you make changes to how you spend your time? ◆ Create an empty space on a wall or shelf in your home. When you look at that space, ask God to help you live simply and to keep you attentive to the material needs of others.

Download more questions and activities for families, Christian initiation groups, and other adult groups at http://www.ltp.org/ahw.

Scripture Insights

Today's first reading from Ecclesiastes introduces us to the skeptic of the Old Testament. The preacher, or teacher, who speaks in this book is a man who comes across as having seen it all and tried it all. He is an individual whose instruction might leave us wondering, "So now what?" The Gospel reading paraphrases Ecclesiastes 8:15 ("Therefore I praised joy, because there is nothing better for mortals under the sun than to eat and to drink and to be joyful.") when the landowner says to himself, "you have so many good things stored up for many years, rest, eat, drink, be merry!" (Luke 12:19).

The opening line in the first reading, "Vanity of vanities" (1:2), is significant. The Hebrew word can mean vapor, breath, meaninglessness, and even transitoriness. It is a superlative form of the word, and thus, whichever translation is preferred, it carries with it an intensity. Like our first reading, the responsorial psalm recognizes the limitation of human life.

Luke's Gospel passage for today is a reminder that human beings can be very petty. The man who comes to Jesus through the crowd is upset because of a legal dispute with his brother. Jesus responds by telling the man a parable that demonstrates how ridiculous it is to hoard what one has received.

◆ Have you ever felt that life is futile? That human life does not have a specific purpose? As you reflect on the first reading, ask God to be with you in your moments of darkness. Listen to how God responds to you. Keep in mind that God's voice is likely to speak within your heart.

◆ Paul tells the Colossians that they "have taken off the old self with its practices and have put on the new self." Have you discarded any poor practices, habits, or attitudes so that you can take on ones that are more life-giving?

◆ How can you express gratitude to God for the blessings you have received and share those blessings with others? Offer words of thanksgiving for the gifts you have been given.

READING I *Wisdom 18:6–9*

The night of the passover was known
    beforehand to our fathers,
  that, with sure knowledge of the oaths in
    which they put their faith,
  they might have courage.
Your people awaited the salvation of the just
  and the destruction of their foes.
For when you punished our adversaries,
  in this you glorified us whom you
    had summoned.
For in secret the holy children of the good were
    offering sacrifice
  and putting into effect with one accord the
    divine institution.

RESPONSORIAL PSALM
Psalm 33:1, 12, 18–19, 20–22 (12b)

R. Blessed the people the Lord has chosen to
    be his own.

Exult, you just, in the LORD;
  praise from the upright is fitting.
Blessed the nation whose God is the LORD,
  the people he has chosen for his own
    inheritance. R.

See, the eyes of the LORD are upon those who
    fear him,
  upon those who hope for his kindness,
to deliver them from death
  and preserve them in spite of famine. R.

Our soul waits for the LORD,
  who is our help and our shield.
May your kindness, O LORD, be upon us
  who have put our hope in you. R.

READING II *Hebrews 11:1–2, 8–12*

Longer: Hebrews 11:1-2, 8-19

Brothers and sisters: Faith is the realization of what is hoped for and evidence of things not seen. Because of it the ancients were well attested.

By faith Abraham obeyed when he was called to go out to a place that he was to receive as an inheritance; he went out, not knowing where he was to go. By faith he sojourned in the promised land as in a foreign country, dwelling in tents with Isaac and Jacob, heirs of the same promise; for he was looking forward to the city with foundations, whose architect and maker is God. By faith he received power to generate, even though he was past the normal age—and Sarah herself was sterile—for he thought that the one who had made the promise was trustworthy. So it was that there came forth from one man, himself as good as dead, descendants as numerous as the stars in the sky and as countless as the sands on the seashore.

GOSPEL *Luke 12:32–48*

Shorter: Luke 12:35–40

Jesus said to his disciples: "Do not be afraid any longer, little flock, for your Father is pleased to give you the kingdom. Sell your belongings and give alms. Provide money bags for yourselves that do not wear out, an inexhaustible treasure in heaven that no thief can reach nor moth destroy. For where your treasure is, there also will your heart be.

"Gird your loins and light your lamps and be like servants who await their master's return from a wedding, ready to open immediately when he comes and knocks. Blessed are those servants whom the master finds vigilant on his arrival. Amen, I say to you, he will gird himself, have them recline at table, and proceed to wait on them. And should he come in the second or third watch and find them prepared in this way, blessed are those servants. Be sure of this: if the master of the house had known the hour when the thief was coming, he would not have let his house be broken into. You also must be prepared, for at an hour you do not expect, the Son of Man will come."

Then Peter said, "Lord, is this parable meant for us or for everyone?" And the Lord replied, "Who, then, is the faithful and prudent steward whom the master will put in charge of his servants to distribute the food allowance at the proper time? Blessed is that servant whom his master on arrival finds doing so. Truly, I say to you, the master will put the servant in charge of all his property. But if that servant says to himself, 'My master is delayed in coming,' and begins to beat the menservants and the maidservants, to eat and drink and get drunk, then that servant's master will come on an unexpected day and at an unknown hour and will punish the servant severely and assign him a place with the unfaithful. That servant who knew his master's will but did not make preparations nor act in accord with his will shall be beaten severely; and the servant who was ignorant of his master's will but acted in a way deserving of a severe beating shall be beaten only lightly. Much will be required of the person entrusted with much, and still more will be demanded of the person entrusted with more."

Practice of Hope

We commit ourselves to living according to the Gospel because we hope—we *know*—that one day Christ will come again to bring about the fullness of God's reign. By trying to follow Jesus now, we show God that we want to be with him in his kingdom. ◆ Read Hebrews 11. How does this passage inspire you? ◆ What stories from the lives of the saints further strengthen your commitment to Christ? Are there virtuous habits you set aside because they didn't seem to bear fruit or you got tired of doing them? What life-giving habits should you take up again? What events or situations erode your hope? Do you know others who are struggling? ◆ Host a small gathering and invite people to share moments from their lives that filled them with hope. How do such stories carry you through difficult times?

Download more questions and activities for families, Christian initiation groups, and other adult groups at http://www.ltp.org/ahw.

Scripture Insights

The readings for today invite us to trust in God's ways. The author of the Book of Wisdom reminds us of the faith of our early ancestors, who had been enslaved in Egypt yet trusted that God would lead them to freedom.

In the Letter to the Hebrews, we hear how Abraham, a still earlier ancestor, placed his life in the hands of God, trusting that God would lead him to a new land, where he would become the ancestor of countless believers. Those who claim Abraham as an ancestor in faith include Jews, Muslims, and Christians.

The extensive passage in the reading from the Gospel of Luke can be divided into several parts. In the opening verses, Jesus instructs his disciples about possessions, about being prepared or watchful for the Lord's return, and about responsible leadership. It can be helpful to keep in mind that this instruction takes place while Jesus is on his way to Jerusalem. The first instruction is quite clear. While it was not likely to have been taken literally (to sell everything one has is hardly realistic), it emphasizes that the disciples should not be attached to possessions. The second instruction stresses the importance of being prepared for the Lord's return whenever that will be. Finally, the third instruction offers the disciples a warning about how to use or not use the authority that they have been given. Positions of privilege can lure people to take advantage of others. Such is not the behavior of a disciple of Jesus.

◆ Who in your life has been an example of faithfulness? Express a prayer of gratitude for that individual.

◆ How do you understand the last sentence in today's Gospel?

◆ Ponder the words "For where your treasure is, there also will your heart be." Where is your treasure? Is this a good place for your heart?

READING I *Jeremiah 38:4–6, 8–10*

In those days, the princes said to the king: "Jeremiah ought to be put to death; he is demoralizing the soldiers who are left in this city, and all the people, by speaking such things to them; he is not interested in the welfare of our people, but in their ruin." King Zedekiah answered: "He is in your power"; for the king could do nothing with them. And so they took Jeremiah and threw him into the cistern of Prince Malchiah, which was in the quarters of the guard, letting him down with ropes. There was no water in the cistern, only mud, and Jeremiah sank into the mud.

Ebed-melech, a court official, went there from the palace and said to him: "My lord king, these men have been at fault in all they have done to the prophet Jeremiah, casting him into the cistern. He will die of famine on the spot, for there is no more food in the city." Then the king ordered Ebed-melech the Cushite to take three men along with him, and draw the prophet Jeremiah out of the cistern before he should die.

RESPONSORIAL PSALM
Psalm 40:2, 3, 4, 18 (14b)

R. Lord, come to my aid!

I have waited, waited for the Lord,
    and he stooped toward me.   R.

The LORD heard my cry.
He drew me out of the pit of destruction,
    out of the mud of the swamp;
he set my feet upon a crag;
    he made firm my steps.   R

And he put a new song into my mouth,
    a hymn to our God.
Many shall look on in awe
    and trust in the Lord.   R.

Though I am afflicted and poor,
    yet the LORD thinks of me.
You are my help and my deliverer;
    O my God, hold not back!   R.

READING II *Hebrews 12:1–4*

Brothers and sisters: Since we are surrounded by so great a cloud of witnesses, let us rid ourselves of every burden and sin that clings to us and persevere in running the race that lies before us while keeping our eyes fixed on Jesus, the leader and perfecter of faith. For the sake of the joy that lay before him he endured the cross, despising its shame, and has taken his seat at the right of the throne of God. Consider how he endured such opposition from sinners, in order that you may not grow weary and lose heart. In your struggle against sin you have not yet resisted to the point of shedding blood.

GOSPEL *Luke 12:49–53*

Jesus said to his disciples: "I have come to set the earth on fire, and how I wish it were already blazing! There is a baptism with which I must be baptized, and how great is my anguish until it is accomplished! Do you think that I have come to establish peace on the earth? No, I tell you, but rather division. From now on a household of five will be divided, three against two and two against three; a father will be divided against his son and a son against his father, a mother against her daughter and a daughter against her mother, a mother-in-law against her daughter-in-law and a daughter-in-law against her mother-in-law."

Practice of Faith

When people do God's will, other people sometimes react angrily or even violently. Jeremiah was thrown down a well. Jesus was crucified. Some of Jesus' followers suffered scorn and rejection by family members. ◆ Are there ways in which family members and/or friends make it hard for you to follow Christ? What must you do to bravely but lovingly hold fast to your faith? ◆ Make a list of ordinary people who suffered because of their faith in Jesus. Pray for these people, and ask that they become an encouraging "cloud of witnesses" for you. ◆ Invite some people to pray with you for the protection of people's freedom to worship. The US Conference of Catholic Bishops has links to prayer resources on their website, www.usccb.org/issues-and-action/religious-liberty/index.cfm.

Download more questions and activities for families, Christian initiation groups, and other adult groups at http://www.ltp.org/ahw.

Scripture Insights

Our reading from Jeremiah reminds us that this prophet suffered greatly. The people of Judah did not welcome the words that God commanded Jeremiah to proclaim. The action of the officials who lowered Jeremiah into the cistern was a direct result of their hatred of Jeremiah and his message. During this time, Jeremiah had told the authorities that they should surrender to the Babylonians. This was an unpopular message for a people who would have seen surrender as an act of treason. Yet, another court official, a foreigner, Ebed-melech, whose name means "servant of the king," convinces the king that Jeremiah should be saved.

Today's psalm refrain, "Lord, come to my aid," is an appropriate plea from the mouth of one in Jeremiah's situation. The psalm itself has been classified as a combination of a prayer of thanksgiving and a lament. Since a psalm of thanksgiving tells the story of a past difficulty, we can clearly hear the story of either the psalmist or Jeremiah in this text.

Our Gospel of five verses is a difficult one. Jesus' statement that he has come to bring fire upon the earth might best be understood as some type of purification that needs to take place. And the baptism that Jesus proclaims refers to the death that he will soon face. Most of us are likely to prefer the image of a gentle, tender, and caring Jesus to the one presented to us today. The reality, however, is that to be a follower of Jesus means that we must make many difficult choices, choices that will not always be popular with friends and family.

◆ Read the responsorial psalm from the perspective of Jeremiah. Make this a psalm of your deliverance. When have you waited for the Lord? How has God helped you when you felt stuck?

◆ Today's Gospel reading from Luke sounds harsh. When has the practice of your faith caused tension between you and someone you love?

◆ What similarities do you see between today's reading from Jeremiah and the passage from the Gospel of Luke?

111

READING I *Isaiah 66:18–21*

Thus says the LORD: I know their works and their thoughts, and I come to gather nations of every language; they shall come and see my glory. I will set a sign among them; from them I will send fugitives to the nations: to Tarshish, Put and Lud, Mosoch, Tubal and Javan, to the distant coastlands that have never heard of my fame, or seen my glory; and they shall proclaim my glory among the nations. They shall bring all your brothers and sisters from all the nations as an offering to the LORD, on horses and in chariots, in carts, upon mules and dromedaries, to Jerusalem, my holy mountain, says the LORD, just as the Israelites bring their offering to the house of the LORD in clean vessels. Some of these I will take as priests and Levites, says the LORD.

RESPONSORIAL PSALM
Psalm 117:1, 2 (Mark 16:15)

R. Go out to all the world and tell the
     Good News.
or: Alleluia.

Praise the LORD, all you nations;
    glorify him, all you peoples! R.

For steadfast is his kindness toward us,
    and the fidelity of the LORD endures
      forever. R.

READING II *Hebrews 12:5–7, 11–13*

Brothers and sisters: You have forgotten the exhortation addressed to you as children: "My son, do not disdain the discipline of the Lord or lose heart when reproved by him; for whom the Lord loves, he disciplines; he scourges every son he acknowledges." Endure your trials as "discipline"; God treats you as sons. For what "son" is there whom his father does not discipline? At the time, all discipline seems a cause not for joy but for pain, yet later it brings the peaceful fruit of righteousness to those who are trained by it.

So strengthen your drooping hands and your weak knees. Make straight paths for your feet, that what is lame may not be disjointed but healed.

GOSPEL *Luke 13:22–30*

Jesus passed through towns and villages, teaching as he went and making his way to Jerusalem. Someone asked him, "Lord, will only a few people be saved?" He answered them, "Strive to enter through the narrow gate, for many, I tell you, will attempt to enter but will not be strong enough. After the master of the house has arisen and locked the door, then will you stand outside knocking and saying, 'Lord, open the door for us.' He will say to you in reply, 'I do not know where you are from.' And you will say, 'We ate and drank in your company and you taught in our streets.' Then he will say to you, 'I do not know where you are from. Depart from me, all you evildoers!' And there will be wailing and grinding of teeth when you see Abraham, Isaac, and Jacob and all the prophets in the kingdom of God and you yourselves cast out. And people will come from the east and the west and from the north and the south and will recline at table in the kingdom of God. For behold, some are last who will be first, and some are first who will be last."

Practice of Hope

Jesus opens the door to everyone who strives to live as he did, but joining him in God's kingdom takes sincere and constant effort. We must persist despite whatever challenges we meet. ◆ What is the greatest obstacle you face as you follow Christ? How is this obstacle painful for you to overcome? Share your struggle with the Lord. Listen for the ways God is with you in your struggle. ◆ Make a list of the people you know and their good qualities. Choose two people and send them a note thanking them for the particular ways they reveal God's goodness. ◆ How well do you know the people with whom you gather to celebrate the Eucharist? Introduce yourself to someone. Pray for that person throughout the week.

Download more questions and activities for families, Christian initiation groups, and other adult groups at http://www.ltp.org/ahw.

Scripture Insights

Our readings from Isaiah and Luke focus on the theme of salvation. Is God's saving love offered to only a few? To only the Jews? To a select community? To everyone? According to the closing chapter in the Book of Isaiah, the Lord announces: "I know their works and their thoughts, and I come to gather nations of every language; they shall come and see my glory" (66:18). The text proceeds to make clear that many foreigners will be welcomed on God's holy mountain. This theme of a universal invitation from our saving God is not unusual in this magnificent prophetic book.

"Go out to all the world and tell the Good News," from the closing verses of the Gospel of Mark (16:15), is the refrain for the responsorial psalm from Psalm 117. The psalm, the shortest in the psalter, is itself universal in nature, inviting all nations and all peoples to offer praise to God.

The Gospel passage from Luke invites us to reflect more closely on the message of Jesus as he makes his way to Jerusalem. In a manner not uncommon in Luke, a question is raised. Whose question is this? Is it really from an unknown individual or do many wonder, "Lord, will only a few people be saved" (13:23)? Who will be saved? How will that be determined? Jesus does not give a clear response to the question.

◆ How does the invitation to all to dwell in the kingdom of God reflect God's love? How does that correspond to your love and compassion for people unlike yourself?

◆ Consider learning more about another religious denomination. How do the practices of the tradition resonate with practices of the Catholic faith? How do they differ?

◆ If Jesus were to have answered the question in the Gospel directly, how do you imagine he would have responded? Spend some time reflecting on your answer to this query.

Ordinary Time, Autumn

Prayer before Reading the Word

God of the covenant,
whose promises can never fail,
in every age you place your words
on the lips of the prophets.
We children of this age come to you in faith,
longing to be transformed in Christ
as children of the resurrection.

Give us humility of heart.
Let us cling to your Word
in Moses, the prophets, and the Gospel.
Let each new day be for us
a time to testify to the Gospel.

Through our Lord Jesus Christ, your Son,
who lives and reigns with you
in the unity of the Holy Spirit,
God, for ever and ever. Amen.

Prayer after Reading the Word

O God, author of life and resurrection,
before whom even the dead are alive,
grant that the Word of your Son,
sown in our hearts,
may blossom and bear fruit in every good work,
so that both in life and in death
our hearts may be strengthened
by eternal comfort and good hope.

Through our Lord Jesus Christ, your Son,
who lives and reigns with you
in the unity of the Holy Spirit,
God, for ever and ever. Amen.

Weekday Readings

August 29: *1 Corinthians 2:1–5; Mark 6:17–29*
August 30: *1 Corinthians 2:10b–16; Luke 4:31–37*
August 31: *1 Corinthians 3:1–9; Luke 4:38–44*
September 1: *1 Corinthians 3:18–23; Luke 5:1–11*
September 2: *1 Corinthians 4:1–5; Luke 5:33–39*
September 3: *1 Corinthians 4:6b–15; Luke 6:1–5 (436)*

September 5: *1 Corinthians 5:1–8; Luke 6:6–11*
September 6: *1 Corinthians 6:1–11; Luke 6:12–19*
September 7: *1 Corinthians 7:25–31; Luke 6:20–26*
**September 8: Feast of the Nativity
    of the Blessed Virgin Mary
    Micah 5:1–4a or Romans 8:28–30;
    Matthew 1:1–16, 18–23 or 1:18–23**
September 9: *1 Corinthians 9:16–19, 22b–27; Luke 6:39–42*
September 10: *1 Corinthians 10:14–22; Luke 6:43–49*

September 12: *1 Corinthians 11:17–26, 33; Luke 7:1–10*
September 13: *1 Corinthians 12:12–14, 27–31a; Luke 7:11–17*
**September 14: Feast of the Exaltation of the Holy Cross
    Numbers 21:4b–9; Philippians 2:6–11; John 3:13–17**
September 15: *1 Corinthians 15:1–11; John 19:25–27
    or Luke 2:33–35*
September 16: *1 Corinthians 15:12–20; Luke 8:1–3*
September 17: *1 Corinthians 15:35–37, 42–49; Luke 8:4–15*

September 19: *Proverbs 3:27–34; Luke 8:16–18*
September 20: *Proverbs 21:1–6, 10–13; Luke 8:19–21*
**September 21: Feast of St. Matthew, Apostle and Evangelist
    Ephesians 4:1–7, 11–13; Matthew 9:9–13**
September 22: *Ecclesiastes 1:2–11; Luke 9:7–9*
September 23: *Ecclesiastes 3:1–11; Luke 9:18–22*
September 24: *Ecclesiastes 11:9—12:8; Luke 9:43b–45*

September 26: *Job 1:6–22; Luke 9:46–50*
September 27: *Job 3:1–3, 11–17, 20–23; Luke 9:51–56*
September 28: *Job 9:1–12, 14–16; Luke 9:57–62*
**September 29: Feast of Sts. Michael, Gabriel and
    Raphael, Archangels
    Daniel 7:9–10, 13–14 or Revelation 12:7–12a; John 1:47–51**
September 30: *Job 38:1, 12–21; 40:3–5; Luke 10:13–16*
October 1: *Job 42:1–3, 5–6, 12–17; Luke 10:17–24*

October 3: *Galatians 1:6–12; Luke 10:25–37*
October 4: *Galatians 1:13–24; Luke 10:38–42*
October 5: *Galatians 2:1–2, 7–14; Luke 11:1–4*
October 6: *Galatians 3:1–5; Luke 11:5–13*
October 7: *Galatians 3:7–14; Luke 11:15–26*
October 8: *Galatians 3:22–29; Luke 11:27–28*

October 10: *Galatians 4:22–24, 26–27, 31—5:1; Luke 11:29–32*
October 11: *Galatians 5:1–6; Luke 11:37–41*
October 12: *Galatians 5:18–25; Luke 11:42–46*
October 13: *Ephesians 1:1–10; Luke 11:47–54*
October 14: *Ephesians 1:11–14; Luke 12:1–7*
October 15: *Ephesians 1:15–23; Luke 12:8–12*

October 17: *Ephesians 2:1–10; Luke 12:13–21*
**October 18: Feast of St. Luke, Evangelist
    2 Timothy 4:10–17b; Luke 10:1–9**
October 19: *Ephesians 3:2–12; Luke 12:39–48*
October 20: *Ephesians 3:14–21; Luke 12:49–53*
October 21: *Ephesians 4:1–6; Luke 12:54–59*
October 22. *Ephesians 4:7–16; Luke 13:1 9*

October 24: *Ephesians 4:32—5:8; Luke 13:10–17*
October 25: *Ephesians 5:21–33; Luke 13:18–21*
October 26: *Ephesians 6:1–9; Luke 13:22–30*
October 27: *Ephesians 6:10–20; Luke 13:31–35*
**October 28: Feast of Sts. Simon and Jude, Apostles
    Ephesians 2:19–22; Luke 6:12–16**
October 29: *Philippians 1:18b–26; Luke 14:1, 7–11*

October 31: *Philippians 2:1–4; Luke 14:12–14*
**November 1: Solemnity of All Saints
    Revelation 7:2–4, 9–14; 1 John 3:1–3; Matthew 5:1–12a**
**November 2: Commemoration of All the Faithful Departed
    (All Souls' Day)
    Wisdom 3:1–9; Romans 5:5–11 or Romans 6:3-9;
    John 6:37–40**
November 3: *Philippians 3:3–8a; Luke 15:1–10*
November 4: *Philippians 3:17—4:1; Luke 16:1–8*
November 5: *Philippians 4:10–19; Luke 16:9–15*

November 7: *Titus 1:1–9; Luke 17:1–6*
November 8: *Titus 2:1–8, 11–14; Luke 17:7–10*
**November 9: Feast of the Dedication of the Lateran Basilica
    Ezekiel 47:1–2, 8–9, 12; 1 Corinthians 3:9c–11, 16–17;
    John 2:13–22**
November 10: *Philemon 7–20; Luke 17:20 25*
November 11: *2 John 4–9; Luke 17:26–37*
November 12: *3 John 5–8; Luke 18:1–8*

November 14: *Revelation 1:1–4; 2:1–5; Luke 18:35–43*
November 15: *Revelation 3:1–6, 14–22; Luke 19:1–10*
November 16: *Revelation 4:1–11; Luke 19:11–28*
November 17: *Revelation 5:1–10; Luke 19:41–44*
November 18: *Revelation 10:8–11; Luke 19:45–48*
November 19: *Revelation 11:4–12; Luke 20:27–40*

November 21: *Revelation 14:1–3, 4b–5; Luke 21:1–4*
November 22: *Revelation 14:14–19; Luke 21:5–11*
November 23: *Revelation 15:1–4; Luke 21:12–19*
November 24: *Revelation 18:1–2, 21–23; 19:1–3, 9a;
    Luke 21:20–28*
or, for Thanksgiving Day, any readings from the Lectionary
    for Mass (vol. 4) "In Thanksgiving to God," nos. 943–947
November 25: *Revelation 20:1–4, 11—21:2; Luke 21:29–33*
November 26: *Revelation 22:1–7; Luke 21:34–36*

READING I   *Sirach 3:17–18, 20, 28–29*

My child, conduct your affairs with humility,
    and you will be loved more than a giver
        of gifts.
Humble yourself the more, the greater you are,
    and you will find favor with God.
What is too sublime for you, seek not,
    into things beyond your strength search not.
The mind of a sage appreciates proverbs,
    and an attentive ear is the joy of the wise.
Water quenches a flaming fire,
    and alms atone for sins.

RESPONSORIAL PSALM
Psalm 68:4–5, 6–7, 10–11 (see 11b)

R. God, in your goodness, you have made
        a home for the poor.

The just rejoice and exult before God;
    they are glad and rejoice.
Sing to God, chant praise to his name;
    whose name is the LORD.   R.

The father of orphans and the defender
        of widows
    is God in his holy dwelling.
God gives a home to the forsaken;
    he leads forth prisoners to prosperity.   R.

A bountiful rain you showered down, O God,
        upon your inheritance;
    you restored the land when it languished;
your flock settled in it;
    in your goodness, O God, you provided it for
        the needy.   R.

READING II
Hebrews 12:18–19, 22–24a

Brothers and sisters: You have not approached that which could be touched and a blazing fire and gloomy darkness and storm and a trumpet blast and a voice speaking words such that those who heard begged that no message be further addressed to them. No, you have approached Mount Zion and the city of the living God, the heavenly Jerusalem, and countless angels in festal gathering, and the assembly of the firstborn enrolled in heaven, and God the judge of all, and the spirits of the just made perfect, and Jesus, the mediator of a new covenant, and the sprinkled blood that speaks more eloquently than that of Abel.

GOSPEL   *Luke 14:1, 7–14*

On a sabbath Jesus went to dine at the home of one of the leading Pharisees, and the people there were observing him carefully.

He told a parable to those who had been invited, noticing how they were choosing the places of honor at the table. "When you are invited by someone to a wedding banquet, do not recline at table in the place of honor. A more distinguished guest than you may have been invited by him, and the host who invited both of you may approach you and say, 'Give your place to this man,' and then you would proceed with embarrassment to take the lowest place. Rather, when you are invited, go and take the lowest place so that when the host comes to you he may say, 'My friend, move up to a higher position.' Then you will enjoy the esteem of your companions at the table. For every one who exalts himself will be humbled, but the one who humbles himself will be exalted." Then he said to the host who invited him, "When you hold a lunch or a dinner, do not invite your friends or your brothers or your relatives or your wealthy neighbors, in case they may invite you back and you have repayment. Rather, when you hold a banquet, invite the poor, the crippled, the lame, the blind; blessed indeed will you be because of their inability to repay you. For you will be repaid at the resurrection of the righteous."

Practice of Charity

When we try to win the esteem of others, we often conform ourselves to cultural values instead of welcoming God's love and the way of life that flows from that love. ◆ Spend some time gazing at a crucifix. Pray the Litany of Humility if it is available. How does Jesus' crucifixion contradict what our society tells us is important? ◆ Are there ways in which the crucifixion challenges what is especially important to you? In what ways do you try to project status, youth, or power? What significant change can you make that is countercultural and Gospel-oriented, such as changing how you dress, what you drive, or what you do for entertainment? ◆ If you can afford to, make an anonymous donation to a charity that helps the poor.

Download more questions and activities for families, Christian initiation groups, and other adult groups at http://www.ltp.org/ahw.

Scripture Insights

The reading from Sirach offers us teachings from the Wisdom tradition. The biblical texts identified as "Wisdom" tend to focus on how to live well. Much, if not most, of this material offers instruction. Today's selection from Sirach is a cutting from a larger unit that focuses on the importance of the virtue of humility, a virtue of no less value today than it was at the time this text was composed.

Our reading from Hebrews refers to two mountain scenes or experiences. The first reference is to Mount Sinai, the holy mountain where God was made manifest and entered into a covenant relationship with Israel; the second reference is to Mount Zion and the temple. This latter scene, however, should not be understood as the earthly Jerusalem but as the heavenly Jerusalem, where covenantal promises will be fulfilled.

Luke's Gospel for today offers much for reflection. While Jesus accepted an invitation "to dine at the home of one of the leading Pharisees," we should not miss the rest of this verse that states, "and the people there were observing him" (14:1). The verb used here can imply that the Pharisees were waiting for Jesus to do something in which they could find fault. What will Jesus do? What will he say? Jesus tells a parable. This parable is about a banquet and where people position themselves. Do they select a place of honor? Or do they humbly take a place further from the host, grateful for having been invited to this meal? Jesus then addresses the Pharisee, the host of the dinner. These words also are addressed to us. They confront us with the lavish love of our God. All are welcome at God's banquet.

◆ How do you understand the virtue of humility?

◆ Reread what Jesus says to the host of the wedding banquet. Do you believe that God invites everyone to the kingdom?

◆ How does today's Gospel challenge you to see all people as children of God?

READING I *Wisdom 9:13–18b*

Who can know God's counsel,
or who can conceive what the LORD intends?
For the deliberations of mortals are timid,
and unsure are our plans.
For the corruptible body burdens the soul
and the earthen shelter weighs down the
mind that has many concerns.
And scarce do we guess the things on earth,
and what is within our grasp
we find with difficulty;
but when things are in heaven,
who can search them out?
Or who ever knew your counsel, except you
had given wisdom
and sent your holy spirit from on high?
And thus were the paths of those
on earth made straight.

RESPONSORIAL PSALM
Psalm 90:3–4, 5–6, 12–13, 14 and 17 (1)

R. In every age, O Lord,
you have been our refuge.

You turn man back to dust,
saying, "Return, O children of men."
For a thousand years in your sight
are as yesterday, now that it is past,
or as a watch of the night. R.

You make an end of them in their sleep;
the next morning they are
like the changing grass,
which at dawn springs up anew,
but by evening wilts and fades. R.

Teach us to number our days aright,
that we may gain wisdom of heart.
Return, O LORD! How long?
Have pity on your servants! R.

Fill us at daybreak with your kindness,
that we may shout for joy and gladness
all our days.

And may the gracious care of the LORD our God
be ours;
prosper the work of our hands for us!
Prosper the work of our hands! R.

READING II *Philemon 9–10, 12–17*

I, Paul, an old man, and now also a prisoner for Christ Jesus, urge you on behalf of my child Onesimus, whose father I have become in my imprisonment; I am sending him, that is, my own heart, back to you. I should have liked to retain him for myself, so that he might serve me on your behalf in my imprisonment for the gospel, but I did not want to do anything without your consent, so that the good you do might not be forced but voluntary. Perhaps this is why he was away from you for a while, that you might have him back forever, no longer as a slave but more than a slave, a brother, beloved especially to me, but even more so to you, as a man and in the Lord. So if you regard me as a partner, welcome him as you would me.

GOSPEL *Luke 14:25–33*

Great crowds were traveling with Jesus, and he turned and addressed them, "If anyone comes to me without hating his father and mother, wife and children, brothers and sisters, and even his own life, he cannot be my disciple. Whoever does not carry his own cross and come after me cannot be my disciple. Which of you wishing to construct a tower does not first sit down and calculate the cost to see if there is enough for its completion? Otherwise, after laying the foundation and finding himself unable to finish the work the onlookers should laugh at him and say, 'This one began to build but did not have the resources to finish.' Or what king marching into battle would not first sit down and decide whether with ten thousand troops he can successfully oppose another king advancing upon him with twenty thousand troops? But if not, while he is still far away, he will send a delegation to ask for peace terms. In the same way, anyone of you who does not renounce all his possessions cannot be my disciple."

Practice of Faith

We may think that we love Jesus, but if we are not willing to surrender more and more of our lives to his way of sacrificial love, then we aren't truly his disciples. ◆ Read all of Wisdom 9. Make this prayer your own as you ask God to strengthen and guide your faith. ◆ Is there a significant part of your life in which you aren't fully invested, such as your work or a close relationship? Reflect on this situation or talk with someone such as a spiritual director or your pastor. What changes do you need to make to be more committed? ◆ As we try to commit ourselves more fully to Christ, others are bound to human masters. Slavery isn't a thing of the past. Learn about human trafficking at www .usccb.org/about/anti-trafficking-program/index. cfm. What could you do to prevent human trafficking and help victims rebuild their lives?

Download more questions and activities for families, Christian initiation groups, and other adult groups at http://www.ltp.org/ahw.

Scripture Insights

Today's Gospel reading from Luke, like last Sunday's Gospel, draws our attention to discipleship. While last week's text took place at a table, the setting of today's passage is quite different. Jesus is on his way to Jerusalem, where he will be crucified. Crowds followed Jesus as he made his way to his death and his resurrection.

Jesus' words to the people seem shocking. Does Jesus really want us to hate our parents, our spouse, our siblings? Is this what it takes to be a disciple? Doesn't this contradict Jesus' teaching on love? Aren't disciples supposed to love one another, even those who hate us? Three times in this text, we hear that unless a person does or does not do something that person "cannot be my disciple" (14:26, 27, 33). In essence, Jesus states that we must hate our family, carry our cross, and renounce our possessions.

It is helpful to be aware of several literary aspects in this puzzling passage. First of all, some commentators are quick to point out that the saying about hating family members is a "Semitic hyperbole." In other words, it is an exaggerated statement intended to make a point emphatically (consider how even today, when upset, someone might say, "I could just kill him!" or "I could wring her neck!"). Jesus is emphasizing that if one chooses to be his disciple, the road ahead will not be easy. There will be a price to pay, and that price is high. Second, the Greek verb that is translated "hate" might best be understood as "prefers." Thus, the text could be understood as stating, "Whoever prefers family over me, cannot be my disciple." Again, to be a disciple of Jesus means be ready to follow him without compromise.

◆ What does the Gospel tell you about the cost of discipleship? What have you given up to more closely follow Christ?

◆ How do you balance the command to love all people with what Jesus expresses in this Gospel?

◆ What questions does this Gospel passage stir up in you? Write these questions down and pray over them.

September 11, 2022

READING I *Exodus 32:7–11, 13–14*

The LORD said to Moses, "Go down at once to your people, whom you brought out of the land of Egypt, for they have become depraved. They have soon turned aside from the way I pointed out to them, making for themselves a molten calf and worshiping it, sacrificing to it and crying out, 'This is your God, O Israel, who brought you out of the land of Egypt!' I see how stiff-necked this people is," continued the LORD to Moses. "Let me alone, then, that my wrath may blaze up against them to consume them. Then I will make of you a great nation."

But Moses implored the LORD, his God, saying, "Why, O LORD, should your wrath blaze up against your own people, whom you brought out of the land of Egypt with such great power and with so strong a hand? Remember your servants Abraham, Isaac, and Israel, and how you swore to them by your own self, saying, 'I will make your descendants as numerous as the stars in the sky; and all this land that I promised, I will give your descendants as their perpetual heritage.'" So the LORD relented in the punishment he had threatened to inflict on his people.

READING II *1 Timothy 1:12–17*

Beloved: I am grateful to him who has strengthened me, Christ Jesus our Lord, because he considered me trustworthy in appointing me to the ministry. I was once a blasphemer and a persecutor and arrogant, but I have been mercifully treated because I acted out of ignorance in my unbelief. Indeed, the grace of our Lord has been abundant, along with the faith and love that are in Christ Jesus. This saying is trustworthy and deserves full acceptance: Christ Jesus came into the world to save sinners. Of these I am the foremost. But for that reason I was mercifully treated, so that in me, as the foremost, Christ Jesus might display all his patience as an example for those who would come to believe in him for everlasting life. To the king of ages, incorruptible, invisible, the only God, honor and glory forever and ever. Amen.

GOSPEL *Luke 15:1–32*

Shorter: Luke 15:1–10

Tax collectors and sinners were all drawing near to listen to Jesus, but the Pharisees and scribes began to complain, saying, "This man welcomes sinners and eats with them." So to them he addressed this parable. "What man among you having a hundred sheep and losing one of them would not leave the ninety-nine in the desert and go after the lost one until he finds it? And when he does find it, he sets it on his shoulders with great joy and, upon his arrival home, he calls together his friends and neighbors and says to them, 'Rejoice with me because I have found my lost sheep.' I tell you, in just the same way there will be more joy in heaven over one sinner who repents than over ninety-nine righteous people who have no need of repentance.

"Or what woman having ten coins and losing one would not light a lamp and sweep the house, searching carefully until she finds it? And when she does find it, she calls together her friends and neighbors and says to them, 'Rejoice with me because I have found the coin that I lost.' In just the same way, I tell you, there will be rejoicing among the angels of God over one sinner who repents."

Then he said, "A man had two sons, and the younger son said to his father, 'Father give me the share of your estate that should come to me.' So the father divided the property between them. After a few days, the younger son collected all his belongings and set off to a distant country where he squandered his inheritance on a life of dissipation. When he had freely spent everything, a severe famine struck that country, and he found himself in dire need. So he hired himself out to one of the local citizens who sent him to his farm to tend the swine. And he longed to eat his fill of the pods on which the swine fed, but nobody gave him any. Coming to his senses he thought, 'How many of my father's hired workers have more than enough food to eat, but here am I, dying from hunger. I shall get up and go to my father and I shall say to him, "Father, I have sinned against heaven and against you. I no longer deserve to be called your son; treat me as you would treat one of your hired workers.'" So he got up and went back to his father. While he was still a long way off, his father caught sight of him, and was filled with compassion. He ran to his son, embraced him and kissed him. His son said to him, 'Father, I have sinned against heaven and against you; I no longer deserve to be called your son.' But his father ordered his servants, 'Quickly bring the finest robe and put it on him; put a ring on his finger and sandals on his feet. Take the fattened calf and slaughter it. Then let us celebrate with a feast, because this son of mine was dead, and has come to life again; he was lost, and has been found.' Then the celebration began. Now the older son had been out in the field and, on his way back, as he neared the house, he heard the sound of music and dancing. He called one of the servants and asked what this might mean. The servant said to him, 'Your brother has returned and your father has slaughtered the fattened calf because he has him back safe and sound.' He became angry, and when he refused to enter the house, his father came out and pleaded with him. He said to his father in reply, 'Look, all these years I served you and not once did I disobey your orders; yet you never gave me even a young goat to feast on with my friends. But when your son returns, who swallowed up your property with prostitutes, for him you slaughter the fattened calf.' He said to him, 'My son, you are here with me always; everything I have is yours. But now we must celebrate and rejoice, because your brother was dead and has come to life again; he was lost and has been found.'"

Download more questions and activities for families, Christian initiation groups, and other adult groups at http://www.ltp.org/ahw.

Scripture Insights

One of the themes in today's readings is forgiveness, a need for which each of us is very aware. In the reading from Exodus, we hear that the Israelites sinned by turning away from God and worshiping an idol they had made with their hands. Moses, once again, intercedes for the people by imploring God to remember the saving deeds that God had done on behalf of this chosen people.

Meanwhile, the text from the opening chapter of the First Letter to Timothy presents us with a confession of Paul, the well-known persecutor of the early followers of Jesus. Paul speaks boldly of his arrogance, his sinfulness, and the unbounded mercy of God. It was God's gracious love that touched Paul's heart and transformed him into an apostle.

The responsorial psalm for today does not appear on these two pages, but it is from Psalm 51, perhaps one of the best-known psalms of the psalter. Its opening verse reads, "Have mercy on me, O God, in your goodness; in the greatness of your compassion, wipe out my offense."

Today's Gospel from Luke consists of three parables, each of which is worthy of more attention than we can provide. The first two parables, the shepherd who has lost a sheep and the woman who has lost a coin, are very similar. Both the man and the woman are overjoyed that something lost has been found, and therefore, both celebrate. The well-known parable of the wayward son is a reminder that God's love for each of us, those who have worked tirelessly to be faithful and those who have strayed and are loved, is deeper than we can possibly imagine.

◆ Recall a situation when you knew that only God's saving grace could lift you up from distress. How did feeling God's mercy affect you?

◆ Which of today's three parables captures your imagination? What feelings and images in those parables touch you?

◆ With which of the two sons do you identify? Consider journaling with a sibling about the parable, and be open to the other's experience.

READING I   *Amos 8:4–7*

Hear this, you who trample upon the needy
   and destroy the poor of the land!
"When will the new moon be over," you ask,
   "that we may sell our grain,
   and the sabbath, that we may display
      the wheat?
We will diminish the ephah,
   add to the shekel,
   and fix our scales for cheating!
We will buy the lowly for silver,
   and the poor for a pair of sandals;
   even the refuse of the wheat we will sell!"
The LORD has sworn by the pride of Jacob:
   Never will I forget a thing they have done!

RESPONSORIAL PSALM
Psalm 113:1–2, 4–6, 7–8 (see 1a, 7b)

R. Praise the Lord, who lifts up the poor.
or: Alleluia.

Praise, you servants of the LORD,
   praise the name of the LORD.
Blessed be the name of the LORD
   both now and forever.   R.

High above all nations is the LORD;
   above the heavens is his glory.
Who is like the LORD, our God,
      who is enthroned on high
   and looks upon the heavens
      and the earth below?   R.

He raises up the lowly from the dust;
   from the dunghill he lifts up the poor
to seat them with princes,
   with the princes of his own people.   R.

READING II   *1 Timothy 2:1–8*

Beloved: First of all, I ask that supplications, prayers, petitions and thanksgivings be offered for everyone, for kings and for all in authority, that we may lead a quiet and tranquil life in all devotion and dignity. This is good and pleasing to God our savior, who wills everyone to be saved and to come to knowledge of the truth.

For there is one God.
There is also one mediator between God
      and men,
   the man Christ Jesus,
who gave himself as ransom for all.

This was the testimony at the proper time. For this I was appointed preacher and apostle—I am speaking the truth, I am not lying—, teacher of the Gentiles in faith and truth.

   It is my wish, then, that in every place the men should pray, lifting up holy hands, without anger or argument.

GOSPEL   *Luke 16:1–13*

Shorter: Luke 16:10–13

Jesus said to his disciples, "A rich man had a steward who was reported to him for squandering his property. He summoned him and said, 'What is this I hear about you? Prepare a full account of your stewardship, because you can no longer be my steward.' The steward said to himself, 'What shall I do, now that my master is taking the position of steward away from me? I am not strong enough to dig and I am ashamed to beg. I know what I shall do so that, when I am removed from the stewardship, they may welcome me into their homes.' He called in his master's debtors one by one. To the first he said, 'How much do you owe my master?' He replied, 'One hundred measures of olive oil.' He said to him, 'Here is your promissory note. Sit down and quickly write one for fifty.' Then to another the steward said, 'And you, how much do you owe?' He replied, 'One hundred kors of wheat.' The steward said to him, 'Here is your promissory note; write one for eighty.' And the master commended that dishonest steward for acting prudently.

   "For the children of this world are more prudent in dealing with their own generation than are the children of light. I tell you, make friends for yourselves with dishonest wealth, so that when it fails, you will be welcomed into eternal dwellings. The person who is trustworthy in very small matters is also trustworthy in great ones; and the person who is dishonest in very small matters is also dishonest in great ones. If, therefore, you are not trustworthy with dishonest wealth, who will trust you with true wealth? If you are not trustworthy with what belongs to another, who will give you what is yours? No servant can serve two masters. He will either hate one and love the other, or be devoted to one and despise the other. You cannot serve both God and mammon."

Practice of Hope

Attachment to wealth reveals that we aren't truly devoted to God, whose Son gave away his very life for us. We who hope to enter the fullness of God's kingdom must live as if we were in it now. ◆ Do you sometimes hesitate to help those in need? Imagine that Jesus is sitting with you. Talk with him about why you sometimes do not help people when you could. ◆ Do you have an investment portfolio? Do your investments reflect a concern for social justice? If not, consider socially responsible investing. Learn more from the Forum for Sustainable and Responsible Investment at www.ussif.org. ◆ Do you buy products such as coffee or clothing that don't provide the producer with a living wage? Try switching to a product that has received fair trade certification. Visit www.fairtradecertified.org to learn about your options.

Download more questions and activities for families, Christian initiation groups, and other adult groups at http://www.ltp.org/ahw.

Scripture Insights

Today's reading from the prophet Amos depicts the injustice of sellers in the marketplace. The poor are treated unjustly, something God will not forget. In contrast to the actions in the marketplace, the responsorial psalm for today emphasizes what God does on behalf of the poor. God "raises up the lowly from the dust; / from the dunghill he lifts up the poor / to seat them with princes, / with the princes of his own people" (113:7). The psalm expresses a special love for the poor, for those who are treated unfairly.

The passage from the First Letter to Timothy invites us to reflect on communal intercessory prayer. It is right that we pray for one another, even those individuals with whom we may have disagreements. When we pray, we ought to ask God for blessings on those we love and on those toward whom we hold no affection.

Today's parable from Luke is challenging and not very easy to understand. While the steward is recognized as being quite clever, he is looking out for himself, no one else. Yes, the men who owed the steward's master must have been happy for the reduction of their debt. The steward lowers their payment because he wants to have some people to turn to when he is fired. At the very end of this parable, we find insight into its meaning: "No servant can serve two masters. He will either hate one and love the other, or be devoted to one and despise the other. You cannot serve both God and mammon" (16:13).

◆ How do you see the poor taken advantage of in your community? What might you do to help change the plight of the poor in your city?

◆ Be attentive to the universal prayer, also called the prayer of the faithful, in your parish. How do the petitions invite you to show compassion?

◆ What does today's Gospel passage invite you to do? If you had the opportunity, what would you like to ask the steward?

123

READING I *Amos 6:1a, 4–7*

Thus says the LORD, God of hosts:
Woe to the complacent in Zion!
Lying upon beds of ivory,
    stretched comfortably on their couches,
they eat lambs taken from the flock,
    and calves from the stall!
Improvising to the music of the harp,
    like David, they devise their
        own accompaniment.
They drink wine from bowls
    and anoint themselves with the best oils;
    yet they are not made ill
        by the collapse of Joseph!
Therefore, now they shall be
        the first to go into exile,
    and their wanton revelry shall be done
        away with.

RESPONSORIAL PSALM
Psalm 146:7, 8–9, 9–10 (1b)

R. Praise the Lord, my soul!
or: Alleluia.

Blessed is he who keeps faith forever,
    secures justice for the oppressed,
    gives food to the hungry.
The LORD sets captives free. R.

The LORD gives sight to the blind;
    the LORD raises up those
        who were bowed down.
The LORD loves the just;
    the LORD protects strangers. R.

The fatherless and the widow he sustains,
    but the way of the wicked he thwarts.
The LORD shall reign forever;
    your God, O Zion, through
        all generations. Alleluia. R.

READING II *1 Timothy 6:11–16*

But you, man of God, pursue righteousness, devotion, faith, love, patience, and gentleness. Compete well for the faith. Lay hold of eternal life, to which you were called when you made the noble confession in the presence of many witnesses. I charge you before God, who gives life to all things, and before Christ Jesus, who gave testimony under Pontius Pilate for the noble confession, to keep the commandment without stain or reproach until the appearance of our Lord Jesus Christ that the blessed and only ruler will make manifest at the proper time, the King of kings and Lord of lords, who alone has immortality, who dwells in unapproachable light, and whom no human being has seen or can see. To him be honor and eternal power. Amen.

GOSPEL *Luke 16:19–31*

Jesus said to the Pharisees: "There was a rich man who dressed in purple garments and fine linen and dined sumptuously each day. And lying at his door was a poor man named Lazarus, covered with sores, who would gladly have eaten his fill of the scraps that fell from the rich man's table. Dogs even used to come and lick his sores. When the poor man died, he was carried away by angels to the bosom of Abraham. The rich man also died and was buried, and from the netherworld, where he was in torment, he raised his eyes and saw Abraham far off and Lazarus at his side. And he cried out, 'Father Abraham, have pity on me. Send Lazarus to dip the tip of his finger in water and cool my tongue, for I am suffering torment in these flames.' Abraham replied, 'My child, remember that you received what was good during your lifetime while Lazarus likewise received what was bad; but now he is comforted here, whereas you are tormented. Moreover, between us and you a great chasm is established to prevent anyone from crossing who might wish to go from our side to yours or from your side to ours.' He said, 'Then I beg you, father, send him to my father's house, for I have five brothers, so that he may warn them, lest they too come to this place of torment.' But Abraham replied, 'They have Moses and the prophets. Let them listen to them.' He said, 'Oh no, father Abraham, but if someone from the dead goes to them, they will repent.' Then Abraham said, 'If they will not listen to Moses and the prophets, neither will they be persuaded if someone should rise from the dead.'"

Practice of Charity

Overconsumption harms us, other people, and the environment. Do you consume too much food or spend too much time using social media or watching television? Cut down on your intake this week. ♦ Spend time instead praying for those who go without enough food, water, or adequate housing. ♦ How aware are you of the needs of the members of your faith community? Talk with your pastor or other minister about ways you can support one or two people, from taking someone to an appointment to visiting and praying with someone. ♦ Look for ways to reduce your use of the earth's resources and to protect those resources. Recycle what you can. Use reusable grocery bags. Switch to biodegradable products and cleaning products that are less toxic to the environment and to you and your family.

Download more questions and activities for families, Christian initiation groups, and other adult groups at http://www.ltp.org/ahw.

Scripture Insights

Today's readings from the prophet Amos and the Gospel of Luke require more than one quick read. Otherwise, we might interpret these two texts to be a strong condemnation against all material wealth or even comfort. That is not to say that these texts do not have anything to say about this. What Amos speaks against quite strongly is the complacency of those he addresses. When we are comfortable, it can be easy to forget the plight of others. Amos is expressing distress over those people who have become "complacent."

Before turning to today's Gospel, it is helpful for us to be aware of several verses of Luke that do not appear in either last week's or this week's lectionary. Last week's passage concluded with the words, "You cannot serve God and mammon" (Luke 16:13). Immediately afterward, the Gospel states, "The Pharisees, who loved money, heard all these things and sneered at him." Thus, we may interpret today's Gospel as being addressed to both the Pharisees and the disciples. What is the cost of discipleship?

Today, Luke presents us with two men. The unnamed man is wealthy, well-fed, draped in rich garments, and comfortable; Lazarus is poor, starving, clothed in sores, and lying outside the door of the rich man. When the men die, their plights continue to be the opposite of each other. While the rich man experiences torment, Lazarus rests in "the bosom of Abraham" (16:22). The text indicates that both men are acquainted with Abraham, and thus, both are likely men of Israel. That being the case, the rich man, according to the law, was responsible for attending to Lazarus, which he did not do.

♦ If both the Pharisees and Jesus' disciples heard this parable, what lesson do you think each group might have gleaned from Jesus?

♦ Once again, today's Scripture texts invite us to reflect on what it means to be a disciple of Jesus. Are your material possessions more important to you than sharing your food with the hungry or offering comfort to those who suffer?

♦ How does working for justice equate with keeping the faith?

October 2, 2022

READING I *Habakkuk 1:2–3; 2:2–4*

How long, O LORD? I cry for help
   but you do not listen!
I cry out to you, "Violence!"
   but you do not intervene.
Why do you let me see ruin;
   why must I look at misery?
Destruction and violence are before me;
   there is strife, and clamorous discord.
Then the LORD answered me and said:
   Write down the vision clearly upon the tablets,
   so that one can read it readily.
For the vision still has its time,
   presses on to fulfillment,
      and will not disappoint;
if it delays, wait for it,
   it will surely come, it will not be late.
The rash one has no integrity;
   but the just one, because of
      his faith, shall live.

RESPONSORIAL PSALM
Psalm 95:1–2, 6–7, 8–9 (8)

R. If today you hear his voice, harden not
      your hearts.

Come, let us sing joyfully to the LORD;
   let us acclaim the Rock of our salvation.
Let us come into his presence with thanksgiving;
   let us joyfully sing psalms to him. R.

Come, let us bow down in worship;
   let us kneel before the LORD who made us.
For he is our God,
   and we are the people he shepherds, the flock
      he guides. R.

Oh, that today you would hear his voice:
   "Harden not your hearts as at Meribah,
   as in the day of Massah in the desert,
where your fathers tempted me;
   they tested me though they had seen
      my works." R.

READING II *2 Timothy 1:6–8, 13–14*

Beloved: I remind you, to stir into flame the gift of God that you have through the imposition of my hands. For God did not give us a spirit of cowardice but rather of power and love and self-control. So do not be ashamed of your testimony to our Lord, nor of me, a prisoner for his sake; but bear your share of hardship for the gospel with the strength that comes from God.

Take as your norm the sound words that you heard from me, in the faith and love that are in Christ Jesus. Guard this rich trust with the help of the Holy Spirit that dwells within us.

GOSPEL *Luke 17:5–10*

The apostles said to the Lord, "Increase our faith." The Lord replied, "If you have faith the size of a mustard seed, you would say to this mulberry tree, 'Be uprooted and planted in the sea,' and it would obey you.

"Who among you would say to your servant who has just come in from plowing or tending sheep in the field, 'Come here immediately and take your place at table'? Would he not rather say to him, 'Prepare something for me to eat. Put on your apron and wait on me while I eat and drink. You may eat and drink when I am finished'? Is he grateful to that servant because he did what was commanded? So should it be with you. When you have done all you have been commanded, say, 'We are unprofitable servants; we have done what we were obliged to do.'"

Practice of Faith

In our walk with Christ, we seek to surrender more and more of ourselves to him who held nothing back from us. ◆ Learn the Suscipe, a prayer by St. Ignatius of Loyola: "Take, Lord, and receive all my liberty, my memory, my understanding, and my entire will, all that I have and call my own. You have given all to me. To you, O Lord, I return it. Everything is yours; do with it what you will. Give me only your love and your grace, that is enough for me." Offer this prayer at least one time each day this week. ◆ Strengthen your faith by joining a weekly prayer group or taking advantage of a retreat opportunity. ◆ Choose a country or region of the world afflicted by war. Go to daily Mass or pray the Rosary for everyone affected by the violence, both victims and perpetrators.

Download more questions and activities for families, Christian initiation groups, and other adult groups at http://www.ltp.org/ahw.

Scripture Insights

Once again, today's readings invite us to reflect on the themes of faith and discipleship. Note that our Gospel passage from Luke is addressed to the apostles, individuals chosen by Jesus to accompany him. Today's text contains two distinct units: the first two verses focus on faith, while the following verses are a type of parable that invites us to ponder the meaning of discipleship.

The apostles' request for an increase in faith may be a response to what Jesus had said in the verses immediately prior to what we hear today. In those verses, Jesus instructs his followers about forgiveness. If someone sins against them seven times in one day, they are to forgive that person seven times. Perhaps the apostles requested an increase in faith so that they could forgive in the manner in which Jesus instructed them to forgive. In addition to recognizing that Jesus uses hyperbole, it is helpful to know that the Greek construction of Jesus' words indicates that the faith of the apostles is already capable of doing great deeds.

The second portion of the Gospel text can be very difficult for faithful women and men of the twenty-first century to understand. At the time of Jesus, it was not unusual for someone to have a servant (or as the *New Revised Standard Version* of the Bible translates this, "slave"). Within the Scriptures, the connotation of "servant" is not always understood negatively. While the role of the servant in today's Gospel may strike a negative chord in us, it is helpful to keep in mind that both Jesus and his mother, Mary, along with many other persons in the Bible are referred to as servants of God.

◆ God assures the despairing Habakkuk that he only needs to wait. Can you identify with the cry of the prophet? Are you able to wait patiently for God's response to you?

◆ How comfortable are you with identifying yourself as a disciple of Jesus? A servant of Jesus?

◆ How do you understand your Christian responsibility toward your neighbor?

READING I *2 Kings 5:14–17*

Naaman went down and plunged into the Jordan seven times at the word of Elisha, the man of God. His flesh became again like the flesh of a little child, and he was clean of his leprosy.

Naaman returned with his whole retinue to the man of God. On his arrival he stood before Elisha and said, "Now I know that there is no God in all the earth, except in Israel. Please accept a gift from your servant."

Elisha replied, "As the LORD lives whom I serve, I will not take it"; and despite Naaman's urging, he still refused. Naaman said: "If you will not accept, please let me, your servant, have two mule-loads of earth, for I will no longer offer holocaust or sacrifice to any other god except to the LORD."

RESPONSORIAL PSALM
Psalm 98:1, 2–3, 3–4 (see 2b)

R. The Lord has revealed to the nations his
    saving power.

Sing to the LORD a new song,
    for he has done wondrous deeds;
his right hand has won victory for him,
    his holy arm.   R.

The LORD has made his salvation known:
    in the sight of the nations he has revealed
        his justice.
He has remembered his kindness and
        his faithfulness
    toward the house of Israel.   R.

All the ends of the earth have seen
    the salvation by our God.
Sing joyfully to the LORD, all you lands:
    break into song; sing praise.   R.

READING II *2 Timothy 2:8–13*

Beloved: Remember Jesus Christ, raised from the dead, a descendant of David: such is my gospel, for which I am suffering, even to the point of chains, like a criminal. But the word of God is not chained. Therefore, I bear with everything for the sake of those who are chosen, so that they too may obtain the salvation that is in Christ Jesus, together with eternal glory. This saying is trustworthy:

If we have died with him
    we shall also live with him;
if we persevere
    we shall also reign with him.
But if we deny him
    he will deny us.
If we are unfaithful
    he remains faithful,
        for he cannot deny himself.

GOSPEL *Luke 17:11–19*

As Jesus continued his journey to Jerusalem, he traveled through Samaria and Galilee. As he was entering a village, ten lepers met him. They stood at a distance from him and raised their voices, saying, "Jesus, Master! Have pity on us!" And when he saw them, he said, "Go show yourselves to the priests." As they were going they were cleansed. And one of them, realizing he had been healed, returned, glorifying God in a loud voice; and he fell at the feet of Jesus and thanked him. He was a Samaritan. Jesus said in reply, "Ten were cleansed, were they not? Where are the other nine? Has none but this foreigner returned to give thanks to God?" Then he said to him, "Stand up and go; your faith has saved you."

Practice of Faith

In both the reading from Second Kings and the Gospel, people received the gift of healing. While that healing inspired a new or deeper faith in some, others missed the opportunity to grow in their relationship with God. ◆ Imagine that you are one of the lepers in today's Gospel account. What was your life like as a leper? How did Jesus change your life? How did you react to being healed? Why did or didn't you return to thank him? ◆ Make a list of things for which you are thankful. Spend time simply reflecting on and experiencing gratitude. ◆ When you are at Mass, listen for all the moments in which we give thanks. Are there moments you had not noticed before? In what ways does your experience of gratitude help you participate more fully in the liturgy?

Download more questions and activities for families, Christian initiation groups, and other adult groups at http://www.ltp.org/ahw.

Scripture Insights

Today's readings from Second Kings and the Gospel invite us to reflect on how we respond to God's saving deeds. In each of these readings, we find an individual who recognizes the goodness and healing power of God. In the first instance, Naaman, a Syrian, was a man of high regard in his native land. At the suggestion of his servant girl, and with the permission of his master, Naaman went to Israel to be cleansed of his leprosy. The prophet Elisha had directed Naaman to plunge into the Jordan seven times. Although Naaman's initial reaction to this instruction was one of disgust, he did as he was told, and "his flesh became again like the flesh of a little child, and he was clean of his leprosy" (2 Kings 5:14). Naaman's response was one of belief in and gratitude for the God of Israel. In the Gospel from Luke, we are told of ten men who, upon seeing Jesus, call out to him and ask for pity. Jesus' response is simple: "Go show yourselves to the priests." As the ten were obeying this command, "they were cleansed" (17:14). One man, a Samaritan, returned to Jesus and glorified God.

While much could be said of each story, what the texts tell us is quite clear. Not everyone responds in the same way to the merciful actions of God. In both of these Scripture readings, the individuals cleansed of their leprosy were foreigners, not men of Israel. Yet both of them returned to express their gratitude and their recognition of the saving power of God.

◆ At the time of Naaman and the time of Jesus, leprosy was a disease that resulted in people becoming outcasts of the community. Who are the outcasts in our society? In your neighborhood?

◆ Upon seeing the lepers, Jesus gave these individuals an instruction that would free them. Are there people who call to you that you choose not to see?

◆ Having experienced God's blessing, the individuals in today's readings immediately express their gratitude. When do you give thanks to God?

129

READING I *Exodus 17:8–13*

In those days, Amalek came and waged war against Israel. Moses, therefore, said to Joshua, "Pick out certain men, and tomorrow go out and engage Amalek in battle. I will be standing on top of the hill with the staff of God in my hand." So Joshua did as Moses told him: he engaged Amalek in battle after Moses had climbed to the top of the hill with Aaron and Hur. As long as Moses kept his hands raised up, Israel had the better of the fight, but when he let his hands rest, Amalek had the better of the fight. Moses' hands, however, grew tired; so they put a rock in place for him to sit on. Meanwhile Aaron and Hur supported his hands, one on one side and one on the other, so that his hands remained steady till sunset. And Joshua mowed down Amalek and his people with the edge of the sword.

RESPONSORIAL PSALM
Psalm 121:1–2, 3–4, 5–6, 7–8 (see 2)

R. Our help is from the Lord, who made heaven
      and earth.

I lift up my eyes toward the mountains;
    whence shall help come to me?
My help is from the LORD,
    who made heaven and earth. R.

May he not suffer your foot to slip;
    may he slumber not who guards you:
indeed he neither slumbers nor sleeps,
    the guardian of Israel. R.

The LORD is your guardian;
        the LORD is your shade;
he is beside you at your right hand.
The sun shall not harm you by day,
    nor the moon by night. R.

The LORD will guard you from all evil;
    he will guard your life.
The LORD will guard your coming and
        your going,
    both now and forever. R.

READING II *2 Timothy 3:14—4:2*

Beloved: Remain faithful to what you have learned and believed, because you know from whom you learned it, and that from infancy you have known the sacred Scriptures, which are capable of giving you wisdom for salvation through faith in Christ Jesus. All Scripture is inspired by God and is useful for teaching, for refutation, for correction, and for training in righteousness, so that one who belongs to God may be competent, equipped for every good work.

I charge you in the presence of God and of Christ Jesus, who will judge the living and the dead, and by his appearing and his kingly power: proclaim the word; be persistent whether it is convenient or inconvenient; convince, reprimand, encourage through all patience and teaching.

GOSPEL *Luke 18:1–8*

Jesus told his disciples a parable about the necessity for them to pray always without becoming weary. He said, "There was a judge in a certain town who neither feared God nor respected any human being. And a widow in that town used to come to him and say, 'Render a just decision for me against my adversary.' For a long time the judge was unwilling, but eventually he thought, 'While it is true that I neither fear God nor respect any human being, because this widow keeps bothering me I shall deliver a just decision for her lest she finally come and strike me.'" The Lord said, "Pay attention to what the dishonest judge says. Will not God then secure the rights of his chosen ones who call out to him day and night? Will he be slow to answer them? I tell you, he will see to it that justice is done for them speedily. But when the Son of Man comes, will he find faith on earth?"

Practice of Faith

Jesus instructs the disciples to pray always. If we want to draw closer to God, we must persist in our prayer. ✦ Each time that you pray this week, raise your arms upward and outward, palms up. This gesture signifies offering. What do you offer God? What do you receive from God? The more time we spend in prayer, the more likely our prayer will change. ✦ Look back at how you have prayed over the years. What are high points in your prayer life? What are low points? What was happening in your life at those times? How might your prayer need to change now? ✦ Form a prayer group or buddy system in which members check in with each other to share their prayer, their struggles in prayer, and new ways of praying.

Download more questions and activities for families, Christian initiation groups, and other adult groups at http://www.ltp.org/ahw.

Scripture Insights

Today's readings present us with some most interesting texts. Our first reading from Exodus speaks of Moses' persistence to praying for Israel's success in battle. Note, however, Moses would not have succeeded had he not had the support of Aaron and Hur.

The Gospel text for today is unique to Luke, a parable often identified as that of "the unjust judge" or "the persistent widow." What an engaging parable! Preachers frequently focus on the character of the judge, and, therefore, listeners are inclined to associate the judge with God. Listeners might conclude that their own prayer is not strong enough and that perhaps, if they just prayed harder or more often, God would answer their prayer as they want it answered. But we must ask: Is this how God acts? Is this how God listens to prayer? Does God count how frequently we pray?

Another way of looking at this parable is to focus on the character of the widow. Biblical scholar Barbara Reid has called the woman "an icon for what it means to do the work of justice." The unnamed widow in this story repeatedly approaches the unjust judge. She is persistent in her demand for justice. Why is this text often presented as the widow badgering the judge? This widow is requesting (according to the Greek text, "over and over") justice.

✦ Can you identify with the widow in today's Gospel? Have you ever had the experience of making a request over and over to someone who did not hear you?

✦ In today's first reading, Israel's success is dependent on Moses keeping his arms held high. He could not have done this without the assistance of Aaron and Hur. How have you needed the support of others in your spiritual life?

✦ Persistence is a theme in today's three Scripture texts. What do you think is the meaning of the passage from the Second Letter to Timothy: "proclaim the word; be persistent whether it is convenient or inconvenient; convince, reprimand, encourage through all patience and teaching"?

READING I *Sirach 35:12–14, 16–18*

The LORD is a God of justice,
   who knows no favorites.
Though not unduly partial toward the weak,
   yet he hears the cry of the oppressed.
The Lord is not deaf to the wail of the orphan,
   nor to the widow when she pours out
      her complaint.
The one who serves God willingly is heard;
   his petition reaches the heavens.
The prayer of the lowly pierces the clouds;
   it does not rest till it reaches its goal,
nor will it withdraw till the
      Most High responds,
   judges justly and affirms the right,
and the Lord will not delay.

RESPONSORIAL PSALM
Psalm 34:2–3, 17–18, 19, 23 (7a)

R. The Lord hears the cry of the poor.

I will bless the LORD at all times;
   his praise shall be ever in my mouth.
Let my soul glory in the LORD;
   the lowly will hear me and be glad. R.

The LORD confronts the evildoers,
   to destroy remembrance of them from
      the earth.
When the just cry out, the LORD hears them,
   and from all their distress
      he rescues them. R.

The LORD is close to the brokenhearted;
   and those who are crushed in spirit he saves.
The LORD redeems the lives of his servants;
   no one incurs guilt who takes refuge
      in him. R.

READING II *2 Timothy 4:6–8, 16–18*

Beloved: I am already being poured out like a libation, and the time of my departure is at hand. I have competed well; I have finished the race; I have kept the faith. From now on the crown of righteousness awaits me, which the Lord, the just judge, will award to me on that day, and not only to me, but to all who have longed for his appearance.

At my first defense no one appeared on my behalf, but everyone deserted me. May it not be held against them! But the Lord stood by me and gave me strength, so that through me the proclamation might be completed and all the Gentiles might hear it. And I was rescued from the lion's mouth. The Lord will rescue me from every evil threat and will bring me safe to his heavenly kingdom. To him be glory forever and ever. Amen.

GOSPEL *Luke 18:9–14*

Jesus addressed this parable to those who were convinced of their own righteousness and despised everyone else. "Two people went up to the temple area to pray; one was a Pharisee and the other was a tax collector. The Pharisee took up his position and spoke this prayer to himself, 'O God, I thank you that I am not like the rest of humanity—greedy, dishonest, adulterous—or even like this tax collector. I fast twice a week, and I pay tithes on my whole income.' But the tax collector stood off at a distance and would not even raise his eyes to heaven but beat his breast and prayed, 'O God, be merciful to me a sinner.' I tell you, the latter went home justified, not the former; for whoever exalts himself will be humbled, and the one who humbles himself will be exalted."

Practice of Hope

Today's Gospel passage is the inspiration for the Jesus Prayer: "Lord Jesus Christ, Son of God, have mercy on me, a sinner." Offer the Jesus Prayer throughout your day. Receive God's mercy and strength. Use these words to pray with and for those who struggle to know and do what is right, especially those trapped in difficult situations. ♦ Sometimes we may act like the tax collector, but at other times, like the Pharisee, doing the right things but thinking too highly of ourselves. ♦ Use the Examen, a prayer developed by St. Ignatius of Loyola. Recognize that you are in God's presence. Give thanks for something that happened today, no matter how small. Pray for the Spirit's guidance. ♦ Reflect on a moment today in which you did not act with love. Confess your need for God's mercy and help as you strive to grow in holiness.

Download more questions and activities for families, Christian initiation groups, and other adult groups at http://www.ltp.org/ahw.

Scripture Insights

Once again, today's Scriptures focus our attention on prayer. The first reading from the Book of Sirach and the responsorial psalm remind us that God hears the cry of the oppressed, the orphan, the widow, the lowly, and the poor. This does not mean that God does not listen to the prayer of all people, but God is especially attentive to people in great need, people who know that they rely on God for their very existence. As the final strophe of the psalm declares: "The LORD is close to the broken-hearted; / and those who are crushed in spirit he saves. / The LORD redeems the lives of his servants; / no one incurs guilt who takes refuge in him" (Psalm 34:19, 23).

In the text of the Second Letter to Timothy, the author (most probably a follower of St. Paul, who writes as if he were Paul) recognizes his utter dependence on God when he proclaims that the Lord "stood by me and gave me strength" (4:17). It is obvious that such a declaration comes from someone who has a firm relationship with God.

The parable in today's Gospel presents us with two contrasting figures, a Pharisee and a tax collector. Members of the Pharisaic sect identified themselves as strict observers of the law, while tax collectors were understood as individuals collaborating with the Roman establishment. The Pharisee in this parable thanks God that he is not like other people, particularly those whom he would consider "lowlifes." Meanwhile, the tax collector recognizes that he is a sinner and pleads for God's mercy. Which prayer is more sincere?

♦ Reread today's Gospel passage. Have there been times in your life when your prayers resembled that of the Pharisee? The tax collector?

♦ Slowly pray today's responsorial psalm. How does this text invite you to reconsider what it means to be poor?

♦ Catholic social teaching encourages the faithful to be attentive to the needs of the marginalized. How does what is called "the preferential option for the poor" reflect God's love?

READING I *Wisdom 11:22—12:2*

Before the LORD the whole universe is as a
　　grain from a balance
　　or a drop of morning dew come down upon
　　　　the earth.
But you have mercy on all, because you can
　　do all things;
　　and you overlook people's sins that they
　　　　may repent.
For you love all things that are
　　and loathe nothing that you have made;
　　for what you hated, you would not
　　　　have fashioned.
And how could a thing remain, unless you
　　willed it;
　　or be preserved, had it not been called
　　　　forth by you?
But you spare all things, because they are yours,
　　O LORD and lover of souls,
　　for your imperishable spirit is in all things!
Therefore you rebuke offenders little by little,
　　warn them and remind them of the sins they
　　　　are committing,
　　that they may abandon their wickedness and
　　　　believe in you, O LORD!

RESPONSORIAL PSALM *Psalm 145:1–2, 8–9, 10–11, 13, 14 (see 1)*

R. I will praise your name for ever, my king
　　and my God.

I will extol you, O my God and King;
　　and I will bless your name forever and ever.
Every day I will bless you;
　　and I will praise your name forever
　　　　and ever. R.

The LORD is gracious and merciful,
　　slow to anger and of great kindness.
The LORD is good to all,
　　and compassionate toward all his works. R.

Let all your works give you thanks, O LORD,
　　and let your faithful ones bless you.
Let them discourse of the glory of your kingdom
　　and speak of your might. R.

The LORD is faithful in all his words
　　and holy in all his works.
The LORD lifts up all who are falling
　　and raises up all who are bowed down. R.

READING II *2 Thessalonians 1:11—2:2*

Brothers and sisters: We always pray for you, that our God may make you worthy of his calling and powerfully bring to fulfillment every good purpose and every effort of faith, that the name of our Lord Jesus may be glorified in you, and you in him, in accord with the grace of our God and Lord Jesus Christ.

We ask you, brothers and sisters, with regard to the coming of our Lord Jesus Christ and our assembling with him, not to be shaken out of your minds suddenly, or to be alarmed either by a "spirit," or by an oral statement, or by a letter allegedly from us to the effect that the day of the Lord is at hand.

GOSPEL *Luke 19:1–10*

At that time, Jesus came to Jericho and intended to pass through the town. Now a man there named Zacchaeus, who was a chief tax collector and also a wealthy man, was seeking to see who Jesus was; but he could not see him because of the crowd, for he was short in stature. So he ran ahead and climbed a sycamore tree in order to see Jesus, who was about to pass that way. When he reached the place, Jesus looked up and said, "Zacchaeus, come down quickly, for today I must stay at your house." And he came down quickly and received him with joy. When they all saw this, they began to grumble, saying, "He has gone to stay at the house of a sinner." But Zacchaeus stood there and said to the Lord, "Behold, half of my possessions, Lord, I shall give to the poor, and if I have extorted anything from anyone I shall repay it four times over." And Jesus said to him, "Today salvation has come to this house because this man too is a descendant of Abraham. For the Son of Man has come to seek and to save what was lost."

Practice of Charity

Sometimes we don't see the goodness that is within and around us. Who do you think God sees when looking at you? Are you like Zacchaeus, eager for God to find you, or are there parts of yourself that you are trying to hide from God? ◆ Imagine what it was like for Zacchaeus. Feel the joy of welcoming Jesus' presence within you. As Zacchaeus tried to see Jesus, people in the crowd might have deliberately prevented him. ◆ Zacchaeus oversaw the collection of taxes for Rome, and so people condemned him as a sinner. Is there someone whose relationship with God you might have misjudged? Pray for that person. What might that person's relationship with God really be? ◆ If you can, spend some time outside. Reflect on all that God has fashioned. Cherish the things God has made, from the largest to the smallest.

Download more questions and activities for families, Christian initiation groups, and other adult groups at http://www.ltp.org/ahw.

Scripture Insights

In today's first reading from the Book of Wisdom, we hear that God loves all that God has created. What an affirmation of the goodness of the entire cosmos! Additionally, the author of this text emphasizes that God is both merciful and forgiving. This depiction of God is affirmed in today's responsorial psalm.

Meanwhile, the author of the Second Letter to the Thessalonians reminds the community that the coming of the Lord Jesus is not likely to take place soon. It seems that there were rumors circulating that the Lord would return in the near future. And while the Lord's return would take place, the author wants the community to live out their faith until that unknown time.

Luke's Gospel provides the only account of the tax collector named Zacchaeus. Since the Romans depended on the tax collectors to acquire funds, the Jews often despised them. This small tax collector "was seeking to see who Jesus was; but he could not see him because of the crowd, for he was short in stature" (19:3). How disturbed the crowd must have been when they heard that Jesus would stay in the home of Zacchaeus! And how shocked Zacchaeus must have been at this news!

Once again, we have a Gospel story that depicts Jesus in a way that we might find surprising. Jesus does not follow the common practice of despising a tax collector. While Zacchaeus sought Jesus, Jesus sought Zacchaeus. And the response of this tax collector is one of immediate repentance. He offers half of his possessions to the poor and then proclaims that he will repay fourfold anyone whom he has wronged.

Confronted with the love of Jesus, Zacchaeus recognizes who he is and desires to be different. In seeking Jesus, Zacchaeus was found.

◆ Reread today's passage from Wisdom. Reflect on the words "You have mercy on all." Consider the ways that God has been merciful to you.

◆ Have you, like Zacchaeus, sought to see Jesus? How have you pursued him?

◆ Reflect on Jesus' words to Zacchaeus. How would you respond if Jesus told you that he wanted to dine with you this evening?

READING I   *2 Maccabees 7:1–2, 9–14*

It happened that seven brothers with their mother were arrested and tortured with whips and scourges by the king, to force them to eat pork in violation of God's law. One of the brothers, speaking for the others, said: "What do you expect to achieve by questioning us? We are ready to die rather than transgress the laws of our ancestors."

At the point of death he said: "You accursed fiend, you are depriving us of this present life, but the King of the world will raise us up to live again forever. It is for his laws that we are dying."

After him the third suffered their cruel sport. He put out his tongue at once when told to do so, and bravely held out his hands, as he spoke these noble words: "It was from Heaven that I received these; for the sake of his laws I disdain them; from him I hope to receive them again." Even the king and his attendants marveled at the young man's courage, because he regarded his sufferings as nothing.

After he had died, they tortured and maltreated the fourth brother in the same way. When he was near death, he said, "It is my choice to die at the hands of men with the hope God gives of being raised up by him; but for you, there will be no resurrection to life."

RESPONSORIAL PSALM
Psalm 17:1, 5–6, 8, 15 (15b)

R. Lord, when your glory appears,
    my joy will be full.

Hear, O LORD, a just suit;
    attend to my outcry;
    hearken to my prayer from lips
        without deceit. R.

My steps have been steadfast in your paths,
    my feet have not faltered.
I call upon you, for you will answer me, O God;
    incline your ear to me; hear my word. R.

Keep me as the apple of your eye,
    hide me in the shadow of your wings.
But I in justice shall behold your face;
    on waking I shall be content in
        your presence. R.

READING II   *2 Thessalonians 2:16—3:5*

Brothers and sisters: May our Lord Jesus Christ himself and God our Father, who has loved us and given us everlasting encouragement and good hope through his grace, encourage your hearts and strengthen them in every good deed and word.

Finally, brothers and sisters, pray for us, so that the word of the Lord may speed forward and be glorified, as it did among you, and that we may be delivered from perverse and wicked people, for not all have faith. But the Lord is faithful; he will strengthen you and guard you from the evil one. We are confident of you in the Lord that what we instruct you, you are doing and will continue to do. May the Lord direct your hearts to the love of God and to the endurance of Christ.

GOSPEL   *Luke 20:27–38*

Shorter: Luke 20:27, 34–38

Some Sadducees, those who deny that there is a resurrection, came forward and put this question to Jesus, saying, "Teacher, Moses wrote for us, *If someone's brother dies leaving a wife but no child, his brother must take the wife and raise up descendants for his brother.* Now there were seven brothers; the first married a woman but died childless. Then the second and the third married her, and likewise all the seven died childless. Finally the woman also died. Now at the resurrection whose wife will that woman be? For all seven had been married to her." Jesus said to them, "The children of this age marry and remarry; but those who are deemed worthy to attain to the coming age and to the resurrection of the dead neither marry nor are given in marriage. They can no longer die, for they are like angels; and they are the children of God because they are the ones who will rise. That the dead will rise even Moses made known in the passage about the bush, when he called out 'Lord,' the God of Abraham, the God of Isaac, and the God of Jacob; and he is not God of the dead, but of the living, for to him all are alive."

Practice of Hope

At the time of Jesus, not all Jews believed in an afterlife. The seven brothers in the first reading believed in the resurrection of the just, whereas others, such as the Sadducees, did not. Jesus' resurrection ensures that there is new life to come. ◆ What stories, paintings, and other art strengthen your hope in the life to come? Choose an image of the risen Jesus. Pray with this image, asking God to complete his glorification of all creation. ◆ Are you scared of death? Share your fears with the Lord. What should you do to prepare for death, not only spiritually, but in other aspects of your life? ◆ During November we especially remember those who have died. Pray today's responsorial psalm on behalf of those who have died, especially those who died young or who died a violent death.

Download more questions and activities for families, Christian initiation groups, and other adult groups at http://www.ltp.org/ahw.

Scripture Insights

Today's readings can be better understood when placed within their historical context. The first reading from the Second Book of Maccabees recounts the circumstances of Judaism in the latter part of the second century before Christ. It was during this time that belief in the resurrection from the dead was emerging within parts of Judaism. Not all Jews believed in resurrection. Among those that believed in the resurrection were the Pharisees; among those that did not believe in the resurrection were the Sadducees. While there were other sects within Judaism, it is these two groups that are often referred to in the Gospels.

Today's first reading is part of a text that recounts the story of a mother and her seven sons. Each member of this family was killed for refusing to disobey the law by eating food that was forbidden them to eat. Each bravely faced death rather than break God's command, and each believed that God would raise them to new life.

Our Gospel from Luke, written in the first century, presents a story of some Sadducees, who placed a question to Jesus regarding the resurrection and marriage.

While the Sadducees did not believe in the resurrection, they confronted Jesus with a situation that forced him to respond. Another teaching of Judaism, and one held by the Sadducees, was that, when a male sibling died without offspring, it was the responsibility of the next brother to provide a child for his sibling's widow. When they confront Jesus with the question, "at the resurrection whose wife will that woman be?" (20:33), Jesus is compelled to respond to the Sadducees in a manner to which they were accustomed. He refers to another portion of Scripture to emphasize the point that God is the God of the living, not of the dead.

◆ Reflect on when you were faced with a decision that would go against your beliefs. How did you confront this difficulty?

◆ Reread today's responsorial psalm. Which lines in this psalm speak to your heart?

◆ How do you envision the resurrection?

READING I *Malachi 3:19–20a*

Lo, the day is coming, blazing like an oven,
    when all the proud and all evildoers will
        be stubble,
and the day that is coming will set them on fire,
    leaving them neither root nor branch,
    says the LORD of hosts.
But for you who fear my name, there will arise
    the sun of justice with its healing rays.

RESPONSORIAL PSALM
Psalm 98:5–6, 7–8, 9 (see 9)

R. The Lord comes to rule the earth with justice.

Sing praise to the LORD with the harp,
    with the harp and melodious song.
With trumpets and the sound of the horn
    sing joyfully before the King, the LORD.   R.

Let the sea and what fills it resound,
    the world and those who dwell in it;
let the rivers clap their hands,
    the mountains shout with them for joy.   R.

Before the LORD, for he comes,
    for he comes to rule the earth;
he will rule the world with justice
    and the peoples with equity.   R.

READING II *2 Thessalonians 3:7–12*

Brothers and sisters: You know how one must imitate us. For we did not act in a disorderly way among you, nor did we eat food received free from anyone. On the contrary, in toil and drudgery, night and day we worked, so as not to burden any of you. Not that we do not have the right. Rather, we wanted to present ourselves as a model for you, so that you might imitate us. In fact, when we were with you, we instructed you that if anyone was unwilling to work, neither should that one eat. We hear that some are conducting themselves among you in a disorderly way, by not keeping busy but minding the business of others. Such people we instruct and urge in the Lord Jesus Christ to work quietly and to eat their own food.

GOSPEL *Luke 21:5–19*

While some people were speaking about how the temple was adorned with costly stones and votive offerings, Jesus said, "All that you see here—the days will come when there will not be left a stone upon another stone that will not be thrown down."

Then they asked him, "Teacher, when will this happen? And what sign will there be when all these things are about to happen?" He answered, "See that you not be deceived, for many will come in my name, saying, 'I am he,' and 'The time has come.' Do not follow them! When you hear of wars and insurrections, do not be terrified; for such things must happen first, but it will not immediately be the end." Then he said to them, "Nation will rise against nation, and kingdom against kingdom. There will be powerful earthquakes, famines and plagues from place to place; and awesome sights and mighty signs will come from the sky.

"Before all this happens, however, they will seize and persecute you, they will hand you over to the synagogues and to prisons, and they will have you led before kings and governors because of my name. It will lead to your giving testimony. Remember, you are not to prepare your defense beforehand, for I myself shall give you a wisdom in speaking that all your adversaries will be powerless to resist or refute. You will even be handed over by parents, brothers, relatives and friends, and they will put some of you to death. You will be hated by all because of my name, but not a hair on your head will be destroyed. By your perseverance you will secure your lives."

Practice of Faith

We entrust our lives to Christ and remain steadfast in faith despite whatever comes our way, be it devastating natural events, violence, or ridicule. ◆ For some, the delay of Christ's return became a spiritual challenge in itself. Do times of hardship strengthen or weaken your faith? Why do you think you respond this way? How might these difficult times help you see and connect with God in new ways? ◆ Read paragraphs 1042–1050 of the *Catechism of the Catholic Church*. How are these passages familiar? Are there passages that surprise you? ◆ In our second reading, St. Paul urges people not to get so caught up in expectations about the world ending that they neglect their work. What task have you been putting off? Complete this work today as an offering to the Lord.

Download more questions and activities for families, Christian initiation groups, and other adult groups at http://www.ltp.org/ahw.

Scripture Insights

Nearing the end of the liturgical year, we read biblical texts that often are referred to as telling of the end times. In the brief first reading from the prophet Malachi, we hear of a day when evildoers will be treated differently from those who reverence God's name. This day, sometimes called "the day of the Lord," is a day of judgment. By no means is Israel exempt from this judgment.

Today's Gospel from Luke turns our attention to the future. Jesus begins by speaking about the destruction of the temple, followed by a reference to the destruction of Jerusalem and then the coming of the Son of Man.

Referring to the temple, Jesus states, "All that you see here—the days will come when there will not be left a stone upon another stone that will not be thrown down." Those present wanted to know when this would happen and what sign would alert them to this event. It is likely that those listening to Jesus considered the destruction of the temple and the end times as the same. Jesus instructs the people that these two events are not the same.

Today's Gospel text is not easy to understand. While the early followers of Jesus may have associated the destruction of the temple with the end times, we most certainly do not. We believe that the kingdom of God has broken into our world through the paschal mystery. But that kingdom has yet to be fully realized. We wait in hope.

◆ Reread the text from Malachi. Does this passage give you comfort or make you fearful? If you have reverence for the name of God, you can take comfort in the saving hand of God.

◆ As you read today's excerpt from 2 Thessalonians, consider whether you imitate the early followers of Jesus. How do you do this?

◆ Spend some time reflecting on the refrain from today's psalm: "The Lord comes to rule the earth with justice."

Reading I *2 Samuel 5:1–3*

In those days, all the tribes of Israel came to David in Hebron and said: "Here we are, your bone and your flesh. In days past, when Saul was our king, it was you who led the Israelites out and brought them back. And the LORD said to you, 'You shall shepherd my people Israel and shall be commander of Israel.'" When all the elders of Israel came to David in Hebron, King David made an agreement with them there before the LORD, and they anointed him king of Israel.

Responsorial Psalm
Psalm 122:1–2, 3–4, 4–5 (see 1)

R. Let us go rejoicing to the house of the Lord.

I rejoiced because they said to me,
   "We will go up to the house of the LORD."
And now we have set foot
   within your gates, O Jerusalem.   R.

Jerusalem, built as a city
   with compact unity.
To it the tribes go up,
   the tribes of the LORD.   R.

According to the decree for Israel,
   to give thanks to the name of the LORD.
In it are set up judgment seats,
   seats for the house of David.   R.

Reading II *Colossians 1:12–20*

Brothers and sisters: Let us give thanks to the Father, who has made you fit to share in the inheritance of the holy ones in light. He delivered us from the power of darkness and transferred us to the kingdom of his beloved Son, in whom we have redemption, the forgiveness of sins.

He is the image of the invisible God, / the firstborn of all creation. / For in him were created all things in heaven and on earth, / the visible and the invisible, / whether thrones or dominions or principalities or powers; / all things were created through him and for him. / He is before all things, / and in him all things hold together. / He is the head of the body, the church. / He is the beginning, the firstborn from the dead, / that in all things he himself might be preeminent. / For in him all the fullness was pleased to dwell, / and through him to reconcile all things for him, / making peace by the blood of his cross / through him, whether those on earth or those in heaven.

Gospel *Luke 23:35–43*

The rulers sneered at Jesus and said, "He saved others, let him save himself if he is the chosen one, the Christ of God." Even the soldiers jeered at him. As they approached to offer him wine they called out, "If you are King of the Jews, save yourself." Above him there was an inscription that read, "This is the King of the Jews."

Now one of the criminals hanging there reviled Jesus, saying, "Are you not the Christ? Save yourself and us." The other, however, rebuking him, said in reply, "Have you no fear of God, for you are subject to the same condemnation? And indeed, we have been condemned justly, for the sentence we received corresponds to our crimes, but this man has done nothing criminal." Then he said, "Jesus, remember me when you come into your kingdom." He replied to him, "Amen, I say to you, today you will be with me in Paradise."

Practice of Charity

"All the tribes of Israel" supported David as they chose him as their king. Jesus' only support is from a convicted criminal. ◆ Jesus and that criminal look like failures in the eyes of the onlookers. When have you failed at something? Is everything that you consider a failure truly a failure? Bring your failures before God. How is God helping you grow from these experiences? ◆ Spend some time at a cemetery. Pray for those who are buried there. Ask God to forgive their sins and bring them into his kingdom. ◆ The Church formally opposes the death penalty. What more could you do to learn about and take action on this issue? Find valuable resources at usccb.org/death-penalty and catholicsmobilizing.org. Consider hosting a discussion group using the US Conference of Catholic Bishops' statement *A Culture of Life and the Penalty of Death.*

Download more questions and activities for families, Christian initiation groups, and other adult groups at http://www.ltp.org/ahw.

Scripture Insights

Today's solemn feast occurs on the last Sunday of the liturgical year. Next week the new liturgical year will be welcomed with the celebration of the First Sunday of Advent.

The Solemnity of Our Lord Jesus Christ, King of the Universe, invites us to reflect on Jesus in ways that most of us are unaccustomed to doing. Today's texts stretch our minds and our hearts to ponder what it means to recognize Jesus as the Christ, the firstborn of all creation.

In the selection from the Second Book of Samuel, we hear that David was both recognized by the people and appointed by God to be king of Israel. The responsorial psalm emphasizes the great delight that Israel had in visiting their holy city, Jerusalem, the home of both the united monarchy, established with King David, and the temple, built by the son of David, King Solomon. The song is one of tremendous delight!

Luke's Gospel text for today's feast invites us to consider what it means for Jesus to be king. He is on the cross. He has been crucified. While Jesus hangs there, the rulers and the soldiers sneer at him, and above his head the inscription reads, "This is the King of the Jews." The scene is filled with irony. Those who use this title for Jesus do so to mock him. Yet, all the while, we, and one of the criminals, know the truth. Jesus is, indeed, the King of Jews. This is no ordinary kingship. The kingship of Jesus, the Christ, is made known not in extravagant robes and ceremonies but in the embrace and the humiliation of the cross.

◆ What was it about King David that caused him to be popular among the people?

◆ Reread today's passage from Colossians. Which lines invite you to probe more deeply the mystery of Jesus?

◆ Imagine that you were to encounter Jesus on earth today. What kind of king is he?